The New England Gardener's

BOOK OF LISTS

Karan Davis Cutler

Series Editor
Lois Trigg Chaplin

Taylor Trade Publishing
Dallas, Texas

For my husband, Steve, a native New England list-maker who is not a gardener but willingly supports my horticultural endeavors—on paper and on our fifteen acres in northern Vermont.

Designed by David Timmons

Published by Taylor Publishing Company
1550 West Mockingbird Lane
Dallas, Texas 75235
www.taylorpub.com

Library of Congress Cataloging-in-Publication Data is available.

10 9   8   7   6   5   4   3   2   1

Printed in the United States of America

CONTENTS

ACKNOWLEDGMENTS

Naming all those who helped in this project would produce the longest list in the book. Rather than create that list and chance overlooking someone, let me just say how grateful I am for the help I received from gardeners living throughout New England (and elsewhere). Many contributors were already acquaintances, but many were not. Like Blanche Dubois in *A Streetcar Named Desire*, I "depended on the kindness of strangers." I hope those strangers are now friends.

I also would like to thank Lois Trigg Chaplin, author of *The Southern Gardener's Book of Lists*, and the patient and capable editors at Taylor Publishing Company, Michael Emmerich, Fred Francis, and Eileen Smith. They've done their best to catch my errors; whatever mistakes may have slipped through are entirely mine.

INTRODUCTION

When I began working on this book, I thought I knew a fair amount about what plants would thrive in my and other New England gardens. But thanks to the generosity of others, I've learned twice what I knew. Over the last eighteen months, I've taken advantage of the expertise of seed sellers and nursery owners, plant breeders, university professors, Extension agents, garden writers and editors, and dozens of backyard gardeners.

It didn't come as a surprise to me that gardeners are a helpful lot. My mother was the gardener when I was growing up, forever giving neighbors divisions of daylilies and bearded iris. Now ninety-five, she still gardens—in southern California rather than southern Illinois—and passes out leaves and slips to anyone who registers an interest.

My first ornamental garden was an entirely hand-me-down affair, composed of plants discarded by a friend, a woman of immense energy and taste and the creator of one of the loveliest small gardens in northern Ohio. Like the English writer Vita Sackville-West, Carol Campbell was ruthless and rooted out any plant that was incompatible or unsuccessful. I was the heir to her strong views and cultivated her cast-offs as well as her passion for gardening.

Garden generosity isn't anything new, of course. In 1735, the Englishman Peter Collinson wrote to his friend John Custis, the Virginian with whom he often exchanged seeds and plants: "I think there is no Greater pleasure than to be Communicative and oblige others.... Wee Brothers of the Spade find it very necessary to share." Wee Sisters do too.

Garden books, too, are about being "communicative," about sharing ideas and experiences, collaborating. "I merely wish to talk to you on paper," is how Mrs. E.W. Earle began *Pot-Pourri From a Surrey Garden* (1897). Authors anxious to convey their thoughts also learn theirs is no exclusive on sharing. Writing is interactive, full of give and take. Years ago I did a short article about vegetables containing nitrates, and a reader wrote to tell me that, "You are stupid and if you smoked more dope, you might make sense." Except for the dope part, I suspected it was one of my children writing under an assumed name.

Most gardeners are as generous with their praise as with their criticism. One woman, for instance, wrote to tell me that I erred in an article, and that Anna Comstock's *Handbook of Nature-Study* was written in 1911, not 1939. Then she softened her censure, going on to explain that the book was also one of her favorites, that she had discovered it while a college student, and that she was delighted to see me refer to it. Another reader of the magazine I edited, a man in his nineties from southern Vermont, wrote: "I liked your article, but I was amazed to read that your bleeding hearts don't self-sow. Mine do—I bought them at the Woolworth store in the 1930s. You're welcome to a sample. Come and help yourself," he added, giving me directions to his house. "Go on in through the side gate—I won't be home—and dig up whatever you see that you don't have. I will like thinking of them growing in your garden."

"No one can garden alone," Elizabeth Lawrence observed. Her *Gardening for Love*, published posthumously in 1987, celebrates the connections made by "hard-working farm women who are never too tired ... to gather seeds, to dig and pack plants, and to send them off with friendly letters." I hope you think of this book as a friendly letter filled with ideas from other New England gardeners. The lists it contains are testaments to the pleasure of sharing our work.

While gardeners and gardens are individual and idiosyncratic, gardening, ultimately, is communal. Welcome to the club.

GARDENING IN NEW ENGLAND

One of the brightest gems in the New England weather," Mark Twain remarked in a speech in 1876, "is the dazzling uncertainty of it." Twain supposedly is also the source of the often-quoted observation that if you don't like the weather in New England, wait an hour.

We New Englanders—residents of Rhode Island, Connecticut, Massachusetts, Maine, New Hampshire, and Vermont—know that Twain's comments still apply. And they apply not only to differences in time but in space. In my state of Vermont, it can be hailing one minute, sunny the next. What's more, it can be raining in Burlington at the same time that Morrisville, only 40 miles to the northeast, is having a blizzard.

PLANTS AND HARDINESS

The 40-mile drive that takes me from Burlington to Morrisville also takes me from hardiness Zone 5 to Zone 3. Hardiness zones were devised by the U.S. Department of Agriculture to help gardeners choose plants that would survive in their locations. The current map divides North America into eleven zones based on the lowest temperatures that can be expected during a year. Zone 1 is the coldest (an average minimum temperature below -50 degrees F) and Zone 11 (an average minimum temperature above 40 degrees F) is the warmest. Zones 2 through 10 are subdivided into two subzones; "a" subzones average 5 degrees colder than "b" subzones.

As you can see from the map, New England ranges from a chilly Zone 3 to a balmy Zone 7 on Cape Cod, but the majority of us garden in Zones 4, 5, or 6. Because so few New Englanders have reliable Zone 7 conditions, no plants hardy only as far north as Zone 7 have been included. At the same time, I have noted when plants are hardy to Zone 2—a darn good sign that they'll also survive in the frigid conditions with which Zone 3 gardeners cope. The hardiness zone rating is only one consideration when selecting plants for your garden, but it's an important one. Gardeners in our region who plant bougainvillea, hardy to Zone 9, will find only a dead vine next spring.

CRANESBILL

Gardeners in northern Maine, New Hampshire, and Vermont—where summers are cool and short, and winters are icy cold and seem to last forever—are the most limited in what they can grow. When you look at garden books, seed and plant catalogs, or nursery tags, you won't find many that read "Zone 3." But one of the

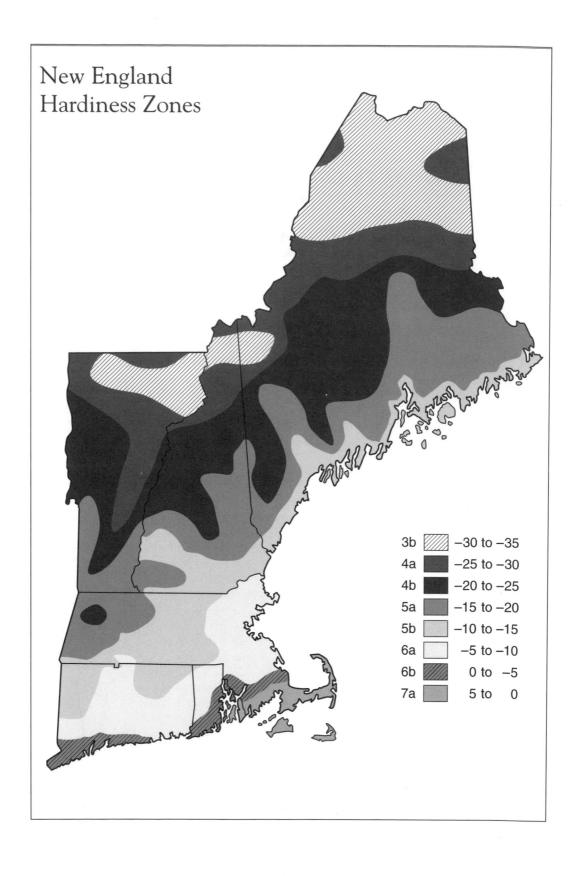

New England
Hardiness Zones

3b	/////	−30 to −35
4a		−25 to −30
4b		−20 to −25
5a		−15 to −20
5b		−10 to −15
6a		−5 to −10
6b		0 to −5
7a		5 to 0

things I've learned in my own garden and from contributors to this book is that many plants are far tougher than the standard references indicate. For example, *Corydalis lutea*, that small perennial with fernlike foliage and bright yellow flowers, is regularly cited as being hardy to Zone 5, but I've been growing it for several years in my Zone 4a garden.

It's not just that zone designations can be wrong. It's that factors other than minimum low temperature, the sole basis of the USDA zones, affect a plant's hardiness.

- Genetics: Plant hardiness is genetically determined, which explains why different strains or cultivars of the same species can have different tolerances. Plants also make genetic adaptions to climate over time. One reason to purchase locally grown plants is that nurseries typically use the most vigorous and hardy plants for propagation.
- Soil: Plants growing in a site that collects water often die over the winter from root rot, not from cold temperatures. If the drainage is good in your garden, you may be able to grow plants designated at least one hardiness zone warmer than your own.
- Wind: Protection from or exposure to winter winds, which makes the air feel colder than the thermometer reads, can mean a difference of one hardiness zone. For example, if you're in Zone 4 but your garden is exposed, you may want to play it safe and purchase only plants rated hardy for Zone 3.
- Snowcover: Snow works as a mulch in winter, keeping the soil temperature stable and protecting the plant parts it covers. (It explains your forsythia having blooms only on its lowest branches.) A reliable and deep snowcover can mean the difference of one, even two, hardiness zones.
- Plant Vigor: Plants that are stressed during the growing season—not enough or too much light, food, heat, or moisture—will be less hardy.

Although there may be a bit of "pushing the hardiness envelope," the plant hardiness zone ratings in this book are based on first-hand experience. They tend to be lower than those given in most garden books. Plants that are on the borderline between two zones and marked 4/5 or 5/6, for example, are iffy in the colder zone.

Moreover, plants that are grown at the cold-extreme of their range may survive but be smaller or less productive. Here in northern Vermont, I can grow many of the rhododendrons that thrive in southern Connecticut, but mine are 4 feet tall, not 15. Friends farther north in Greensboro, Vermont, report that wisteria survives winters in their Zone 3 garden. The bad news is that their vine never blooms.

Within every hardiness zone are hundreds of "microclimates," smaller areas where conditions are different from the prevailing climate. It may be a matter of elevation. The higher you are, the colder the winter and the cooler the summer. The general rule is that every 300 feet of elevation equals ten fewer growing days.

Latitude also makes a difference. Both Bar Harbor, Maine, and Boston, Massachusetts, are designated Zone 6, but a 'Red Jade' crabapple will flower about a week earlier in Boston than it does in Bar Harbor; for every degree of latitude there is a three to four day difference in flowering time. Living next to a large body of water, salt or fresh, moderates climate, as does living in an urban setting, or in a protected exposure.

To be sure which plants will excel in your garden requires some homework. Talk to other gardeners in the area—the closer they live to you the better. Visit nearby gardens and nurseries, and keep notes about what plants thrive in the neighborhood. Make sure you know the dates of average first and last frost in your area, which will also give you the length of your growing season. Get some information about annual rainfall and mean temperatures in summer. Your Extension Service or local airport may have these numbers, or check your local library for a copy of *Climates of the United States*, a two-volume compilation of climate data for every state. Gardeners who travel the information highway can log on to the National Weather Service (www.nws.noaa.gov) for climate information.

Whenever you can, buy plants that have been grown locally or grown in a climate like yours. Finally, if you're an extremely cautious sort, choose plants hardy to the zones colder than your own, especially if you're planting an expensive shrub or tree.

IDENTIFYING AND FINDING PLANTS

Ahhh, those *#&%@!! botanical names. As you probably remember from science class, they were the result of the same common names being used for different plants and of dozens of different common names being used for the same plant. The eventual answer to such cognomen crises was the binomial system devised by the Swedish naturalist Carolus Linnaeus (1707–1778).

Thanks to Linnaeus, every plant now has a two-word name: a genus name (for the large group to which the plant belongs) and a species name (which distinguishes a plant from the others in its group, or genus). For example, the genus name for maples that grow in the wild—there are more than 150—is *Acer*, Latin for the maple tree. The species name of the sugar maple, one of the 150, is *saccharum*, which is Latin for sweet. So the botanical, or scientific, name for New England's arboreal icon is *Acer saccharum*. When botanical names are written, they appear in italics or are underlined, and the genus is capitalized.

Many plants have a third, or cultivar, name. The word "cultivar" comes from the term "cultivated variety," a plant bred or selected in cultivation. Cultivar names are capitalized and placed in single quotations. *Acer saccharum* 'Temple's Upright,' for example, has a columnar form, tall but only 15 feet wide. *Acer saccharum* 'Fairview' is nearly as broad as it is tall, while *Acer saccharum* 'Flax Mill Majesty' is an especially fast-growing sugar maple.

Don't turn your back on common names, which are wonderfully evocative, but to ensure you're buying what you think you're buying, use the complete botanical name: the genus, species, and any cultivar name. I'm the first to agree that remembering and pronouncing the botanical names isn't easy. If it's any comfort, remember that botanical names often are manufactured Latin, not the Latin they taught in high school. No one knows whether the Romans said ACE-er or AH-cer, or even a-CER. There are rules, of course, but what's important is that you get the maple tree you want.

While many of the plants listed in this book are familiar, many are not common fare. They won't be waiting for you at the local garden center. You may have to ask your nursery to find them, or to recommend another nursery or seed company where you can buy them. In addition to fine general nurseries, New England is rich with companies that specialize in groups of plants, such as conifers, or even a single species, such as tree peonies. The Yellow Pages list most of them, but if you're looking for unusual daylilies and there's no source in your area, check out the seed and plant companies listed in "The Mail-Order Garden" section of this book. Anything you want is only a postage stamp away.

A last word: Although hundreds of plants are mentioned in this book, many thousands more aren't included. It's not that they are less desirable or don't grow well in New England—they just didn't happen to be someone's favorite or fit the criteria for a particular list. As helpful as I hope these lists will be, they are only a place to begin.

BULBS

Few places in North America are more congenial to growing bulbs than New England. Not the tender species, of course. We can't leave freesias in the ground year-round. But hardy bulbs are as happy as clams in the slightly acid, good-draining soils on which most New England houses sit. All this shouldn't be a surprise, since many of the most popular hardy bulbs are native to northern hemisphere climates that are similar to ours.

> Safe in the earth they lie, serenely waiting;
> They never speak to north winds or to snow,
> Perfume and color in the dark creating,
> Fit for the sunlit world they will know.

Those lines are from the American poet Louise Driscoll, and how well they describe hardy bulbs. The term "bulb" is used loosely by most of us and includes a large number of plants, many of which are not true bulbs at all. Tulips and lilies are *true bulbs*, as are onions. They grow from an enlarged underground stem that is wrapped in modified leaves, or scales. True bulbs have pointed tops, another way to recognize them, and they multiply by dividing (which is something that doesn't work in math class).

Corms, which look like bulbs, are what you're handling when you purchase gladioli, crocuses, and winter aconites. Instead of dividing, as a bulb does, they form a new corm on top of the old one, which shrivels and dies, or they may produce cormels, or mini-corms, around the base of the new corm—another technique for multiplying. *Rhizomes* also are modified stems, but instead of sending shoots straight up from the top as bulbs do, they sprout mostly from the sides, spreading horizontally. Bearded iris and cannas grow from rhizomes. If you grow dahlias or caladiums, you're working with *tubers*, which are swollen roots that taper at each end.

New England gardeners are acquainted with the wonderful array of hardy spring bulbs, but what most of us haven't done is to take advantage of the summer- and fall-flowering bulbs that thrive in our region. Although some are too tender to survive winter, many of them, such as lilies, excel here. Non-hardy bulbous plants, such as dahlias, gladioli, cannas, and tuberous begonias, can be grown as annuals: set out in spring after the danger of frost is past, dug in autumn, stored indoors in a cool, dry place during the winter months, then replanted in spring.

If the prospect of digging and storing bulbs in autumn—at exactly the same time you're trying to save the last few tomatoes and pick the surviving basil and asters—is one task too many, do as I do and let them perish. Fortunately, many popular tender species are available from nurseries each spring; a six-pack of dahlias is only slightly more expensive than a six-pack of marigolds.

Hardy bulbs demand good drainage—soppy conditions are sure death—which is why they thrive when planted on hillsides and in raised beds. If you have good snowcover, or mulch heavily, and plant deep in a protected site that drains well, you may succeed with bulbs that are rated at least one hardiness zone less cold than yours. Lewis and Nancy Hill, Vermont gardeners and the authors of *Bulbs: Four Seasons of Beautiful Blooms* (1994), grow *Lycoris squamigera*, magic lily, in their Zone 3 garden, although most garden encyclopedias indicate it's hardy only to Zone 6.

For the best results, enrich your soil with compost or a complete organic fertilizer before you plant bulbs, and spread a layer of organic mulch over the planting. Bulbs usually come with recommended planting depths, but in case the instructions are missing, the general rule is to set bulbs so that their tops are two to three times as deep as their diameter, a little deeper in sandy soil, slightly less deep in heavy, clay soil. Tulips are the exception: Set them in holes that are between 6 and 8 inches deep.

Top dress bulbs with more compost or a balanced fertilizer in spring, but stay away from bonemeal, which attracts assorted wildlife and your neighbor's dog. Remove any seed pods—they siphon energy from the bulb—and let the foliage die back naturally after the flowers fade. Those leaves are pumping food into the bulb to produce next year's blooms.

NARCISSUS FOR NATURALIZING

Not as long-lived as peonies, perhaps, but narcissus—which are commonly called daffodils—are a close second when it comes to horticultural staying-power. Not only do they have built-in longevity—it's in the genes—but they are practically never troubled by disease and altogether uninteresting to rodents. When the experts talk about narcissus for naturalizing, they are referring to vigorous, tough species and cultivars that will survive and multiply year after year with little or no attention.

One caveat: Plant narcissus in well-drained soil.

The classes of flower forms—the terms in the second column of this list—were devised by the Royal Horticultural Society. Definitions of each class are usually provided in mail-order bulb catalogs, or see "Who's What?" on page 9 of this book.

NARCISSUS

Hardy to Zone 3	Flower form	Color
'Accent'	large-cupped	pink and white
'Actaea'	poeticus	white and red
'Arctic Gold'	trumpet	yellow
'Audubon'	small-cupped	white and pink
'Bell Song'	jonquilla	white and pink
'Bravoure'	trumpet	yellow and white
'Bridal Crown'	double	cream and saffron
'Bunting'	jonquilla	yellow and orange
'Camelot'	large-cupped	yellow
'Cantabile'	poeticus	white and red
'Ceylon'	large-cupped	red and yellow
'Meeting'	double	yellow
'Misty Glen'	large-cupped	white
'Pipit'	jonquilla	yellow
'Primeur'	trumpet	yellow
'Rijnveld's Early Sensation'	trumpet	yellow
'Saint Keverne'	large-cupped	yellow
'Sir Winston Churchill'	double	white and orange
Hoop petticoat (*N. bulbocodium*)	species	yellow
Tenby daffodil (*N. obvallaris*)	species	yellow
Pheasant's eye (*N. poeticus*)	species	white and red

Hardy to Zone 4

'Canarybird'	tazetta	yellow
'Hillstar'	jonquilla	yellow and white
'Ice Wings'	triandrus	white
'Lauren Koster'	tazetta	white and yellow
'Scarlet Gem'	tazetta	yellow and red

Who's What?

The experts know that all jonquils are narcissus, but not all narcissus are jonquils. Confused? It gets worse when the catalogs begin talking about tazettas and doubles and poet's narcissus. Fortunately for us, Britain's Royal Horticultural Society came to the rescue by dividing the genus into twelve groups, which are primarily based on the length and shape of the flower's corona, or tubular cup. In addition to the division names, other terms you may encounter include *bicolor* (the corona is one color, the petals another); *corolla* (a collective term for the petals); *perianth* (a collective term for the corona and corolla); and *reflexed* (the petals are backswept, or recurved). As for the term *daffodil*, it's the common name for any *Narcissus*.

Division I	trumpet daffodils: corona longer than the petals; one flower per stem.
Division II	large-cupped daffodils: corona more than one-third the length of the petals; one flower per stem.
Division III	small-cupped daffodils: corona not more than one-third the length of the petals; one flower per stem.
Division IV	double-flowered daffodils: twice as many petals and/or double corona; one or more flowers per stem.
Division V	triandrus daffodils: small, severely nodding blooms with reflexed petals; several flowers per stem.
Division VI	cyclamineus daffodils: extremely reflexed petals, like a cyclamen's; one flower per stem.
Division VII	jonquilla daffodils: small corona; fragrant; two to three flowers per stem.
Division VIII	tazetta daffodils: small corona; fragrant; four or more flowers per stem.
Division IX	poeticus daffodils: white petals with small, disc-shaped corona marked with red; fragrant; one flower per stem.
Division X	species and wild daffodils: forms found in the wild, usually with small flowers and short stems.
Division XI	split-corona daffodils: flat corona segmented, or split; one flower per stem; also known as butterfly daffodils.
Division XII	miscellaneous daffodils: daffodils not included in Divisions I to XI.

SMALL MIRACLES

Not everyone has five acres and room for "a host of golden daffodils," or even a minihost of golden daffodils. For gardeners with modest yards who still want to enjoy the blooms of hardy spring bulbs, this list provides a place to begin. (Some of these bulbs are hardy even to Zone 2.) Most of these plants only grow a foot or less and are delicately sized and shaped. Be sure they have good drainage, are planted in organically rich soil, and are kept weed-free and well-mulched in winter if your snowfall is meager. Although it's small, you may want to avoid star of Bethlehem (*Ornithogalum umbellatum*), a hardy, fragrant, greenish-white American native that spreads faster than gossip.

Leek lily (*Allium moly*)	3, 4, 5, 6
Windflower (*Anemone blanda* cvs.)	4/5, 6
Italian arum (*Arum italicum*)	5, 6
Glory of the snow (*Chionodoxa luciliae*)	3, 4, 5, 6
Crocus (*Crocus* spp. and cvs.)	3, 4, 5, 6
Winter aconite (*Eranthis hyemalis*)	3, 4, 5, 6
Yellow adder's tongue (*Erythronium americanum*)	2, 3, 4, 5, 6
Checkered lily (*Fritillaria meleagris*)	3, 4, 5, 6
Common snowdrop (*Galanthus nivalis* and cvs.)	3, 4, 5, 6
Spring starflower (*Ipheion uniflorum* and cvs.)	5, 6
Grape hyacinth (*Muscari* spp.)	3, 4, 5, 6
Striped squill (*Puschkinia scilloides*)	3, 4, 5, 6
Siberian squill (*Scilla siberica*)	2, 3, 4, 5, 6
Tulip (*Tulipa batalinii* cvs.)	5, 6
'Lilac Wonder' tulip (*Tulipa saxatilis*)	5, 6

SNOWDROP

HOW SWEET IT IS: FRAGRANT NARCISSUS

If take-your-breath-away beautiful isn't enough to satisfy you, you can add another sense to your spring garden by planting fragrant *Narcissus* cultivars. The flowers on this list will not only smell good, but they offer different colors and forms, everything from large-cupped daffodils to diminutive yellow jonquils. The classes of flower forms were devised by the Royal Horticultural Society; definitions of each class are usually listed in mail-order bulb catalogs, or see "Who's What?" on page 9. Be sure to plant at least two or three of these flowers near your house or a walkway, where you can enjoy their fragrance every day.

Hardy to Zone 3	Flower form	Color
'Actaea'	poeticus	white and red
'Big Gun'	large-cupped	white and orange-yellow
'Bridal Crown'	double	cream and saffron
'Cantabile'	poeticus	white and red
'Carlton'	large-cupped	yellow and orange/red
'Eastern Dawn'	large-cupped	apricot-pink
'Edna Earl'	small-cupped	white and yellow-orange
'Felindre'	poeticus	white, yellow and red
'Gigantic Star'	large-cupped	yellow
'Louise de Coligny'	large-cupped	white and yellow-pink
'Meeting'	double	yellow
'Milan'	poeticus	white, yellow and red
'Pipit'	jonquilla	yellow and white
'Sinopel'	small-cupped	white and lime green
'Sir Winston Churchill'	double	white and orange
'Sweet Charity'	large-cupped	cream and orange
'Yellow Cheerfulness'	double	yellow

Hardy to Zone 4		
'Abba'	double	white and orange
'Canarybird'	tazetta	yellow
'Cheerfulness'	double	white and yellow
'Falconet'	tazetta	yellow and red

'Geranium'	tazetta	white and orange
'Hillstar'	jonquilla	yellow and white
'Hoopoe'	tazetta	yellow and orange
'Ice Wings'	triandrus	white
'Mondragon'	split-corona	yellow and tangerine
'Petrel'	triandrus	white
'Sweetness'	jonquilla	yellow
'Trevithian'	jonquilla	yellow
'Tripartite'	split-corona	yellow

Hardy to Zone 5

'Buffawn'	jonquilla	yellow
'Canary'	jonquilla	yellow and white
'Fruit Cup'	jonquilla	white and yellow

PERENNIAL TULIPS

Long-lived" is a relative term when it comes to tulips, which are famous for being glorious in their first season, disappointing in their second, and missing in their third. Tulip breeding, which has focused on better color, size, and disease resistance, has meant that most cultivars are garden transients. Some have more staying-power than others, however, and usually are referred to as "perennial tulips" in bulb catalogs. Listed below are long-lived *Tulipa* cultivars recommended by the Netherlands Flower Bulb Information Center, all hardy to Zone 3 if given winter protection. But be warned: Even with a topdressing of compost each spring, long-lived probably means between three and five years.

'Kees Nelis'	'Oxford'
'Aladdin'	'Striped Apeldoorn'
'Maytime'	'Candela' (*T. fosteriana*)
'Red Shine'	'Orange Emperor' (*T. fosteriana*)
'White Triumphator'	'Purissima' (*T. fosteriana*)
'Apeldoorn's Elite'	'Red Emperor' (*T. fosteriana*)
'Beauty of Apeldoorn'	'Red Riding Hood' (*T. greigii*)
'Golden Apeldoorn'	'Toronto' (*T. greigii*)

 Despite being long-lived, many of our favorite bulbous plants are endangered, or threatened with extinction, because of over-collection and loss of habitat. Cultivated plants—those with a cultivar name, such as 'Red Riding Hood' tulip, or 'Connecticut King' lily—are in no danger. Buy cultivated bulbs and plant them with abandon—and with a clear conscience. It is species bulbs, usually small flowers, such as nodding trillium (*Trillium cernuum*) and winter aconite (*Eranthis hyemalis*), that are propagated in tiny numbers or not at all. Unless sellers will provide written verification of the origin of their stock, stick to bulbs with cultivar names. Be wary: "Nursery Grown" doesn't mean nursery propagated.

HEIRLOOM HYACINTHS

Dutch, or garden, hyacinths have a formal, old-fashioned look to them that correlates nicely with their long history. A favorite flower of Madame de Pompadour, they were cultivated well before the eighteenth century. In fact, Dutch breeders started breeding *Hyacinthus orientalis*, the parents of today's showy hybrids, in the late 1500s. If you're interested in heirloom flowers, in growing plants your great-grandparents knew and loved, this list is a good place to start. All these nineteenth-century hyacinths are hardy to Zone 4—even Zone 3 if you plant them in well-draining soil and mulch them in winter.

'Bismarck'	blue
'Chestnut Flower'	pink
'City of Haarlem'	yellow
'General Köhler'	blue
'L'Innocence'	white
'La Victoire'	magenta
'Lady Derby'	pink
'Lord Balfour'	dark violet

COLOR CHIC

According to the horticultural mavens of hues and tones, orange and purple are *au courant*. To keep your spring garden stylish, the Netherlands Flower Bulb Information Center, the U.S. representatives of the Dutch flower-bulb industry, recommends these brightly colored bulbs. All orange? All purple? Some of both? It's entirely up to you.

Orange Flowers

'The Premier' crown imperial fritillaria (*Fritillaria imperialis*)	5, 6
'Gipsy Queen' hyacinth (*Hyacinthus*)	4, 5, 6
'Ballerina' tulip (*Tulipa*)	3, 4, 5, 6
'Best Seller' tulip (*Tulipa*)	3, 4, 5, 6
'Little Princess' tulip (*Tulipa*)	3, 4, 5, 6
'Orange Emperor' tulip (*Tulipa*)	3, 4, 5, 6
'Orange Sun' tulip (*Tulipa*)	3, 4, 5, 6
'Prinses Irene' tulip (*Tulipa*)	3, 4, 5, 6

Purple Flowers

'Peter Stuyvesant' hyacinth (*Hyacinthus*)	4, 5, 6
'George' reticulata iris (*Iris reticulata*)	3, 4, 5, 6
Grape hyacinth (*Muscari latifolium*)	4, 5, 6
'Arabian Mystery' tulip (*Tulipa*)	3, 4, 5, 6
'Attila' tulip (*Tulipa*)	3, 4, 5, 6
'Black Parrot' tulip (*Tulipa*)	3, 4, 5, 6

TRUMPETING TRUMPET DAFFODILS

To most New England gardeners, the word "daffodil" means a trumpet daffodil, a member of that group of foot-tall plants with glorious all-yellow flowers. Most trumpet *Narcissus*, designated as Division I by England's Royal Horticultural Society, have one bloom per stem and are easily recognized by a long corona, or tubular "trumpet." 'King Alfred', which has been around more than 100 years, is still the very definition of Wordsworth's "golden host," but there is a huge number of other and better trumpet cultivars. The names on this list, if planted in organically rich, well-draining soil and given winter protection, are hardy to Zone 3.

'Arctic Gold'	yellow
'Bestseller'	yellow
'Bravoure'	yellow and white

'Dutch Master'	yellow
'Foresight'	white and yellow
'Golden Spur'	yellow
'Holland Sensation'	yellow and white
'Honeybird'	yellow
'Kassell's Gold'	yellow
'King Alfred'	yellow
'Las Vegas'	yellow and white
'Lemon Gold'	yellow
'Lumar Sea'	yellow and white
'Marieke'	yellow
'Mondoc'	yellow
'Mount Hood'	white
'Mrs. E. H. Krelage'	white and yellow
'New Generation'	yellow and white
'Primeur'	yellow
'Red Curtain'	yellow and red/orange
'Rijnveld's Early Sensation'	yellow
'Solo'	yellow
'Spellbinder'	yellow
'Tpopolino'	dwarf cream and yellow
'Unsurpassable'	yellow
'White Ideal'	white

WHERE HAVE ALL THE FLOWERS GONE?
If your daffodils don't bloom next spring, it is because:

- **you purchased "economy" bulbs (less than 1 and one-quarter inch in diameter) that are too small to bloom the first year**
- **you planted too deep or in soil that was too heavy and wet**
- **you planted too late in the year**
- **your site didn't get enough sun or water**
- **your soil lacked adequate nutrients**

SCENTS OF SPRING

Does not the scent of the primrose, the violet and the cowslip sometimes transport us to the banks and meads where we first found them," English vicar Samuel Reynolds Hole wrote more than 100 years ago. Hole could have added the giant snowdrop or the yellow fritillary to his list, although they and many other hardy spring bulbs aren't famous for their fragrance, as the violet is. Most names on this list are gently scented when brought indoors. The exception? Dutch hyacinths, which explode with sweetness.

Naples onion (*Allium neapolitanum*)	5, 6
Yellow fritillary (*Fritillaria pudica*)	2, 3, 4, 5, 6
Giant snowdrop (*Galanthus elwesii*)	3, 4, 5, 6
Common snowdrop (*Galanthus nivalis* and cvs.)	3, 4, 5, 6
Spanish bluebell (*Hyacinthoides hispanica*)	4, 5, 6
English bluebell (*Hyacinthoides non-scripta*)	4, 5, 6
Dutch hyacinth (*Hyacinthus orientalis* cvs.)	3, 4, 5, 6
Spring starflower (*Ipheion uniflorum* and cvs.)	5, 6

Iris (*Iris histrioides* cvs.)	5, 6
Grape hyacinth (*Muscari armeniacum* and cvs.)	4, 5, 6
'Album' grape hyacinth (*Muscari botryoides*)	3, 4, 5, 6
'Plumosum' tassel grape hyacinth (*Muscari comosum*)	4, 5, 6

NARCISSUS FOR AN OLD-FASHIONED GARDEN

If you want to replicate an old garden and are looking for historically appropriate *Narcissus*, this is the list for you. Be warned that not all of these cultivars are choice. 'Falaise', one of the first double narcissus, or daffodils, is described as "rather nondescript" by one critic. But many *are* choice, including 'King Alfred', which set the standard for yellow trumpet daffodils for decades and dates back to 1899.

These are suggestions from Scott Kunst, an heirloom-bulb specialist and owner of Old House Gardens, a mail-order nursery in Michigan. "Some people think *heirloom* means worn-out and boring," Scott notes, "but I know the past is full of spectacular, unusual bulbs for the ornamental garden. At least a few of them belong in every gardener's yard."

The classes of flower forms—the terms in the second column in this list—were devised by the Royal Horticultural Society. Definitions of each class are usually listed in mail-order bulb catalogs, or see "Who's What?" on page 9.

'Actaea'	poeticus	3, 4, 5, 6
'Butter and Eggs'	double	5, 6
'Carbineer'	small cup	4, 5, 6
'Carlton'	small cup	3, 4, 5, 6
'Falaise'	double	4, 5, 6
'Golden Spur'	trumpet	3, 4, 5, 6
'King Alfred'	trumpet	3, 4, 5, 6
'Queen of the North'	small cup	4, 5, 6
'Scarlet Gem'	tazetta	4, 5, 6
'W. P. Milner'	miniature trumpet	4, 5, 6
'Mount Hood'	trumpet	3, 4, 5, 6
'Seagull'	small cup	4, 5, 6

COLD-HARDY TULIPS

TULIP

Unlike narcissus, which can survive the worst of winters, tulips (*Tulipa*) aren't known for their cold-hardiness, although most cultivars do well throughout New England. For gardeners shivering in the coldest spots in our region, here are a group of mid- to late-season bloomers that will brighten spring in Zone 3 gardens, and possibly Zone 2 with good drainage and winter protection. Several tulip types are represented, including two of those wild-and-crazy parrot tulips. The list comes from hardiness trials carried out in Minnesota, another spot in the country that knows plenty about miserably cold weather.

'Black Parrot'	purple	3, 4, 5, 6
'Blue Parrot'	violet	3, 4, 5, 6
'Golden Harvest'	lemon yellow	3, 4, 5, 6
'Mme. Lefeber' 'Red Emperor'	fire-red	3, 4, 5, 6
'Mount Tacoma'	white	3, 4, 5, 6
'Queen of Night'	dark maroon	3, 4, 5, 6
Kolpakowskiana tulip (*T. kolpakowskiana*)	white and red	3, 4, 5, 6

'Fusilier' (*T. praestans*)	red	3, 4, 5, 6
Tarda tulip (*T. tarda*)	white and yellow	3, 4, 5, 6

SMALL SCENTS: FRAGRANT MINIATURE NARCISSUS

Need something pretty for the spring garden? Something small? Something fragrant? Any of the miniature *Narcissus* listed below will fit that bill, all Lilliputian blooms guaranteed to enchant. All are yellow except for 'New Baby', a bicolor yellow and white.

Take care when planting miniature daffodils—make sure you set them in a sunny, well-drained spot, one where they won't be overrun by more vigorous plants, and keep them weeded. Beyond that, they need no special care; treat them as you would any *Narcissus*. The classes of flower forms, the terms in the second column of this list, were devised by the Royal Horticultural Society; definitions of each class are usually listed in mail-order bulb catalogs, or see "Who's What?" on page 9.

'Baby Moon'	jonquilla	5, 6
'Chit Chat'	jonquilla	5, 6
'New Baby'	jonquilla	5, 6
'Pencrebar'	double	4, 5, 6
'Sun Disc'	jonquilla	4, 5, 6
'Sundial'	jonquilla	4, 5, 6

GETTING IT TOGETHER: BULB COMBINATIONS

Debbie Van Bourgondien—an eighth-generation member of the Van Bourgondien nursery family—plants thousands of bulbs every year. (Hey, she gets them free!) Almost all hardy spring bulb species do better in New England than anywhere else in the country, she says, so we Yankees can concentrate on finding cultivars that combine effectively in the garden. Among her favorite combinations are these four; all of the cultivars are hardy to Zone 3.

A Sunny Combination:
'Orange Emperor' tulip (*Tulipa*)	orange
'Fortissimo' narcissus (*Narcissus*)	yellow and orange
'Barrett Browning' narcissus (*Narcissus*)	white and orange/red

Bordered by:
'Blue Spike' grape hyacinth (*Muscari armeniacum*)	blue

A Pastel Garden:
'Angélique' tulip (*Tulipa*)	pink
'Palmares' narcissus (*Narcissus*)	white and pink

Bordered by:
'Blue Spike' grape hyacinth (*Muscari armeniacum*)	blue

An Early Flowering Combination:
'February Gold' narcissus (*Narcissus*)	yellow

Bordered by:
'Fusilier' tulip (*Tulipa praestans*)	red

A White Garden:
'Ice Follies' narcissus (*Narcissus*)
'Mount Hood' narcissus (*Narcissus*)
'White Emperor' tulip (*Tulipa*)

Bordered by:
'Carnegie' hyacinth (*Hyacinthus orientalis*)

"Ferns—especially Christmas fern, lady fern, and maidenhair fern—make wonderful companions for hardy spring bulbs and lilies in garden beds and borders. And if you garden in an especially cold location, you can convince some of your bulbs to flower early by planting them in a sunny, protected spot."
Lewis Hill, garden writer, Greensboro, Vermont

SPRING'S SHADY CHARACTERS

Almost no hardy flowering plants thrive in full shade, but many flowers can be grown in dappled light. Kathy Bond Borie, who gardens in Richmond, Vermont, likes to plant small spring bulbs under deciduous trees, because they are up and blooming before the tree leaves appear, then are perfectly happy to ripen their foliage in shady conditions. Bond Borie, who is a staff member at the National Gardening Association, warns against planting bulbs beneath shallow-rooted trees and shrubs "that will hog the nutrients and moisture in the soil."

Windflower (*Anemone blanda*)	4/5, 6
'Alba' wood anemone (*Anemone nemorosa*)	5, 6
Anemone (*Anemone ranunculiodes*)	5, 6
Arum (*Arum italicum*)	5, 6
Glory of the snow (*Chionodoxa luciliae*)	3, 4, 5, 6
Snow crocus (*Crocus chrysanthus*)	3, 4, 5, 6
Winter aconite (*Eranthis hyemalis*)	3, 4, 5, 6
Yellow adder's tongue (*Erythronium americanum*)	2, 3, 4, 5, 6
European dog's-tooth violet (*Erythronium dens-cansis*)	3, 4, 5, 6
Giant snowdrop (*Galanthus elwesii*)	3, 4, 5, 6
Common snowdrop (*Galanthus nivalis* and cvs.)	3, 4, 5, 6
Spanish bluebell (*Hyacinthoides hispanica*)	4, 5, 6
English bluebell (*Hyacinthoides non-scripta*)	4, 5, 6
Siberian squill (*Scilla siberica*)	2, 3, 4, 5, 6

THE ROSE OF ROOTS: ORNAMENTAL ALLIUMS

Not all onions belong in the vegetable garden—and even some of those traditionally grown in the vegetable garden also deserve to be planted in ornamental beds and borders. Hardy alliums are pest-free, dependable, and underappreciated bulbs that bloom in late spring and summer. Many have globelike flowers, with colors ranging from pale pink to deep purple as well as white and yellow; plant heights range from 6 inches to 3 feet. Nearly all species prefer a sunny, well-drained location, but check the calendar before you plant: According to a South American legend, alliums set out on Good Friday won't grow.

ALLIUM

'Purple Sensation' ornamental garlic (*Allium aflatunense*)	purple	4, 5, 6
Wild leek (*Allium ampeloprasum*)	white, pink, rose	3, 4, 5, 6
Blue globe onion (*Allium caeruleum*)	blue	3, 4, 5, 6
Lady's leek (*Allium cernuum*)	pink	3, 4, 5, 6
Stars of Persia (*Allium cristophii*)	lavender	5, 6
Nodding onion (*Allium cyathophorum* var. *farreri*)	reddish-purple	3, 4, 5, 6
Welsh onion (*Allium fistulosum*)	cream	2, 3, 4, 5, 6
'Globemaster' giant allium (*Allium giganteum*)	purple-violet	3/4, 5, 6
Leek lily (*Allium moly*)	yellow	
Naples onion (*Allium neapolitanum*)	white	5, 6
Allium nutans	rose	2, 3, 4, 5, 6
Allium oreophilum	purple-pink	3/4, 5, 6
Allium paniculatum	white	2, 3, 4, 5, 6
Rosenback onion (*Allium rosenbachianum*)	rose-purple	4, 5, 6
Common garden chive (*Allium schoenoprasum*)	purple, pink	2, 3, 4, 5, 6
Allium schubertii	pink	4/5, 6
Drumstick allium (*Allium sphaerocephalon*)	purple-maroon	3, 4, 5, 6

A (WHITE) HOST OF DAFFODILS

A garden of white daffodils? Yes, with apologies to Wordsworth and a bow to Englishwoman Vita Sackville-West, who popularized creating a white garden. You don't have to copy Sackville-West's garden conceit, a bed of nothing but white daffodils; instead, scatter these white bloomers throughout your garden to accent other colors. The classes of flower forms—the terms in the second column—were devised by the Royal Horticultural Society; definitions of each class are usually listed in mail-order bulb catalogs, or see "Who's What?" on page 9.

'Beersheba'	trumpet	3, 4, 5, 6
'Cool Crystal'	small-cupped	3, 4, 5, 6
'Easter Moon'	large-cupped	3, 4, 5, 6
'Empress of Ireland'	trumpet	3, 4, 5, 6
'Gay Song'	double	3, 4, 5, 6
'Ice Wings'	triandrus	4, 5, 6
'Jenny'	cyclamineus	4, 5, 6
'Misty Glen'	large-cupped	3, 4, 5, 6
'Mount Hood'	trumpet	3, 4, 5, 6
'Obdam'	double	3, 4, 5, 6
'Stainless'	large-cupped	3, 4, 5, 6
'Thalia'	triandrus	3, 4, 5, 6
'Tracey'	cyclamineus	4, 5, 6
'Tresamble'	triandrus	3, 4, 5, 6
'White Ideal'	trumpet	3, 4, 5, 6
'White Plume'	large-cupped	3, 4, 5, 6

RODENT RESISTANT

New England gardeners are all too familiar with woodchucks, mice, and other underground wildlife dining on their garden plants. Moles, by the way, are innocent. They're carnivores, unlike their vole cousins who are vegetarians *par excellence*. No one will go so far as to say that these are plants that rodents *never* munch, but these will be the absolutely last bulbous plants to attract the underground crowd. They'll be around long after the tulips and lilies are toast.

Allium (*Allium* spp.)	3, 4, 5, 6
Lily-of-the-valley (*Convallaria majalis*)	3, 4, 5, 6
Winter aconite (*Eranthis hyemalis*)	3, 4, 5, 6
Fritillary (*Fritillaria* spp.)	3, 4, 5, 6
Snowdrop (*Galanthus* spp.)	3, 4, 5, 6
Hyacinth (*Hyacinthus* spp.)	4, 5, 6
Narcissus/daffodil (*Narcissus* cvs.)	3, 4, 5, 6
Siberian squill (*Scilla siberica*)	2, 3, 4, 5, 6

Too Tender to Survive New England Winters

Lily-of-the-Nile (*Agapanthus africanus*)	Dahlia (*Dahlia* cvs.)
Poppy anemone (*Anemone coronaria*)	Gladiolus (*Gladiolus* cvs.)
Canna (*Canna* cvs.)	Persian buttercup (*Ranunculus asiaticus*)

"To discourage voles from lunching on your tulip bulbs, drop a mothball into each planting hole."
Kathy Bond Borie, editor, National Gardening Association, Richmond, Vermont

FRAGRANT PEACOCKS: ADDING SCENT TO THE TULIP GARDEN

Tulips (*Tulipa*), often called the "peacocks and parrots" of flowering spring bulbs, aren't famous for fragrance. Yet some cultivars, including those listed below, are nicely scented. All are hardy to Zone 3 if protected in winter by snowcover or a generous layer of organic mulch. Tulips have been classified into fifteen groups by bulb growers. The term in the second column of this list is the group to which the cultivar belongs. You can find definitions of the groups in most mail-order bulb catalogs, or in garden books, such as *Bulbs: Four Seasons of Beautiful Bloomers* (1994) by Vermonters Lewis and Nancy Hill.

'Abba'	double early	red
'Apricot Beauty'	single early	salmon
'Ballerina'	lily-flowering	red, yellow and orange
'Beauty Queen'	single early	salmon
'Bellona'	triumph	yellow
'Couleur Cardinal'	triumph	scarlet/plum
'Daydream'	Darwin hybrid	yellow-orange
'Dillenburg'	single late	terra-cotta
'Electra'	double early	rose-pink
'Generaal de Wet'	single early	orange and yellow
'Holland's Glory'	Darwin hybrid	orange-red
'Monsella'	double early	yellow and red
'Monte Carlo'	double early	yellow
'Oranjezon'	Darwin hybrid	orange
'Prince of Austria'	single early	red

'Prinses Irene'	triumph	orange and purple
'Salmon Pearl'	triumph	rose-coral and gold
'Schoonoord'	double early	white
'Silverstream'	Darwin hybrid	creamy yellow
'Vivex'	Darwin hybrid	carmine rose

RESORTING TO FORCE: NARCISSUS FOR WINTER BLOOM

Blooms in winter are spirit-lifters in New England, reminders that spring will come. Brent and Becky Heath, who grow hundreds of different *Narcissus* at their retail nursery, Brent and Becky's Bulbs, recommend these cultivars for forcing in their book *Daffodils for American Gardens* (1995). All these *Narcissus*, unlike the tender paper-white (*Narcissus papyraceus*), can be transplanted to the garden after they flower or when the ground thaws. 'Abba' and 'Bridal Crown' are fragrant. The classes of flower forms, the terms in the second column of this list, were devised by the Royal Horticultural Society; definitions of each class are usually listed in mail-order bulb catalogs, or see "Who's What?" on page 9.

Hardy to Zone 3

'Bridal Crown'	double	cream and saffron
'Ice Follies'	large-cupped	white and yellow
'Johann Strauss'	large-cupped	white and orange
'Pipit'	jonquilla	yellow and white
'Rijnveld's Early Sensation'	trumpet	yellow
Tenby daffodil	species	yellow

Hardy to Zone 4

'Abba'	double	white and orange
'Garden Princess'	cyclamineus	yellow
'Jumblie'	miniature	yellow and orange
'Little Beauty'	miniature trumpet	white and yellow
'Little Gem'	miniature trumpet	yellow
'Tête-à-Tête'	miniature miscellaneous	yellow and orange
'W. P. Milner'	miniature trumpet	cream

Gardeners refer to it as "forcing," but coaxing is a more friendly term. In either case, the aim is to control the bloom time of a plant. Most New Englanders are familiar with paper whites, but they aren't the only bulbs that we can get to flower before the snow melts. To trick hardy spring bulbs, pot them up in a moist soil mix in fall, and store them for at least twelve weeks in a cold place (between 35 and 40 degrees F). Then bring them out of storage and set them in a cool place (60-65 degrees F) in bright light. Once the flower buds appear, move the pot out of direct sunlight to extend the blooming period.

FAVORITE LILIES FROM A VERMONT NURSERY

This list of LA lilies comes from George and Gail Africa, who run the Vermont Flower Farm in Marshfield, Vermont. LA lilies aren't botanical refugees from California; they are a new group of hybrids, offspring from crossing *Lilium longiflorum* and Asiatic lilies. These handsome, sweet-smelling children have the best traits of both parents: showy, upfacing blooms, fine fragrance, good hardiness, and glorious colors.

LA hybrids bloom in late summer, are strong growers, 3 feet or taller, and show good resistance to diseases. According to the Africas, they are extremely hardy, perfect for New England gardens, even those in Zone 3.

'Best-Seller'	apricot
'Club House'	cantaloupe
'Dream'	pink
'Royal Highness'	peach
'Science Fiction'	red-maroon
'Twilight Life'	rose-purple

George Africa and his wife Gail own the Vermont Flower Farm. "I keep it simple with visitors and customers new to LA lilies," George explains, "and say they are the result of longiflorums, the Easter Lily type, crossed with the colors of the Asiatics. Among my favorites is 'Science Fiction'. When I first grew it, I walked by it for days trying to place the fragrance. I finally settled at the smell of little red cinnamon heart candies. I also like especially the Oriental 'Scheherazade'. Many in the lily organizations don't care for it because it is somewhat down-facing, but one we have growing by the back door is 6 feet tall and has 16 blooms."

BEARDED LADIES: TALL IRIS FOR NEW ENGLAND GARDENS

Bearded iris, which grow from rhizomes, aren't as popular with garden designers as they used to be, but they're still popular with gardeners. The most difficult thing about growing these glorious flowers is knowing where to start. (From a financial perspective, it's knowing where to stop!) There are tens of thousands of cultivars, including blends, bitones, plicatas, variegatas, and more. This short list, selected from favorite tall cultivars (35 to 40 inches) singled out by members of the American Iris Society, is a starting place.

Depending on where you live, "early" cultivars can begin flowering in May, and "late" cultivars may wait until July 1 to bloom. For most of us, however, June is iris month.

All of the iris in this list are hardy to Zone 3. A note to New England gardeners living in the coldest parts of our region: Iris with dark-colored flowers tend to be more hardy than cultivars with light blooms.

Iris	Bloom period	Color
'Before the Storm'	midseason	black
'Beverly Sills'	midseason	coral pink
'Dusky Challenger'	late	dark purple
'Going My Way'	midseason	purple
'Honky Tonk Blues'	midseason	blue and white
'Hot Fudge'	midseason	burgundy and yellow
'Joyce Terry'	midseason	yellow/white falls
'Laced Cotton'	late	white
'Mary Frances'	midseason	blue
'Superstition'	midseason	black
'Thornbird'	midseason	tan
'Titan's Glory'	midseason	dark violet
'Vanity'	early	pink
'Victoria Falls'	midseason	blue

The late Josephine Nuese gardened in Connecticut. Her classic book *The Country Garden* (1970) is a goldmine of reliable information for New England gardeners. About bearded iris she writes that they like light soil enriched with bone meal. "And it is easy to remember how deeply to plant if you keep in mind the old as-a-duck-swims rule. This means that the top of the rhizome should ride just above ground level."

COLD COMFORT: ASIATIC LILIES

Classed by the American and British lily societies in Division I, Asiatic lilies (*Lilium*) are a godsend to northern gardeners. They bloom in summer and do best in well-drained sites that receive plenty of sun. There are Asiatic lilies with downward- and outward-facing flowers, but the blooms of these relatively new cultivars face upward. All grow about 3 feet tall and, according to Nigel Strohman, owner of The Lily Nook, all are hardy to Zone 2. Typically available for purchase in the fall, these cold-tolerant beauties have everything but fragrance.

'Adelina'	yellow and gold
'America'	burgundy rose
'Antarctica'	white
'Compass'	melon orange
'Grand Cru'	yellow with red center
'Malta'	lavender pink
'Menton'	peach
'Monte Negro'	dark red
'Pulsar'	white
'Shiraz'	pink
'Tangerine'	orange
'Windsong'	wine and gold bicolor

Ellen Gallager lives in the far northern White Mountains, the region of New Hampshire known as The Great North Woods. "Although I grow many hybrids in my garden, the species lilies have become my favorites. And *Lilium cernuum* is my absolute favorite. It is a small, early downfacing vibrant pink that blooms well before any other lily. It tends to rot easily in wet soil, so make sure that it is planted in exceptionally well-drained location."

MADE IN JAPAN: *IRIS JAPONICA*

According to Jody Camille, who runs Mountain River Flower Farm *waaay* up north in West Dummer, New Hampshire, Japanese iris (*Iris*) are still under-appreciated by gardeners despite their "stunning flattened, beardless flowers, elegant foliage, and suitability to New England, even in its coldest parts." Japanese iris are also versatile and can be planted singly or in masses; choose among the landscaping cultivars if you're going to plant by the dozen.

Camille is engaged in an ongoing hybridization program with Currier McEwen, an international authority on the species, to grow cultivars hardy enough for northern zones. For early flowers, her favorite is 'Sapphire Star', a red and blue-lavender cultivar; to close the Japanese iris season, plant 'August Emperor', which is red-violet with blue shading. While we're waiting for her new cultivars, Camille recommends these iris for fellow Yankees. All are hardy to Zone 3.

Landscaping Cultivars

'Acclaim'	red-violet with blue shading
'Accountable'	white with red-violet splashes
'Azure Perfection'	red-violet
'Sapphire Star'	bicolor red and blue-lavender

Blue and Purple Cultivars

'Evening Episode'	dark lavender-blue
'Mist Falls'	lavender-blue with white sanding
'Summer Storm'	dark purple

White Cultivars

'Frilled Enchantment'	white with narrow rose edge
'Prairie Edge'	white with red-violet edges
'Snowy Hills'	white
'White Parachute'	white

Red Cultivars

'Acclaim'	red
'Crystal Halo'	red
'Raspberry Gem'	red

Veined Cultivars

'Beni Tsubaki'	red-violet with white veining
'Caprician Butterfly'	white with blue-purple veining
'Mai Oji'	blue with white veining
'Ruffled Dimity'	dark blue veining

According to legend, Iris, whose rainbow bridge connected heaven and earth, was in such a rush to claim her reward—a flower bearing her name—from Zeus's wife Hera, she left a few drops in the vial as she hurriedly poured the magic potion creating the iris flower on earth. That's why there is no true red iris.

ORIENTAL SHADES AND SCENTS: MORE LILIES FOR NEW ENGLAND GARDENS

Oriental lilies (*Lilium*) produce some of the world's most spectacular flowers. Their huge blooms appear in late summer and perfume the air with powerful fragrances. This baker's half-dozen of favorites comes from George and Gail Africa, who run a retail nursery, Vermont Flower Farm, in Marshfield, Vermont. 'Acapulco', George notes, is even more show-stopping when planted near purple flowers, such as gayfeather (*Liatris* spp.) and coneflowers (*Echinacea purpurea*). Technically, 'Black Beauty' and 'Scheherazade' are part of a new group of lilies called orienpets, crosses between trumpets, aurelians, and orientals.

All are hardy to Zone 4. If the snow isn't several feet deep in your garden in winter, be sure to give all these lilies good protection in winter.

'Acapulco'	rose-pink
'Black Beauty'	crimson

LILY

'Cascade'	white and rose
'Journey's End'	rose-red
'Marco Polo'	pink
'Scheherazade'	burgundy andwhite
'White Stargazer'	white

 "Lilies are surprisingly cold hardy. We haven't had any problems with Vermont winters despite what some journals say. Trumpets seem to do better in raised beds, and all lilies need to avoid wet spots."
George Africa, owner, Vermont Flower Farm, Marshfield, Vermont

GLAD TIDINGS

Gary Adams runs a retail and mail-order nursery in Agawam, Massachusetts, Pleasant Valley Glads. He's been in the business of growing and selling gladioli (*Gladiolus*)—and dahlias and tuberoses—for more than forty years. He also sells cut flowers, if you're in the neighborhood.

The glads in this list are recently bred cultivars that Adams recommends you add to your garden. Give them full sun and well-drained, organically rich soil—and change their location each year to discourage disease and pest problems. Gladioli, remember, are not hardy in New England; dig the corms in autumn and store in a cool, dark place indoors until it's safe to replant in spring.

'Becky's Beauty'	light red
'Jennis's Joy'	black
'Light Light'	orange and yellow
'Mileesh'	ruffled tan
'Ornament'	ruffled black-red
'Peachy Keen'	ruffled salmon and gold
'Redheat'	ruffled red
'Regal Robe'	ruffled purple
'Ruth Ann'	ruffled white
'Wild Thing'	ruffled two-tone rose

CANNAS AND DAHLIAS: GHOSTS OF SUMMERS PAST

You don't have to live in a three-story, eighteen-room Victorian house to plant these summer-flowering heirloom cannas and dahlias, cultivars that were popular in gardens around 1900. Alas, all these flowers are tender, unable to survive a winter in New England—they will come back next year, but only if you dig them in autumn and store them in a cool, dark location until spring. These are recommendations from Scott Kunst, the proprietor of Old House Gardens, a Michigan mail-order nursery specializing in heirloom bulbs.

Canna

'Florence Vaughan'	yellow and orange
'Königen Charlotte'	red and yellow
'Prince Charmant'	pink
'Richard Wallace'	yellow
'Roi Humbert'	scarlet

Dahlia

'Betty Anne'	pink
'Bishop of Llandaff'	scarlet

'Mary Munns'	deep lavender
'Stolz von Berlin'	lavender-rose
'Thomas A. Edison'	deep purple
'Yellow Gem'	yellow

GLAD TO BE FIRST: EARLY FLOWERING GLADIOLI

Gladioli (*Gladiolus*) often are dismissed as being too stiff and formal to fit well in beds and borders, even dismissed as "lower class" by hoi-polloi gardeners. Yet few flowers are better suited for the vase, and gladioli also look great in the garden if well placed. The familiar hybrids—which bloom in every color except true blue—are not hardy in New England, but you can plant early flowering cultivars like the ones on this list in spring for cutting in about seventy-five days. To have blooms next year, dig the corms in late fall, allow them to dry, and store in a dark, cool, dry place for replanting next spring.

'Apache'	smoky and cream
'Atlantis'	deep blue with white throat
'Aubrey Lane'	two-tone yellow
'Black Stone'	black red
'Brown Beauty'	chocolate brown
'Bull's Eye'	yellow with red blotch
'Early Shirley'	salmon pink with white blotch
'First Snow'	white
'Gold Struck'	golden yellow
'High Seas'	lavender-blue with white throat
'Lavender Spire'	light blue with white throat
'Nate'	rose with rose and white blotch
'Ornament'	black-red
'Picasso'	rosy purple
'Plum Tart'	purple
'Pretty Woman'	orange with yellow center
'Redcoat'	red with white
'Repartee'	white with red throat blotch
'Scarlet Fever'	red
'Stormy Moon'	smoky with salmon throat
'Trinket'	white with yellow blotch
'White Ice'	white

"When bulbs arrive too late to plant outdoors, you can often salvage them by potting them close together in deep flats and storing them in a root cellar or cold frame until spring. Or try what one of our friends did with her tulip bulbs—put them in a paper bag and store them in an unheated garage. In early spring, soak them overnight in water and plant outdoors as soon as the ground can be worked. They may not flower the first year, but they should be back on schedule their second season in the garden."
Lewis and Nancy Hill, garden authors, Greensboro, Vermont

DAHLIA MANIA

Dahlias (*Dahlia*) are a little like potato chips: It's hard to stop after just one. In fact, it's hard to stop after a couple dozen—just ask Gary Adams, who runs Pleasant Valley Glads, a retail and mail-order nursery in Agawam, Massachusetts, that sells dahlias and tuberoses as well as gladioli. Adams grows all forms of dahlias, including formal decoratives, informal decoratives, cactuses, semi-cactuses, waterlilies, incurves, and more. There are cultivars with blooms the size of dinner plates all the way down to miniatures. The cultivars on this list have sensible-sized flowers, 4 inches or less in diameter, and fit beautifully in perennial beds and borders. Be sure to remove spent blooms to keep your plants flowering until the first frost.

DAHLIA

'All Triumph'	white semi-cactus
'Alpen Buttercup'	yellow formal decorative
'Barbarry Symbol'	red formal decorative
'Blended Beauty'	dark red and white cactus
'Brookside J. Cooley'	yellow informal decorative
'Buffie G'	apricot-peach formal decorative
'Hockley Nymph'	white informal decorative
'Mary Jo'	pink semi-cactus
'Pineapple Lollipop'	yellow formal decorative
'Prom Queen'	white and lavender informal decorative

LATE BLOOMERS

When New England gardeners think of bulbs, they think of spring, of brightly colored crocuses, daffodils, tulips, and more. Fall is the time to plant bulbs, not to enjoy their blooms. Surprise, surprise! There is a basketful of bulbous plants that flower in late summer and fall, hardy gems that give the term "late bloomer" new meaning. Planting times vary—bulbs will be available at nurseries and through the mail at the right time—but be sure to mark where you plant. Most autumn-flowering bulbs sprout in spring and then die back. They reappear, often without leaves, when it's time to bloom, so it's fitting that some carry common names like naked lady and magic lily.

Magic lily (*Amaryllis belladonna*)	3/4, 5, 6
'Autumn Queen' meadow saffron (*Colchicum*)	3, 4, 5, 6
Meadow saffron (*Colchicum autumnale* and cvs.)	4, 5, 6
Autumn crocus (*Colchicum byzantinum*)	4, 5, 6
Showy autumn crocus (*Colchicum speciosum* and cvs.)	4, 5, 6
Saffron crocus (*Crocus sativus*)	5, 6
Autumn snowflake (*Leucojum autumnale*)	5, 6
Resurrection lily/naked lady (*Lycoris squamigera*)	4, 5, 6
Magic lily (*Lycoris squamigera*)	3/4, 5, 6

ANNUALS, BIENNIALS, AND TENDER PERENNIALS

Like many terrific things in this world, annual flowers don't get nearly enough respect. Nor do biennials and tender perennials. Annuals, in particular, are relegated to the role of "fillers," stopgap sources of color while the ever-praised perennials laze their way into bloom. Yet there are annual flowers for every taste: refined hues and bold, ground-huggers and skyscrapers, huge blooms and small. There are plants for dry spots and damp, for large spaces and small, for sun and for partial shade.

Their uses are as diverse as the flowers themselves. Easiest to plant is a tidy edging of a single flower—lobelia, say—or an eye-catching patch of fire-engine-red salvia fronting a stone wall. Or an equally bold bed of zinnias, cultivars ranging from pink and rose to crimson. Or perhaps a row of larkspur, tucked between the pole beans and the tomatoes, sown just for cutting.

Slightly more complicated are borders and beds filled with many kinds of annuals. What about a white garden filled with baby's breath, candytuft, cosmos, nicotiana, petunias, spider flowers, and zinnias, an annual version of the perennial icon made famous by Englishwoman Vita Sackville-West? Or a fragrant garden crowded with dianthus, evening stocks, evening primroses, four o'clocks, heliotropes, mignonettes, and sweet alyssum? Or a garden for winter bouquets, planted with bells of Ireland, cockscomb, globe amaranth, statice, and strawflowers? Annuals are also model residents for containers—window boxes, pots, planters, and hanging baskets.

The perennial-touting garden books are correct, of course: Annuals *are* superb for filling holes between permanent plantings and for adding color when perennial borders and rock gardens are "between." They may be used in designs that are either doggedly formal or entirely casual.

For the gardener, there are advantages to growing annuals, plants that take care of business in one growing season. They race at breakneck speed to flower; some, such as marigolds, bloom about ten weeks from germination. Most flower freely and ceaselessly, far longer than most perennials, and many boast superb foliage.

Annuals are mostly disease- and pest-free, easy to cultivate, and inexpensive, too: A single plant of the latest daylily, fresh from the breeder, may cost $75 or more, whereas a seed packet of the new marigold runs around $2—and the packet contains fifty seeds.

Most annuals prefer average, near-neutral soil that is well drained and only moderately fertile. A few species like damp conditions, but far more flourish in dry locations. Above all, go easy on fertilizer. Some flowers, such as portulaca, thrive only in relatively infertile conditions—what gardeners call "lean" soil—and most annuals respond to heavy doses of nitrogen-rich fertilizer by producing oversize leaves and precious few blooms.

To keep your flowers blooming, be sure to deadhead (remove the spent blossoms). Or you may want to let a few cultivars go to seed and collect them for next year's garden. If the plants aren't hybrids, their seeds will produce blooms exactly like the ones you've been enjoying. Annuals, it turns out, *can* last longer than a year.

Biennials and tender perennials do last longer than a year, but only if you can provide the conditions they need. Specifically, biennials, such as pansies, stock, and hollyhock, last two years: during their first season they produce leaves, then overwinter, and in their second season they produce flowers, set seeds, and die. That schedule is problematic for many gardeners, especially those with small plots and no space to waste on plants that won't flower for another eighteen months.

The secret to "annualizing" biennials is to sow seeds every year so that some plants in your garden are always in their second season. Commercial breeders are working to shorten the time it takes biennials to produce their first blooms. 'Foxy', a *Digitalis purpurea* cultivar, is one of their successes. Rather than 365 days, it takes 150 days to produce its first flowers, then reblooms the following year.

Tender perennials, such as impatiens, coleus, and zonal geraniums, last indefinitely where the temperatures never sink near or below freezing—or if you move your plants indoors in winter. That's too much trouble for most of us, as is sowing their seeds indoors many months before the last spring frost. Fortunately, commercial flower producers provide nurseries and garden centers with truckloads of tender perennials each spring, which allows New England gardeners to grow them as if they were annuals.

Since annuals live only one season, and biennials and tender perennials are normally handled by northeastern gardeners as annuals, no hardiness zone ratings are included in this chapter.

ANNUALS THAT DON'T LIKE THE HEAT

While many of the most common annual flowers are heat lovers, there are also species that thrive in the cooler conditions that New England summers often offer, especially at higher elevations and in the far northern parts of our region. Here are a few of the choice flowers—annuals, biennials, and tender perennials grown as annuals—for gardeners who live where air conditioners are as rare as robins in December.

Snapdragon (*Antirrhinum majus*)
Pot marigold (*Calendula officinalis*)
Rocky Mountain garland (*Clarkia elegans*)
Pinks (*Dianthus chinensis*)
Sweet pea (*Lathyrus odoratus*)
Honesty/money plant (*Lunaria annua*)
Common stock/gilly flower (*Matthiola incana*)
Nemesia (*Nemesia strumosa*)
Flowering tobacco (*Nicotiana alata*)
Love-in-a-mist (*Nigella damascena*)
Iceland poppy (*Papaver nudicaule*)
Shirley poppy/Flanders Field poppy (*Papaver rhoeas*)
Painted tongue (*Salpiglossis sinuata*)
Pincushion flower (*Scabiosa atropurpurea*)
Poor man's orchid (*Schizanthus wisetonensis*)
Pansy (*Viola wittrockiana*)

SNAPDRAGON

BACKGROUND MUSIC: TALL PLANTS FOR BEDS AND BORDERS

Tall annuals and biennials are essential in beds and borders. They not only form attractive backdrops, they shelter smaller neighbors from sun and wind. Tall plants sown in rows can create boundaries; grouped, they can obscure eyesores. Like many flowers, tall species are most effective when planted in large, informal displays, but even a single hollyhock is eye-catching. The plants in this list vary in height, reaching 3 feet and up. For skyscraping height, add sunflowers, *Helianthus annuus*, to your garden—'Russian Giant' grows 12 feet and higher. (See the Sunflower Sampler in this chapter.)

Hollyhock (*Alcea rosea*)	4–6 feet
Joseph's coat (*Amaranthus tricolor*)	3–4 feet
Bishop's flower/false Queen Anne's lace (*Ammi majus*)	3 feet
Rose mallow (*Anisodontea hypomandarum*)	3–5 feet
Sweet Annie (*Artemisia annua*)	2–5 feet
Angel's trumpet/datura (*Brugmansia aurea*)	5–10 feet
Wheat celosia (*Celosia spicata*)	3 feet
Basket flower (*Centaurea americana* 'Aloha')	3–5 feet
Plumed thistle (*Cirsium japonicum*)	3–5 feet
Spider flower (*Cleome hassleriana*)	3–6 feet
Larkspur (*Consolida ajacis*)	3–4 feet
Cosmos (*Cosmos bipinnatus*)	3–5 feet
Yellow cosmos (*Cosmos sulphureus*)	3–5 feet
Common foxglove (*Digitalis purpurea* 'Gloxinioides')	3–4 feet
Snow-on-the-mountain/ghost weed (*Euphorbia marginata*)	3 feet
Annual mallow (*Lavatera trimestris* 'Loveliness')	3–4 feet
Hartweg lupine (*Lupinus hartwegii*)	3 feet
Flowering tobacco (*Nicotiana sylvestris*)	3–5 feet
Evening primrose (*Oenothera biennis*)	3–5 feet
Scotch thistle (*Onopordum acanthium*)	3–9 feet
Opium poppy (*Papaver somniferum*)	3–4 feet
Purple hedge (*Perilla frutescens*)	3 feet
Prince's feather (*Persicaria orientale*)	3–5 feet
Cape fuchsia (*Phygelius rectus*)	3–5 feet
Castor bean (*Ricinus communis*)	5–10 feet
Mexican sunflower (*Tithonia rotundifolia*)	3–5 feet
Turkish mullein (*Verbascum bombyciferum*)	5–8 feet
Verbena (*Verbena bonariensis*)	3–5 feet

Annuals "are *carpe diem* plants, prepared to seize and make the most of their short day ... the result is an abundance of flower rivaled in the plant kingdom only by forest trees, and a length of blooming time more extensive than almost any perennial can boast."
Wayne Winterrowd, Vermont gardener and author of *Annuals for Connoisseurs* (1992)

SUNFLOWER SAMPLER

The sunflower is chic these days, a far cry from the opinion of English garden writer Alice Morse Earle, who noted a century ago that it "was never a garden flower in olden times, in the sense of being a flower or ornament or beauty." Earle might change her tune if she could see today's cultivars, tall and short with glorious blooms of varied colors, single flowers, multiple flowers, and more. *Helianthus annuus* has come a long way, baby.

These sunflowers are grouped by flower type: single or multiple. Cultivars with single blooms produce one huge flower, and sometimes a few smaller blooms below it. Multiflowered cultivars bear many medium-sized blooms, anywhere from 2 to 5 inches across. The lists are only a sample of what's available, but perhaps they will whet your appetite.

Single Flowers

'Arrowhead'	gold	5–7 feet
'Big Smile'	gold	1–3 feet
'Giant Russian'	gold	7–14 feet
'Moonwalker'	yellow-gold	6–8 feet
'Russian Giant'	yellow	12 feet
'Sunbeam'	yellow-gold	5–7 feet
'Sunrich Lemon'	yellow	3–5 feet
'Sunrich Orange'	orange	3–5 feet
'Taiyo'	yellow	5–6 feet

Multiple Flowers

'Autumn Beauty'	autumn colors	6–8 feet
'Chianti'	wine red	4–5 feet
'Henry Wilde'	yellow-gold	8–10 feet
'Inca Jewels'	autumn colors	5–8 feet
'Italian White'	ivory	5–7 feet
'Kid Stuff'	gold	2–3 feet
'Music Box Mix'	autumn colors	2–4 feet
'Prado Red'	deep red	3–5 feet
'Primrose Yellow'	yellow	8–10 feet
'Sundrops'	yellow	4–5 feet
'Sungold'/'Sol d'Oro'	gold double	4–6 feet
'Teddy Bear'	yellow double	2–3 feet
'Valentine'	yellow	4–6 feet
'Vanilla Ice'	ivory	4–6 feet
'Velvet Queen'	burgundy	5–8 feet

ANNUAL BEAUTY FROM BIENNIALS

Biennial plants, species that produce leaves in their first season, then flower, set seeds, and die in their second year, are often confused with annuals. "Slow annuals," one friend calls them. New England gardeners often can treat biennials as if they were annuals, thanks to commercial growers who sow seeds indoors in early winter to produce plants that will flower in their first summer in the garden. If you're doing the sowing and doing it outdoors in spring, remember that it will be two years before you have flowers.

Be sure to choose a biennial that can survive winter in your garden. All the plants on this list are hardy to *at least Zone 4.*

Hollyhock (*Alcea* spp.)
English daisy (*Bellis perennis*)
Canterbury bells (*Campanula medium*)
Chinese forget-me-not (*Cynoglossum amabile*)
Sweet William (*Dianthus barbatus*)
Common foxglove (*Digitalis purpurea*)

Sweet rocket (*Hesperis* spp.)
Honesty/money plant (*Lunaria annua*)
Forget-me-not (*Myosotis sylvatica*)
Scotch thistle (*Onopordum acanthium*)
Iceland poppy (*Papaver corceum*)
Mullein (*Verbascum bombyciferum*)

SOW DIRECT

If your windowsills and tabletops are already filled with flats of seedlings, save these fast-growing flowers for an outdoor start. All of these annuals are easy to grow from seeds sown in the ground after the last frost date in spring. The plants marked with an asterisk (*) can be sown a week or two before the last frost. Remember that annuals don't want extra comfort—organically rich soil, yes, but too much fertilizer and you'll have too many leaves and too few flowers.

Borage (*Borago officinalis*)*
Pot marigold (*Calendula officinalis*)
Annual tickseed/calliopsis (*Coreopsis tinctoria*)
Cosmos (*Cosmos bipinnatus*)
Snow-on-the-mountain/ghost weed (*Euphorbia marginata*)
Sunflower (*Helianthus annuus*)

Globe/annual candytuft (*Iberis umbellata*)*
Morning glory (*Ipomoea tricolor*)
Annual mallow (*Lavatera trimestris*)*
Night-scented stock (*Matthiola bicornis*)*
Marigold (*Tagetes* spp.)
Mexican sunflower (*Tithonia rotundifolia*)
Nasturtium (*Tropaeolum majus*)
Zinnia (*Zinnia elegans*)

"There should always be a space in your garden for a few annuals. They flower throughout the summer and lend a continuity to the border, fill in gaps, and are especially appreciated in late summer when many of the perennials have finished flowering."
Rachel Kane, owner, Perennial Pleasures Nursery, East Hardwick, Vermont

SHORT AND PROUD OF IT

Low-growing plants are indispensable in the garden, where they thrive on edges of beds and borders, along walkways, in rock gardens and walls—any place they won't be shaded or hidden by taller plants. These diminutives are also the staples of container gardens, ideal for growing in pots, hanging baskets, and window boxes. Many are garden regulars, but that doesn't make them any less lovely. Most must be sown indoors well before the frost-free date, so consult a garden encyclopedia for cultivation details. Some of these plants technically are perennials but are treated as annuals in our region.

Floss flower (*Ageratum houstonianum*)
'Blue Angel' summer forget-me-not (*Anchusa capensis*)
'Little Darling Mixed' dwarf snapdragon (*Antirrhinum majus*)
Wax begonia (*Begonia semperflorens-cultorum* hyb.)
Swan River daisy (*Brachyscome iberidifolia*)
Pot marigold (*Calendula officinalis*)
Crested cockscomb (*Celosia argentea* var. *cristata*)
Plumed cockscomb (*Celosia argentea* var. *plumosa*)
Treasure flower (*Gazania* Mini-star Series)
Lobelia (*Lobelia erinus*)
Sweet alyssum (*Lobularia maritima*)
Sundial Series rose moss (*Portulaca grandiflora*)
Firecracker Series scarlet sage (*Salvia splendens*)
Signet marigold (*Tagetes* Signet Group)
Verbena (*Verbena hybrida* cvs.)
Pansy (*Viola wittrockiana* cvs.)
'Orange Star' Mexican zinnia (*Zinnia haageana*)

SELF-SUCCEEDERS: PLANTS THAT SOW THEMSELVES

Some annuals and biennials you have to sow only once. Self-reliant and determined, they sow themselves and return year after year—often in places you don't expect them. A few flowers on this list won't self-sow in the colder parts of New England, but in Zone 5 and warmer, you'll find seedlings popping up each spring. Experts warn not to expect flowers to self-seed if you've mulched with wood chips or shredded bark. In fact, a gravel mulch is the best medium for encouraging self-seeders to do their thing. Loose, organically rich soil is the runner-up.

COSMOS

Prickly poppy (*Argemone grandiflora*)
Red orache (*Atriplex hortensis* var. *rubra*)
Borage (*Borago officinalis*)
Thorow-wax (*Bupleurum rotundifolium*)
Cornflower/bachelor's buttons (*Centaurea cyanus*)
Bronze-leaved corydalis (*Corydalis ophiocarpa*)
Cosmos (*Cosmos bipinnatus*)
Spiny plume thistle (*Crisium spinosissium*)
Common foxglove (*Digitalis purpurea*)
Snow-on-the-mountain/ghost weed (*Euphorbia marginata*)
Sunflower (*Helianthus annuus*)
Globe/annual candytuft (*Iberis umbellata*)
Sweet alyssum (*Lobularia maritima*)
Honesty/moneywort (*Lunaria annua*)
Rose campion (*Lychnis coronaria*)
Mallow (*Malva sylvestris*)
Forget-me-not (*Myosotis sylvatica*)
Big-flowered evening primrose (*Oenothera glazioviana*)
Shirley poppy/Flanders Field poppy (*Papaver rhoeas*)
Opium poppy (*Papaver somniferum*)
Nasturtium (*Tropaeolum majus*)
Johnny-jump-up (*Viola tricolor*)

ANTIQUE ANNUALS AND BIENNIALS

This is a list of heirloom annuals and biennials, plants our grandparents grew. Heirlooms are increasingly popular these days, both for their simple, old-fashioned charm and for their general vigor in the garden.

Rachel Kane, the owner of Perennial Pleasures Nursery in East Hardwick, Vermont, contributed this list. Kane, who has long been involved in historical restoration work, grows well over 500 old-fashioned flowers and herbs at her Zone 3 location, and almost all the plants and seeds she sells come from her gardens. Also produced at her garden are English cream teas, weather permitting, from Memorial Day until Labor day. Reservations are encouraged—in case you're in her neighborhood.

Love-lies-bleeding (*Amaranthus caudatus*)
Cornflower/bachelor's buttons (*Centaurea cyanus*)
Rocket larkspur (*Consolida orientalis*)
Common foxglove (*Digitalis purpurea*)
Tassel-flower (*Emilia sonchifolia*)
Dame's rocket (*Hesperis matronalis*)

Garden balsam (*Impatiens balsamina*)
Annual mallow (*Lavatera trimestris*)
Curled mallow (*Malva verticillata*)
Common stock/gilly flower (*Matthiola incana*)
Four o'clocks/marvel of Peru (*Mirabilis jalapa*)
Flowering tobacco (*Nicotiana alata*)
Love-in-a-mist (*Nigella damascena*)

'Peony Flowered' opium poppy (*Papaver somniferum*)

Mignonette (*Reseda odorata*)

Pincushion flower (*Scabiosa atropurpurea*)

Peruvian zinnia (*Zinnia peruviana*)

"If you're beginning indoors, don't start old-fashioned annuals (such as cosmos, four o'clocks, tassel flower, nasturtium, and flowering tobacco) too early. Sow about six weeks before your last frost date, or wait until the soil is workable and sow directly outdoors."
Marilyn Barlow, owner, Select Seeds/Antique Flowers, Union, Connecticut

AMBER WAVES: ANNUAL ORNAMENTAL GRASSES

Ornamental grasses add different forms, textures, and colors to the garden—and movement, for they sway gracefully in even the slightest wind. They can be massed or planted singly as dramatic accents. The rage for ornamental grasses hasn't been shared equally by all gardeners, however, as many of the most handsome perennial grass species are not hardy north of Zone 5. If that's the bad news, the good news is there are many annual grasses worthy of a place in New England beds and borders. Moreover, some tender perennials, such as fountain grass, can be treated as an annual in the North. Be warned, though, that many annual grasses self-sow in warmer parts of our region, and you may end up with grass where it's not welcome. (For lists of perennial grasses, see the "Ground Covers, Grasses, and Ferns" chapter.)

Cloud bent grass (*Agrostis nebulosa*)

Wild oat (*Avena sterilis*)

Large quaking grass (*Briza maxima*)

Lesser quaking grass (*Briza minor*)

Chess grass (*Bromus madritensis*)

Foxtail barley (*Hordeum jubatum*)

Hare's tail grass (*Lagurus ovatus*)

Goldentop (*Lamarckia aurea*)

Bowles' golden grass (*Milium effusum* 'Aureum')

'Rubrum' fountain grass (*Pennisetum setaceum*)

Feather top (*Pennisetum villosum*)

Annual beard grass (*Polypogon monspeliensis*)

'Macrochaeta' foxtail millet (*Setaria italica*)

LOVE ME TENDER

Suzy Verrier basks in Zone 6 conditions at her coastal nursery, North Creek Farm, in Phippsburg, Maine. Even her mild climate won't ensure that the tender perennials on this list will survive the winter, although she reports that many self-seed reliably in her garden. Because they bring "a different palette of exotic colors and shapes to the garden," Verrier recommends tender perennials despite their lack of hardiness. New England gardeners should treat them as annuals or overwinter them indoors. "I pot them up and enjoy them indoors until they begin to look ratty," she states. "Then I lop them off and tuck the pots out of sight until it's time to bring them back into the light in anticipation of going outside again."

California poppy (*Eschscholzia californica*)

Weeping lantana (*Lantana montevidensis*)

'Coral Nymph' Texas sage (*Salvia coccinea*)

Autumn sage (*Salvia greggii*)

'Ponytails' feather grass (*Stipa tenuissima*)

Verbena (*Verbena bonariensis*)

'Baby Blue Eyes' Australian violet (*Viola hederacea*)

"If you're moving transplants to the garden, be sure to *harden-off*, or acclimate, your plants before you plant them outdoors. Set them in a sheltered spot for a few hours each day. Bring them in at night. Gradually increase the time they spend outdoors (and the sun they get) until you're leaving them out day and night. Most plants are ready for the garden in a week or ten days."

Jack Chapline, freelance writer and former editor, *Country Journal*, Durham, New Hampshire

ANNUALS AND BIENNIALS FOR DRY CONDITIONS

Do you have a dry, sunny spot to fill with flowers? Here are some annuals and biennials that are willing to bloom even when they're a little thirsty. If the site also has thin, sandy soil, be sure to enrich it with generous amounts of organic matter, such as compost; mulching plants also helps to retain moisture. Remember that even camel-like plants like these need an occasional drink. This list is a place to start if you're looking for bloomers that do well in drier spots. One hint if you want to identify others: Most self-seeding annuals tolerate dry conditions well.

African daisy (*Arctotis* hyb.)
Prickly poppy (*Argemone grandiflora*)
Rock purslane (*Calandrinia grandiflora*)
Pot marigold (*Calendula officinalis*)
Poppy mallow/winecups (*Callirhoe involucrata*)
Madagascar periwinkle (*Catharanthus roseus*)
Cornflower/bachelor's buttons (*Centaurea cyanus*)
Palm Springs daisy (*Cladanthus arabicus*)
Spider flower (*Cleome hassleriana*)
Annual tickseed/calliopsis (*Coreopsis tinctoria*)
Cosmos (*Cosmos bipinnatus*)
African daisy (*Dimorphotheca sinuata*)
Dahlberg daisy (*Dyssodia tenuiloba*)
California poppy (*Eschscholzia californica*)
Blanket flower (*Gaillardia pulchella*)
Globe amaranth (*Gomphrena globosa*)
Strawflower (*Helichrysum bracteatum*)
Statice/sea lavender (*Limonium sinuatum*)
Toadflax (*Linaria macroccana*)
Butter daisy (*Melampodium paludosum*)
Shirley poppy/Flanders Field poppy (*Papaver rhoeas*)
California desert bluebells (*Phacelia campanularia*)
Rose moss (*Portulaca grandiflora*)
Salvia (*Salvia coccinea*)
Marigold (*Tagetes* cvs.)
Verbena (*Verbena* hyb.)

The marigold, *Tagetes* spp., was championed by the late Illinois senator Everett McKinley Dirksen. Famous for his flowery oratory, Dirksen filled the *Congressional Record* with praise for the marigold's beauty and rugged character—"I can think of nothing greater or more inspiring than a field of blooming marigolds tossing their heads in the sunshine and giving a glow to the entire landscape"—but it lost out to the rose as the official U.S. flower.

AM I BLUE?

Blue is the color most sought after by gardeners, the color that garden books say is most difficult to find. Pure blue is rare and a cause for celebration, yet there are more good blue flowers than you might expect. Before you create an all-blue garden with these annuals, biennials, and tender perennials, however, be aware that the revered English garden designer and writer Gertrude Jekyll observed that "any experienced colourist knows that the blue will be more telling—more purely blue—by the juxtaposition of rightly placed complementary colour."

'Blue Danube', 'Blue Mink' floss flower (*Ageratum houstonianum*)
Annual woodruff (*Asperula orientalis*)
Borage (*Borago officinalis*)
'Blue Star' Swan River daisy (*Brachyscome iberidifolia*)
'Blue Bells', 'Blue Troll' bush violet (*Browolia speciosa*)
'Blue Skies' China/annual aster (*Callistephus chinensis*)
Canterbury bells (*Campanula medium*)
'Blue Boy', 'Emperor William' cornflower/bachelor's buttons (*Centaurea cyanus*)
Larkspur (*Consolida ajacis* cvs.)
'Royal Ensign' dwarf morning glory (*Convolvulus tricolor*)
'Firmament' Chinese forget-me-not (*Cynoglossum amabile*)
'Read's Blue' blue daisy (*Felicia amelloides*)
'Heavenly Blue' morning glory (*Ipomoea tricolor*)
'Cambridge Blue', 'Cobalt Blue', 'Blue Moon', 'Crystal Palace' lobelia (*Lobelia erinus*)
Sweet alyssum (*Lobularia maritima* cvs.)
'Royal Blue', 'Blue Bird', 'Blue Basket' forget-me-not (*Myosotis sylvatica*)
'Blue Gem' nemesia (*Nemesia strumosa*)
'Baby Blue Eyes' trailing nemophila (*Nemophila menziesii*)
'Miss Jekyll', 'Oxford Blue', 'Dwarf Moody Blue' love-in-a-mist (*Nigella damascena*)
'Blue Danube', 'Blue Daddy', 'Blue Skies' petunia (*Petunia*)
'Blue Beauty' annual phlox (*Phlox drummondii*)
'Kew Blue' painted tongue (*Salpiglossis sinuata*)
'Blue Bedder' mealycup sage (*Salvia farinacea*)
'Cambridge Blue' meadow clary (*Salvia patens*)
'Baby Lucia', 'True Blue', 'Velour Clear Blue' pansy (*Viola wittrockiana*)

POPEYE'S GIRLS: A CONNECTICUT NURSERYWOMAN'S FAVORITE SWEET PEAS

Bringing the flowers our grandmothers loved into our gardens" is the aim of Marilyn Barlow, owner of Select Seeds/Antique Flowers seed company in Union, Connecticut. Among Barlow's favorite heirlooms are annual sweet peas (*Lathyrus odoratus*), fragrant climbers that were enormously popular with our ancestors. This annual species likes cool conditions and deeply dug, organically rich soil with a neutral pH and plenty of moisture. Seeds should be sown very early in spring when the ground is still cold, so prepare the soil in autumn. All the sweet peas on this list have been cultivated for at least ninety years and some are far older: 'Painted Lady', for example, was introduced in the early 1700s.

	Flower color
'America'	white and red
'Annie Gilroy'	cerise
'Black Knight'	maroon
'Blanche Ferry'	pink and white

SWEET PEA

'Butterfly'	white and mauve
'Captain of the Blues'	mauve
'Countess Cadogan'	violet and blue
'Dorothy Eckford'	white
'Flora Norton'	blue
'Indigo King'	maroon and blue
'Janet Scott'	pink
'Lady Grisel Hamilton'	lavender
'Lord Nelson'	navy blue
'Miss Willmott'	orange-pink
'Painted Lady'	pink and white
'Purple Prince'	purple

SHADY CHARACTERS

Almost no annual flowers bloom well in full shade, but a good number do best in dappled sun or at least with protection during the hot midday. These lovely bloomers, a mix of true annuals, biennials, and tender perennials that New Englanders treat as annuals, thrive out of the sun's glare. Flowers with an asterisk (*) insist on shade during the hottest part of the day.

Not included in this list is *Coleus hybridus*, or flame nettle, which is grown for its foliage, not its blossoms. Coleus foliage is so richly colorful, though, that you may find yourself adding several cultivars to your flower garden. (A list of recommended coleus appears elsewhere in this chapter.)

Annual woodruff (*Asperula orientalis*)*
Wax begonia (*Begonia semperflorens-cultorum* hyb.)*
Tuberous begonia (*Begonia tuberhybrida*)*
Bush violet (*Browallia speciosa*)*
Madagascar periwinkle (*Catharanthus roseus*)*
Wild foxglove (*Ceratotheca triloba*)*
Larkspur (*Consolida ajacis*)
Common foxglove (*Digitalis purpurea*)*
Snow-on-the-mountain/ghost weed (*Euphorbia marginata*)
Fuchsia (*Fuchsia* hyb.)*
Impatiens (*Impatiens walleriana*)*
Violet cress (*Ionopsidum acaule*)
Morning glory (*Ipomoea tricolor*)
Lobelia (*Lobelia erinus*)*
Sweet alyssum (*Lobularia maritima*)
Honesty/moneywort (*Lunaria annua*)
Monkey flower (*Mimulus hybridus*)*
Forget-me-not (*Myosotis sylvatica*)
Baby blue eyes (*Nemophila maculata*)*
Flowering tobacco (*Nicotiana alata*)
Evening primrose (*Oenothera* spp.)
Mignonette (*Reseda odorata*)*
Saponaria (*Saponaria vaccaria*)*
Butterfly flower (*Schizanthus wisetonensis*)
Venus's looking glass (*Specularia speculum*)*
Black-eyed Susan vine (*Thunbergia alata*)
Wishbone flower (*Torenia fournieri*)*
Pansy and viola (*Viola* spp.)

LONG-DISTANCE RUNNERS: PLANTS THAT KEEP ON FLOWERING

Every garden needs flowers that keep on blooming and blooming, the horticultural equivalent of the Energizer bunny. Perennials may come back every year, but few of them bloom for more than a month. For that kind of longevity, you have to plant annuals. The all-time champ is probably impatiens, which already are flowering when you bring them home from the nursery and don't stop until the first frost cuts them down. Impatiens don't even require deadheading (removing spent blossoms), although most annuals will keep blooming far longer if you cut off their faded flowers.

Floss flower (*Ageratum houstonianum*)
Wax begonia (*Begonia semperflorens-cultorum* hyb.)
Spider flower (*Cleome hassleriana*)
Cosmos (*Cosmos bipinnatus*)
Blanket flower (*Gaillardia pulchella*)
Globe amaranth (*Gomphrena globosa*)
'Italian White', 'Inca Jewels', multiflower sunflower (*Helianthus annuus*)
New Guinea impatiens (*Impatiens* New Guinea Group)
Impatiens (*Impatiens walleriana*)
Morning glory (*Ipomoea tricolor*)
Zonal geranium (*Pelargonium* hyb.)
Petunia (*Petunia hybrida*)
Mealycup sage (*Salvia farinacea*)
Scarlet sage (*Salvia splendens*)
Marigold (*Tagetes* spp.)
Mexican sunflower (*Tithonia rotundifolia*)
Zinnia (*Zinnia elegans*)
Mexican zinnia (*Zinnia haageana*)

"Annual flowers are in a hurry to set seeds. To keep plants producing new flowers, be sure to remove all the dead blooms. Pinching back plants that have a tendency to be leggy, such as petunias, also keeps annual plants growing and flowering longer."
David Grist, Gardener's Supply, Burlington, Vermont

COLEUS: VERSATILE FANCY FOLIAGE

Poor old coleus. It didn't have much sex appeal to begin with, and now the taxonomists have renamed it *Solenostemon scutellarioides*, a name that most of us can't pronounce, much less remember. (Previously, its genus name was *Coleus*.) Fortunately, a devoted band of coleus fanciers have kept the faith—and kept breeding cultivars with ever brighter and bolder leaves. Coleus breeders also offer new forms. 'Scarlet Poncho', a deep red edged with gold, has cascading branches, perfect for hanging baskets or window boxes. In contrast, the coleus in the 'Seven Dwarfs Mix'—which includes plants that are all red, red and yellow, salmon and green, ivory and green, cream and lime, lime and red, rose and green, and bronze and green—are only 10 inches tall. Moreover, coleus aren't just for shade anymore: The Sunlover and Solar series can survive sun and heat.

	Foliage color
'Caladium'	white and green
'Palisandra'	near black
'Dazzler'	variegated red, yellow, green, and maroon
'Defiance'	red and gold
'Display'	red and green-yellow
'El Brighto'	pink, green, and yellow
'Indian Frills'	red, green, and yellow
'Molten Lava'	shades of red
'Nettle'	variegated lime green, yellow, pink, and maroon
'Night Skies'	maroon and yellow-green
'Pineapple Queen'	burgundy and gold
'Salmon Lace'	salmon, green, and gold
'Saturn'	maroon and green
'Scarlet Poncho'	red and gold
'The Line'	gold and purple

UPWARD MOBILITY: VINES

Most true vines are tropical natives, perennial climbers that evolved where temperatures stay well above freezing. If you think of vines as botanical plumbing, you understand why they love warm weather. The following list of vines includes a few true annuals, such as Japanese hops, and many tender perennials—moonflower and purple bell vine are two examples—which must be grown as annuals in New England.

Most names on this list benefit by being started indoors four to six weeks before the frost-free date. Be sure to harden-off, or acclimate, young vines before moving them to your garden, and give them something to climb.

Balloon vine/love-in-a-puff (*Cardiospermum halicacabum*)
Cup-and-saucer vine (*Cobaea scandens*)
Marble vine (*Diplocyclos palmatus*)
Chilean glory flower (*Eccremocarpus scaber*)
Wild cucumber (*Echinocystis lobata*)
Japanese hop (*Humulus japonicus*)
Moonflower (*Ipomoea alba*)
Red morning glory (*Ipomoea coccinea*)
Spanish flag (*Ipomoea lobata*)
Star glory (*Ipomoea quamoclit*)
Morning glory (*Ipomoea* spp.)
Hyacinth bean (*Lablab purpureus*)
Bottle gourd (*Lagenaria* spp.)
Sweet pea (*Lathyrus odoratus*)
Climbing snapdragon (*Maurandella antirrhinifolia*)
Scarlet runner bean (*Phaseolus coccineus*)
Purple bell vine (*Rhodochiton atrosanguineum*)
Black-eyed Susan vine (*Thunbergia alata*)
Bengal clock vine (*Thunbergia grandiflora*)
Nasturtium (*Tropaeolum majus*)
Canary creeper (*Tropaeolum peregrinum*)

MORNING GLORY

DOWN EAST ANNUALS

The garden writer A. Carman Clark lives in Union, a midcoast Maine town on the border between Zones 4 and 5. She gardens on ten acres set above a freshwater pond. Her flower gardens date to 1954 and are filled with "a hodgepodge of perennials, biennials, and annuals." Her 25- by 60-foot vegetable garden consists of a series or raised beds so "kids and dogs can roam without anyone yelling, 'Don't walk there.'" Although Clark is especially fond of perennial flowers that take care of themselves—such as delphiniums, asters, Siberian iris, and daylilies—she's also enthusiastic about annuals. This list includes some of her favorites, many of which reseed themselves.

'Sensation Mix' cosmos (*Cosmos bipinnatus*)
'T&M Reselected Hybrid' blanket flower (*Gaillardia grandiflora*)
'Double Mixed' blanket flower (*Gaillardia pulchella*)
'Mixed' common morning glory (*Ipomoea purpurea*)
'Heavenly Blue' morning glory (*Ipomoea tricolor*)
Annual phlox (*Phlox drummondii*)
'Dwarf Jewel Mixed' dwarf nasturtium (*Tropaeolaceae*)
Johnny-jump-up (*Viola tricolor*)

Sydney Eddison, a garden writer who lives in Newtown, Connecticut, is famous for her woodland garden and perennial borders, but she's still a fan of annuals. "Don't underrate annuals. They are a stable, reliable presence in the garden. Once they reach maturity, they stay about the same until frost kills them. Their greatest charm is that they bloom, and bloom, and bloom. And the more you pick them, the more they bloom."

THE KINDEST CUTS: ANNUALS FOR BOUQUETS

There's hardly an annual that doesn't belong in a vase, so choosing only a few is difficult. Cutting them may also be difficult: Once you've created the perfect picture in your garden, you won't want to change it for the sake of a bouquet. That's why many gardeners plant a separate cutting garden, a plot sown strictly for picking. Cutting gardens can be any size or shape, but they're most accessible when their residents are sown in rows.

Flowers for fresh bouquets should be cut in early morning before the dew dries. Early evening is the second-best time. Choose blooms that are almost fully open. Use a clean, sharp knife, and cut as much stem as you can, which will give you more choices when you make arrangements. Stand the stems in a container of warm water immediately after you sever them.

Bishop's flower/false Queen Anne's lace (*Ammi majus*)
Snapdragon (*Antirrhinum majus*)
Pot marigold (*Calendula officinalis*)
China/annual aster (*Callistephus chinensis*)
Plumed cockscomb (*Celosia argentea* var. *plumosa*)
Cornflower/bachelor's buttons (*Centaurea cyanus*)
Garland flower (*Clarkia unguiculata*)
Spider flower (*Cleome hassleriana*)
Larkspur (*Consolida ajacis*)
Annual tickseed/calliopsis (*Coreopsis tinctoria*)
Cosmos (*Cosmos bipinnatus*)
Snow-on-the-mountain/ghost weed (*Euphorbia marginata*)

Prairie gentian (*Eustoma grandiflora*)
Queen Anne's thimbles (*Gilia capiata*)
Baby's breath (*Gypsophila elegans*)
Sunflower (*Helianthus annuus*)
Sweet pea (*Lathyrus odoratus*)
Statice/sea lavender (*Limonium sinuatum*)
Common stock/gilly flower (*Matthiola incana*)
Bells of Ireland (*Moluccella laevis*)
Love-in-a-mist (*Nigella damascena*)
Iceland poppy (*Papaver nudicaule*)
Black-eyed-Susan/gloriosa daisy (*Rudbeckia hirta*)
Clary sage (*Salvia viridis*)
Marigold (*Tagetes* spp.)
Mexican sunflower (*Tithonia rotundifolia*)
Zinnia (*Zinnia elegans*)

"The experts say the best time to cut flowers is midmorning—after the dew has dried but before the sun takes the moisture in the leaves and stems—but I'm never that organized. I think the best time to cut flowers is any time you're in the garden. Whatever the time of day, always carry a pail of water so that the flowers don't wilt between the garden and the house."
Judy Boucher, Cabot, Vermont

PLANTS WITH VARIEGATED FOLIAGE

When it comes to fancy foliage, true geraniums, or *Pelargoniums*, instantly come to mind. Yet there are many more possibilities if you're looking to the leaves to make a statement in your garden or window box. In addition to red-leafed plants, such as coleus and canna 'Ty Ty Red', there are plants with white/silver foliage. *Helichrysum italicum*, or curry plant, not only has gray leaves but is wonderfully pungent. The list that follows includes annuals, biennials, and tender perennials with variegated foliage, green leaves marked with white or cream—or, in the case of caladium, white marked with green. One caveat: Plants with variegated leaves are sometimes less vigorous than other cultivars; you may want to plant these beauties in containers where you can give them a little extra TLC.

'White Peacock' ornamental kale (*Brassica oleracea acephala*)
'Candidum' elephant's ears (*Caladium bicolor*)
'Pretoria' canna (*Canna*)
'Striped Beauty' canna (*Canna*)
'Variegatum' wallflower (*Erysimum linifolium*)
Snow-on-the-mountain/ghost weed (*Euphorbia marginata*)
'Variegata' blue daisy (*Felicia amoena*)
'Variegata' licorice plant (*Helichrysum petiolare*)
'Pink Frost' sweet potato (*Ipomoea batatas*)
'Candy' morning glory (*Ipomoea tricolor*)
'Variegata Alba' honesty/moneywort (*Lunaria annua*)
'Variegata' pineapple mint (*Mentha suaveolens*)
'Variegatum' variegated lemon geranium (*Pelargonium crispum*)
'Variegata' Swedish ivy (*Plectranthus australis*)

'Zanzibarensis' castor bean (*Ricinus communis*)
Our Lady's thistle (*Silybum marianum*)
'Alaska' nasturtium (*Tropaeolum*)
'Variegata' greater periwinkle (*Vinca major*)

WHITE FLOWERS FOR SPECIAL EFFECTS

White flowers aren't a hard sell among gardeners. White is a color that makes other hues bright and shiny; "cleans up other colors" is how Connecticut gardener writer Sydney Eddison expresses it. Several names on this list, including cleome, moonflower, flowering tobacco, and sweet pea, are also fragrant, another good reason to add them to your garden. But don't go overboard. White is so eye-catching that too much will divert attention from other colors. Still, pick and choose at least a hand-ful of plants from this list of white annuals, biennials, and tender perennials. If you're in a Vita Sackville-West mood (she of the famous white garden at Sissinghurst), plant them all.

'White Lustre' prickly poppy/Mexican poppy (*Argemone mexicana*)
'White Splendour' Swan River daisy (*Brachyscome iberidifolia*)
'White Troll' bush violet (*Browallia speciosa*)
'Pacifica White' Madagascar periwinkle (*Catharanthus roseus*)
'Helen Campbell' spider flower (*Cleome hassleriana*)
'Sonata White' cosmos (*Cosmos bipinnatus*)
Baby's breath (*Gypsophila elegans*)
Moonflower (*Ipomoea alba*)
'White Supreme' sweet pea (*Lathyrus odoratus*)
'Mont Blanc' annual mallow (*Lavatera trimestris*)
'Snowball' lobelia (*Lobelia erinus*)
'Carpet of Snow' sweet alyssum (*Lobularia maritima*)
'Alba' honesty/moneywort (*Lunaria annua*)
'Dwarf White Bedder' nicotiana (*Nicotiana alata*)
Flowering tobacco (*Nicotiana sylvestris*)
'Mont Blanc' cupflower (*Nierembergia frutescens*)
'Snowbird' nolana (*Nolana paradoxa*)
'White Cloud' opium poppy (*Papaver somniferum*)
'Alba' zonal geranium (*Pelargonium*)
'Snowdrift' ivy-leaved geranium (*Pelargonium*)
'Celebrity White' petunia (*Petunia*)
'Victoria White' mealycup sage (*Salvia farinacea*)
'Sizzler White' scarlet sage (*Salvia splendens*)
'White Perfection' viola (*Viola cornuta*)
'Cut and Come Again White' zinnia (*Zinnia elegans*)
'Crystal White' Mexican zinnia (*Zinnia haageana*)

Whether they are *hardy annuals* (plants like candytuft and snapdragons, which can withstand a good deal of cold, even a bit of frost) or *half-hardy annuals* (such as marigolds and zinnias, which can tolerate some cold) or *tender annuals* (such as cosmos and impatiens, which wither when the mercury drops near freezing), annual flowers have one thing in common in northern gardens: They live for only one season. They have, as garden writer Richardson Wright put it, "a short life and a merry one."

HANG 'EM HIGH

Few things are more striking than a hanging basket in full flower or a window box or other container overflowing with blooms. All of the plants listed below do well in confined quarters and have the cascading form that complements hanging baskets, window boxes, and other off-the-ground containers. Remember that in sunny locations, container gardens dry out quickly and need to be watered frequently. Some of the flowers on this list, such as impatiens and twining snapdragon, are not true annuals but tender perennials, which are treated as annuals by New England gardeners.

'Phillipsii' pimpernel (*Anagallis monelli*)
'Victoria Falls' twining snapdragon (*Asarina purpusil*)
'Show Angels' tuberous begonia (*Begonia tuberhybrida*)
'Golden Goddess' bidens (*Bidens ferulifolia*)
'Splendor' Swan River daisy (*Brachyscome iberidifolia*)
'Bellissimo' bellflower (*Campanula carpatica*)
'Tropicana' Madagascar periwinkle (*Catharanthus roseus*)
Dwarf morning glory (*Convolvulus tricolor*)
Futura series impatiens (*Impatiens walleriana*)
Cascade series lobelia (*Lobelia erinus*)
Monkey flower (*Mimulus hybridus*)
'Snowstorm' baby blue eyes (*Nemophila menziesii*)
'Summer Showers' ivy-leaf geranium (*Pelargonium*)
'Supercascade Improved' grandiflora petunia (*Petunia*)
'Sun Vale' supertunia/petunia (*Petunia axillaris*)
Rose moss (*Portulaca grandiflora*)
'Scarlet Poncho' coleus (*Solenostemon scutellarioides*)
'Empress of India' nasturtium (*Tropaeolum*)

The flats of annual flowers already in bloom in garden centers are seductive, but all those blossoms stress young plants. To reduce shock, remove all the flowers before you transplant. It's hard to do, but it will redirect the plant's energy to producing a healthy root system and new stems and leaves—and, in the long run, far more flowers.

OH SO SWEET: FRAGRANT PLANTS

The fragrance of the annuals, biennials, and tender perennials on this list ranges from the sweet scent of stock to the pungent aroma of marigolds. Be warned that the blossoms of some fragrant species—mignonette is a good example—are visually unimpressive. Moreover, not all perfume is in the flower. To enjoy the scent of pelargoniums, crush a leaf. Plants with fragrant foliage are marked with an asterisk (*).

A sure giveaway that a plant is fragrant? Some form of the word *odorata* in its botanical name. But buyer beware: Fragrance is something that modern plant breeders often overlook. Read the fine print when choosing a cultivar. Alas, not all sweet alyssum is sweet, although it should be.

Sweet Annie (*Artemisia annua*)*
Angel's trumpet/datura (*Brugmansia aurea*)
Basket flower (*Centaurea americana*)
Royal centaurea (*Centaurea imperialis*)
Palm Springs daisy (*Cladanthus arabicus*)*
Spider flower (*Cleome hassleriana*)
Sweet William (*Dianthus barbatus*)
Annual carnation (*Dianthus caryophyllus*)
Persian violet (*Exacum affine*)
Sweet everlasting (*Gnaphalium obtusifolium*)

Heliotrope (*Heliotropium arborescens*)
Rocket candytuft (*Iberis amara*)
Globe/annual candytuft (*Iberis umbellata*)
Moonflower (*Ipomoea alba*)
Sweet pea (*Lathyrus odoratus*)
Sweet alyssum (*Lobularia maritima*)
Common stock/gilly flower (*Matthiola incana*)

Four o'clock/marvel of Peru (*Mirabilis jalapa*)
Lemon mint (*Monarda citriodora*)*
Flowering tobacco (*Nicotiana alata*)
Evening primrose (*Oenothera biennis*)
Scented geranium (*Pelargonium* spp.)*
Petunia (*Petunia hybrida*)
Mignonette (*Reseda odorata*)
Signet marigold (*Tagetes* Signet Group)

"Annuals are especially useful for new gardens and new gardeners—instant flowers and easy care. And they're ideal for filling bare spots left by spring bulbs."
Sally Williams, publisher, *Garden Literature*, Boston, Massachusetts

ANNUALS FOREVER: PLANTS FOR DRYING

You can extend the life of your garden by planting everlastings. These *immortelles*, which retain their color and form when dried, often have colorful bracts, or modified leaves, rather than petals. For the best results, be sure to pick flowers at midday when they are dry. Remove the lower leaves on the stem, tie several stems together with string, and hang the bunches upside down in a dark location so that their colors won't fade. Once they have dried completely—the time will vary, anywhere from days to more than a month, according to which species you're drying—you can create arrangements and bouquets, and enjoy your garden during the cold New England winter.

Winged everlasting (*Ammobium alatum*)
Swan River daisy (*Brachyscome iberidifolia*)
Strawflower (*Bracteantha bracteata*)
Thorow-wax (*Bupleurum rotundifolium*)
Pot marigold (*Calendula officinalis*)
Crested cockscomb (*Celosia argentea* var. *cristata*)
Plumed cockscomb (*Celosia argentea* var. *plumosa*)
Larkspur (*Consolida ajacis*)
Globe amaranth (*Gomphrena globosa*)
Baby's breath (*Gypsophila elegans*)
Rose everlasting (*Helipterum roseum*)
Statice (*Limonium* spp.)
Yellow ageratum (*Lonas annua*)
Honesty/moneywort (*Lunaria annua*)
Bells of Ireland (*Moluccella laevis*)
Love-in-a-mist (*Nigella damascena*)
Pincushion flower (*Scabiosa stellata*)
Immortelle (*Xeranthemum annuum*)

STRAWFLOWER

PERENNIALS

It takes a leap of faith to believe that the plastic-swaddled perennials in the UPS boxes dropped at my back door will become the horticultural cheesecake served up in four-color nursery catalogues. Rather than "a compact 3 to 4-foot plant ... blessed with glorious sun-golden flowers and delicate ferny leaves that are attractive all season," I am the owner of a 3-inch shoot sulking in a 5-inch pot. There's every promise that my unborn grandchildren will be driving before this perennial blooms.

But close your eyes and take that leap. Not only will most perennials flower in their first season in the garden, but buying perennials—either locally or by mail—is one of the best garden investments you can make. With any luck, perennials *last*. As one wit put it, "they are plants that last forever if they don't die." In fact, some perennials may be around long after you and I are gone, especially if we plant species with octogenarian genes, such as peonies.

When New England gardeners talk about perennials, they mean *herbaceous perennials*, plants whose foliage and stems typically die back in winter but whose roots remain alive in the frozen ground and produce new growth in spring. Perennials are the meat-and-potatoes of beds and borders, but there are perennials and there are perennials. Not all are rugged and tough, although many of them are. Some peter out after a year or two—Shasta daisies and golden columbine (the pale yellow *Aquilegia chrysantha*) are good examples. Other perennials are finicky, requiring very particular conditions and care. The lists in this chapter contain both but are heavily weighted in favor of the rugged and tough—and the beautiful and useful.

The gardener's task, then, is to pick and plant. Picking isn't all that easy, as plant breeders are as enthusiastic about perennials as dogs are about bones. The American Iris Society, for instance, adds around 1,000 new cultivars to its official inventory every year! The lists in this chapter should help with the picking, but other gardeners and local nurseries are also fonts of good advice. You want to be sure to choose perennials that will be hardy—will survive winter—in your garden. The hardiness recommendations in each list will help you choose, but remember that there are many variations, or microclimates, within each hardiness zone. If you live in Zone 3 but don't have reliable snowcover, many perennials rated hardy for your conditions won't survive.

Fall is the traditional time for planting perennials, but that's a legacy from England. Most New England gardeners prefer spring. If you plant in autumn, be sure to do it early enough so that your perennials can establish themselves before the ground freezes. No perennial turns up its nose at organically rich soil. Sun and shade are another matter, with delphiniums demanding the former and bleeding hearts the latter. Water requirements also differ, although most plants prefer good drainage, even those that want plenty of moisture. If you make a serious mistake when choosing a site, your perennials will let you know about it.

More than one garden writer has observed that creating a perennial garden is similar to making a painting, for it involves color, line, form, and texture. Perennials offer great variety of each element: every color imaginable; vertical and horizontal plants; a diversity of forms; and textures as different as the woolly leaves of lamb's ears and the prickly foliage of the globe thistle.

So there is plenty for your horticultural palette, scores and scores of perennials to create a garden painting. Whether you choose perennials for their flowers, or their foliage, or their strong stems, or their disease-resistance—or for all those qualities—be sure to pick the species and cultivars that will be most at home in your garden. Growing plants in conditions they like makes the gardener's work easier.

Take the advice of Vita Sackville-West, English poet and *garden painter extraordinaire*: She advocated planting the "best things … and only the best forms of the best things, by which I mean that everything should be choice and chosen." Fortunately for us, much of the "choice and chosen" grows well in New England.

A HOST A' HOSTAS

Dorothy Pellett, a busy nurserywoman and garden writer, runs a small wholesale nursery, Rock Crest Gardens, just east of Lake Champlain in Charlotte, Vermont. Her country garden is located on the border between Hardiness Zones 4 and 5. The setting gives her downright balmy conditions for growing hostas, most of which are hardy to Zone 3. Pellett looks for "attractive, sturdy leaves and for resistance to slugs" when she's choosing hostas. Names on this list of favorites, which includes small, medium, and large kinds, have both those strengths. All are hardy to Zone 3.

'Carousel'	'Paul's Glory'
'Christmas Tree'	'Queen Josephine'
'Francee'	'Regal Splendor'
'Halcyon'	'Sagae'
'Northern Exposure'	'Second Wind'

Dorothy Pellett, who specializes in hostas and daylilies, runs a small wholesale nursery in Charlotte, Vermont. "Hostas will look their best when grown in dappled shade or with only morning sun. Too much sun will stunt and burn leaves; dense shade, in contrast, will not stimulate growth. And when you are choosing daylily varieties, consider more than flower color. Descriptions of height, size of flower, and number of blooms on each scape (flower stalk) can help in choosing the right ones for you. If they are to be seen up close, eyed and ruffled varieties are appealing."

SUNNY SIDE UP: PERENNIALS FOR FULL SUN

Here are the perennial flowers that worship "that orbed continent, the fire that severs day from night," as Shakespeare (a plantsman who knew cowslip from a columbine and more) put it. These are garden regulars—no exotic cultivars or hard-to-find species on this list. All are guaranteed to succeed if you give them what they want: full sun, organically rich soil, and adequate moisture. To make sure your plants will be back next year, mulch them in early winter, after the ground has frozen, especially if your snowcover is unreliable or scanty.

Yarrow (*Achillea* cvs.)	3, 4, 5, 6
Golden Marguerite (*Anthemis tinctoria*)	3, 4, 5, 6
Columbine (*Aquilegia* spp. and cvs.)	3, 4, 5, 6
Aster (*Aster* spp.)	3, 4, 5, 6
Basket of gold (*Aurinia saxatilis*)	3, 4, 5, 6

ASTER

Blue false indigo (*Baptisia australis*)	2/3, 4, 5, 6
Boltonia (*Boltonia asteroides*)	3, 4, 5, 6
Calamint (*Calamintha nepeta*)	4, 5, 6
Perennial cornflower (*Centaurea montana*)	3, 4, 5, 6
Red valerian (*Centranthus ruber*)	5, 6
Thread-leaf coreopsis (*Coreopsis verticillata*)	3, 4, 5, 6
Delphinium (*Delphinium* cvs.)	3, 4, 5, 6
Cottage pink (*Dianthus plumarius*)	3, 4, 5, 6
Purple coneflower (*Echinacea purpurea*)	3, 4, 5, 6
Globe thistle (*Echinops ritro*)	3, 4, 5, 6
Queen of the prairie (*Filipendula rubra*)	3, 4, 5, 6
Cranesbill/true geranium (*Geranium* spp.)	3, 4, 5, 6
Ox-eye/false sunflower (*Heliopsis helianthoides*)	3, 4, 5, 6
Daylily (*Hemerocallis* cvs.)	3, 4, 5, 6
Japanese iris (*Iris ensata*)	3, 4, 5, 6
Siberian iris (*Iris sibirica*)	3, 4, 5, 6
Lavender (*Lavandula angustifolia*)	4/5, 6
Shasta daisy (*Leucanthemum superbum*)	4, 5, 6
Gayfeather (*Liatris spicata*)	3, 4, 5, 6
Bee balm (*Monarda didyma*)	3, 4, 5, 6
Sundrops (*Oenothera fruticosa*)	4, 5, 6
Peony (*Paeonia* cvs.)	3, 4, 5, 6
Oriental poppy (*Papaver orientale*)	2, 3, 4, 5, 6
Beardlip penstemon (*Penstemon barbatus*)	3, 4, 5, 6
Russian sage (*Perovskia atriplicifolia*)	5, 6
Tall garden phlox (*Phlox paniculata*)	3, 4, 5, 6
Obedient plant (*Physostegia virginiana*)	2, 3, 4, 5, 6
Rudbeckia (*Rudbeckia* spp. and cvs.)	3, 4, 5, 6
Purple sage (*Salvia sylvestris*)	3/4, 5, 6
Sedum/stonecrop (*Sedum* spp.)	3, 4, 5, 6
Lamb's ears (*Stachys byzantina*)	3, 4, 5, 6
Speedwell (*Veronica* spp.)	3, 4, 5, 6

Connecticut garden writer Eleanor Perényi, author of *Green Thoughts: A Writer in the Garden* (1981), believes that perennials are the easiest plants to care for. "Two thirds of them, once established, and with a good supply of compost dumped on them every fall, simply come up, year after year, with no further effort. I never take the beds apart in the English manner; and I don't divide the clumps more often than every seven or eight years, if that. The itch to divide perennials, abetted by garden books, is to be resisted unless the signs that they need it are unmistakable."

HARDY PERENNIALS FOR ZONE 3

In summer, Lewis and Nancy Hill oversee their daylily nursery; in winter, they write books. Good, reliable books. After twenty-five years, enough books to fill a good-sized book shelf. A few of their titles are *Daylilies: The Perfect Perennial, Successful Perennial Gardening, Bulbs: Four Seasons of Beautiful Blooms, Cold-Climate Gardening, Secrets of Plant Propagation,* and *Pruning Simplified.*

The Hills live a couple of miles outside Greensboro, Vermont, a Zone 3 setting where only the hardy can survive. Daylilies are their favorite perennials, they say, "for their beauty, their hardiness, and their independent natures." In addition to daylilies, their list includes perennials that range from maidenhair fern to black-eyed Susan.

American maidenhair fern (*Adiantum pedatum*)
McKana hybrid columbine (*Aquilegia*)
'Fanal' astilbe (*Astilbe*)
Bleeding heart (*Dicentra spectabilis*)
Purple gasplant (*Dictamus albus* var. *purpureus*)
'Decatur Moonlight' daylily (*Hemerocallis*)
'Gentle Shepherd' daylily (*Hemerocallis*)
'Russian Rhapsody' daylily (*Hemerocallis*)
'Strawberry Rose' daylily (*Hemerocallis*)
Hosta (*Hosta* cvs.)
'Enchantment' Asiatic hybrid lily (*Lilium*)
Russell Hybrids, lupine (*Lupinus*)
Tall garden phlox (*Phlox paniculata*)
Black-eyed Susan (*Rudbeckia fulgida*)

THE PRIMROSE PATH

Garden writer Sydney Eddison's Connecticut woodland garden has been featured in many magazines (including *Martha Stewart Living*)—and no wonder. Shaded by huge oaks and planted with scores of native wildflowers and ferns, the highlight comes when the hundreds and hundreds of primroses (*Primula*) that surround the long, stream-fed pond bloom. The list below represents Eddison's favorites "because they grow well in my Zone 6 climate. But most are hardy to Zone 4 with snowcover, perhaps even Zone 3." Many produce flowers in a variety of colors. Eddison already has written enough garden books to fill a shelf but is planning a book on primroses. Until it comes out, try *The Patchwork Garden* (1990), a warm and entertaining account of gardening friendships.

Primula cortusoides	pink to red-violet
Drumstick primrose (*Primula denticulata*)	purple, white, red-purple with yellow eye
Oxslip (*Primula elatior*)	yellow
Japanese primrose (*Primula japonica*)	red-purple to white
Primula kisoana	rose to white
Primula modesta	purple-pink
Hybrid polyanthus primrose (*Primula pruhoniciana*)	yellow, white, blue, red, pink
Primula saxitalis	pink to rose-violet
Primula sieboldii	pink to lavender-blue, white
Cowslip (*Primula veris*)	deep yellow
Common primrose (*Primula vulgaris* and cvs.)	pale yellow; cvs. range from white to violet/purple

 Looking for flowers to interest your kids? According to Marilyn Barlow, owner of Select Seeds, in Union, Connecticut, marsh mallow and balloon flower are two to grow. "My children love marsh mallow. Knowing it was once the source of marshmallow confections was enough to guarantee their devotion. And they can't resist popping the balloon-shaped buds of *Platycodon grandiflorus*."

BACK-ROW BEAUTIES

Handsome perennials that are tall enough to be seen when set at the back of the border, or the middle of the bed, are worth their weight in gold. You'll want to choose plants that not only look good throughout the garden season but that have different bloom times, so that something is always flowering. Be sure each gets a sympathetic location—full sun if it prefers full sun. All of these hardy beauties grow to at least 4 feet tall, but none need staking.

Tall ornamental grasses are another good choice for the back row. Lists of grasses appear in the "Ground Covers, Grasses, and Ferns" chapter.

Hollyhock (*Alcea rosea*)	3, 4, 5, 6
Goatsbeard (*Aruncus dioicus*)	3, 4, 5, 6
'Moerheim's Glory' astilbe (*Astilbe*)	3, 4, 5, 6
Black cohosh (*Cimicifuga racemosa*)	3, 4, 5, 6
'Taplow Blue' globe thistle (*Echinops ritro*)	3, 4, 5, 6
'Gateway' Joe-Pye weed (*Eupatorium fistulosum*)	3/4, 5, 6
'Venusta' queen of the prairie (*Filipendula rubra*)	3, 4, 5, 6
Sneezeweed (*Helenium autumnale*)	3, 4, 5, 6
Perennial sunflower (*Helianthus multiflorus*)	3, 4, 5, 6
Ox-eye/false sunflower (*Heliopsis helianthoides*)	3, 4, 5, 6
'Lord Baltimore' rose mallow (*Hibiscus moscheutos*)	4, 5, 6
Plume poppy (*Macleaya cordata*)	2/3, 4, 5, 6
'Kelway's Coral Plume' plume poppy (*Macleaya microcarpa*)	4, 5, 6
'Atrosanguineum' Chinese/ornamental rhubarb (*Rheum palmatum*)	3/4, 5, 6
'Lavender Mist' meadow rue (*Thalictrum rochebruneanum*)	4, 5, 6
'Southern Charm' mullein (*Verbascum*)	3, 4, 5, 6
Culver's root (*Veronicastrum virginicum*)	3, 4, 5, 6
Adam's needle (*Yucca filamentosa*)	4, 5, 6

PERENNIALS THAT TOLERATE DROUGHT AND COLD WINTERS

No one would characterize New England as desertlike, but many of us have spots in our gardens where the soil dries rock-hard under summer's sun, or where patches of sandy, rocky soil drain way too quickly. If either of these problems is yours, take a look at perennials from this list supplied by Jennifer Bennett. She's the author of *Dry-Land Gardening* (1998), the first book about xeriscaping for regions with cold winters like New England's. Once established, all of these plants will tolerate heat and drought—and, as the zone numbers indicate, cold winters. If you're looking for an ornamental grass, Bennett suggests *Festuca glauca*, blue fescue. Grow it from seed, she advises, and you'll likely get interesting variations.

'Silver Brocade' (*Artemisia stelleriana*)	2, 3, 4, 5, 6
'Fireglow' spurge (*Euphorbia griffithii*)	2, 3, 4, 5, 6
Bigroot cranesbill (*Geranium macrorrhizum*)	3, 4, 5, 6
'Love That Pink' daylily (*Hemerocallis*)	2, 3, 4, 5, 6
Sea lavender (*Limonium latifolium*)	2, 3, 4, 5, 6
Peony (*Paeonia officinalis*)	2, 3, 4, 5, 6
'Mohrchen' sedum/stonecrop (*Sedum*)	2, 3, 4, 5, 6
'Variegatum' sedum/stonecrop (*Sedum kamschaticum*)	2, 3, 4, 5, 6
Speedwell (*Veronica pectinata*)	3, 4, 5, 6

SPEEDWELL

AN ASTILBE SAMPLER FROM THE VERMONT FLOWER FARM

George and Gail Africa, who run the Vermont Flower Farm, a retail perennial nursery located in Marshfield, Vermont, are big fans of astilbes. They grow more than forty cultivars, ranging from 'Moerheim's Glory', an astonishing 6-footer with pink flowers, to the diminutive 10-inch 'Pumila', which sports lilac blooms. The Africas call astilbes "underused perennials." Normally, they explain, astilbes prefer partial shade, but in the cooler parts of New England they also do well in full sun.

Sun or shade, this perennial wants moist, organically rich soil covered with an organic mulch. All of the plants in this list are hardy to Zone 3.

	Flower color	Plant height
'Amethyst'	lilac-rose	2 feet
'Deutschland'	white	2 feet
'Federsee'	carmine red	18 inches
'Granat'	raspberry red	30 inches
'Inshriach Pink'	rose-pink	12 inches
'Moerheim's Glory'	pink	6 feet
'Perkeo'	lavender-rose	8 inches
'Red Sentinel'	crimson red	2 feet
'Sprite'	pink	18 inches
'Visions'	purple	16 inches
'Washington'	white	2 feet

When making a perennial garden, don't waste your money buying ordinary topsoil. It's usually nothing more than sifted dirt (often illegally dug from river beds and banks) that contains almost none of the nutrients that plants need. Instead, purchase "amended topsoil," which contains soil and organic matter. Or add large amounts of organic matter—compost, well-rotted manures, peat moss, cocoa hulls, chopped leaves, chopped straw, pine needles, and more—to your garden site. Whatever the soil problem, adding humus or other organic materials helps.

PERENNIALS THAT THRIVE IN PARTIAL SHADE

Here are perennials that strut their stuff in shade—not darkness, mind you, but dappled light or afternoon shade. There is nothing hard-to-find or rare on this list, just widely available, reliable plants that will thrive in New England gardens. Most perennials do best in slightly acid soil that drains well and has been generously amended with organic matter. It's worth repeating: If you don't have reliable snowcover in your area, be sure to mulch plants after the ground freezes to prevent heaving.

Ladybells (*Adenophora confusa*)	3, 4, 5, 6
Lady's mantle (*Alchemilla mollis*)	3, 4, 5, 6
Japanese anemone (*Anemone hupenhensis* var. *japonica*)	4, 5, 6
Snowdrop anemone (*Anemone sylvestris*)	4, 5, 6
Goatsbeard (*Aruncus dioicus*)	3, 4, 5, 6
European ginger (*Asarum europaeum*)	4, 5, 6
Astilbe (*Astilbe* cvs.)	3, 4, 5, 6
Heartleaf bergenia (*Bergenia cordifolia*)	3, 4, 5, 6
Black cohosh (*Cimicifuga racemosa*)	3, 4, 5, 6
Yellow corydalis (*Corydalis lutea*)	3/4, 5, 6
Maiden pink (*Dianthus deltoides*)	3, 4, 5, 6
Bleeding heart (*Dicentra spectabilis*)	3, 4, 5, 6

Leopard's bane (*Doronicum orientale*)	3, 4, 5, 6
Sweet woodruff (*Galium odoratum*)	3, 4, 5, 6
Bloody cranesbill (*Geranium sanguineum*)	3, 4, 5, 6
Lenten rose (*Helleborus orientalis*)	3, 4, 5, 6
Hosta (*Hosta* cvs.)	3, 4, 5, 6
Spotted dead nettle (*Lamium maculatum*)	4, 5, 6
Bigleaf goldenray (*Ligularia dentata*)	3, 4, 5, 6
Jacob's ladder (*Polemonium caeruleum*)	3, 4, 5, 6
Primrose (*Primula* spp. and cvs.)	3, 4, 5, 6
Bethlehem sage/lungwort (*Pulmonaria saccharata*)	3/4, 5, 6
Featherleaf rodgersia (*Rodgersia pinnata*)	4, 5, 6
False Solomon's seal (*Smilacina racemosa*)	3, 4, 5, 6
Celandine poppy (*Stylophorum diphyllum*)	3/4, 5, 6
Meadow rue (*Thalictrum pubescens*)	3, 4, 5, 6

PERENNIAL PICKS FROM A NEW HAMPSHIRE PLANTSWOMAN

Nancy Maltais, owner of Maltais Flower Farm, a retail and mail-order nursery in Gilmanton, New Hampshire, grows both annuals and perennials. To compensate for her frosty location in Zone 3, she also maintains seven greenhouses. Maltais is famous locally for the size and design of the 1,500 hanging baskets that she produces each year. Her recommendations for your perennial garden include some underplanted flowers, such as mullein, which may hold the record for common names—including hag's taper, candlewick plant, torches, witch's candle, light taper, miner's candle, Aaron's rod, Jacob's staff, hedge taper, shepherd's club, beggar's blanket, blanket leaf, velvet plant, flannel plant, old man's flannel, rag paper, feltwort, bunny's ears, Our Lady's flannel, Adam's flannel, flannel leaf, fluffweed, flannel weed, goose grass, iceleaf, Indian tobacco, Quaker rouge, lamb's tongue, hare's beard, cow's lungwort, lungwort, longwort, and torchwort.

MULLEIN

'Summer Pastels' yarrow (*Achillea*)	3, 4, 5, 6
'Blue Clips' bellflower (*Campanula carpatica*)	3, 4, 5, 6
'Moonbeam' threadleaf tickseed (*Coreopsis*)	3, 4, 5, 6
'Early Sunrise' tickseed (*Coreopsis grandiflora*)	3, 4, 5, 6
'Magnus' purple coneflower (*Echinacea purpurea*)	3, 4, 5, 6
'Burgunder' blanket flower (*Gaillardia grandiflora*)	3, 4, 5, 6
'Palace Purple' coral flower (*Heuchera micrantha*)	3, 4, 5, 6
Lavender (*Lavandula* spp.)	4, 5, 6
Russell Hybrid lupine (*Lupinus*)	3, 4, 5, 6
Soapwort (*Saponaria officinalis*)	3, 4, 5, 6
'Alba' silene (*Silene maritima*)	3/4, 5, 6
'Southern Charm' mullein (*Verbascum*)	3, 4, 5, 6

Nancy Maltais, who owns Maltais Flower Farm in Gilmanton, New Hampshire, recommends this organic concoction to prevent and to remedy insect problems, indoors or out. "It works exceptionally well on aphids."
   mineral oil
   3 cloves garlic, peeled and chopped
   ¼ teaspoon dish detergent
Pour mineral oil over chopped garlic just to cover. Let steep overnight, then strain oil into a small container. Add dish detergent to the garlic oil and mix well. Use one part mixture to 10 parts water as a spray on your plants.

UNDEMANDING PERENNIALS

Footloose and fancy free! That's what you'll be if you stick with plants on this list. There isn't a perennial that needs no care, but these species are about as undemanding as anything you can put in the ground. No spraying, no staking, no nothing. An added advantage: Practically all these plants are hardy throughout New England.

Although they are close to no-care, all of these flowers need to be given the proper amount of light, and all will do better if planted in organically rich soil that drains well.

More plants to keep you fancy-free? Try some hardy ferns and ornamental grasses (lists appear in the "Ground Covers, Grasses, and Ferns" chapter).

Shade tolerant

Canadian wild ginger (*Asarum canadense*)	2, 3, 4, 5, 6
European ginger (*Asarum europaeum*)	4, 5, 6
Astilbe (*Astilbe* cvs.)	3, 4, 5, 6
Hosta (*Hosta* cvs.)	3, 4, 5, 6

Sun loving

Thread-leaf coreopsis (*Coreopsis verticillata*)	3, 4, 5, 6
Purple coneflower (*Echinacea purpurea*)	3, 4, 5, 6
Joe-Pye weed (*Eupatorium fistulosum*)	3, 4, 5, 6
Daylily (*Hemerocallis* cvs.)	3, 4, 5, 6
Siberian iris (*Iris sibirica* cvs.)	3, 4, 5, 6
Peony (*Paeonia* cvs.)	3, 4, 5, 6
'Goldsturm' rudbeckia (*Rudbeckia fulgida* var. *sullivantii*)	3, 4, 5, 6
Sedum/stonecrop (*Sedum* spp.)	3, 4, 5, 6

"A layer of loose, airy mulch spread over the soil prevents erosion, protects plant roots from abrupt changes in temperature, retains moisture by retarding evaporation, and discourages the germination of weed seeds. It is almost impossible to overstate the case for an organic mulch. I say almost only because mulch can provide a haven for small rodents. But the benefits outweigh the risks, and despite vole damage, I continue to mulch my perennial border."
Sydney Eddison, garden writer, Newtown, Connecticut

THE PINNACLE OF PERENNIALS

In 1999, Brant Smith's interest in gardening led him to found Pinnacle Plants, a mail-order perennial and bulb company. Smith, who lives in Essex, Connecticut, is interested in offering other gardeners something different: "'Goldsturm' rudbeckia is a wonderful plant, but it's in every garden center. Our mission is to offer a select number of plants and bulbs that are difficult to find, and in some cases only offered here. These are typically newer cultivars that are superior to better-known plants in their form and vigor and are not widely offered simply because the availability of plants is limited." Here are a dozen truly choice perennials from Smith, all ideal for New England gardens.

'Elise Feldman' snowdrop anemone (*Anemone sylvestris*)	4, 5, 6
'Branford Beauty' lady fern (*Athyrium hybrida*)	3, 4, 5, 6
'Variegata' black horehound (*Ballota nigra*)	3, 4, 5, 6
'Marley's White' Siberian bugloss (*Brunnera macrophylla*)	3, 4, 5, 6

Barrenwort (*Epimedium acuminatum*)	4, 5, 6
'Samobar' cranesbill (*Geranium phaem*)	4, 5, 6
'Petite Marbled Burgundy' coral bells (*Heuchera*)	3, 4, 5, 6
'Dallas Blues' switch grass (*Panicum virgatum*)	5, 6
'Red Dragon' fleece plant (*Persicaria amplexicaule*)	5, 6
'Montrose Tricolor' Canadian phlox (*Phlox divaricata*)	3, 4, 5, 6
'Little Princess' tall garden phlox (*Phlox paniculata*)	3, 4, 5, 6
Fabaria sedum/stonecrop (*Sedum fabari* var. *borderi*)	3, 4, 5, 6

THE (ALMOST) PERMANENT PERENNIAL

Herbaceous perennials, plants that die back in winter and resprout in spring, don't live as long as most trees, vines, and shrubs, but some of them may be around long after your mortgage is paid off. If you want to plant a perennial border that will *really* last, choose from among these widely available flowers. Not surprisingly, most of them are also low-maintenance. For the record, ferns and ornamental grasses are also among the most long-lived herbaceous plants.

Life expectancy 25 or more years

Monkshood (*Aconitum* spp.)	3, 4, 5, 6
Lady's mantle (*Alchemilla* spp.)	3, 4, 5, 6
Wormwood (*Artemisia* spp.)	3, 4, 5, 6
Milkweed (*Asclepias* spp.)	3, 4, 5, 6
Turtlehead (*Chelone* spp.)	3, 4, 5, 6
Daylily (*Hemerocallis* cvs.)	3, 4, 5, 6
Hosta (*Hosta* cvs.)	3, 4, 5, 6
Peony (*Paeonia* cvs.)	3, 4, 5, 6
Lungwort (*Pulmonaria* spp.)	3, 4, 5, 6
Rudbeckia (*Rudbeckia* spp.)	3, 4, 5, 6
Sedum/stonecrop (*Sedum* spp.)	3, 4, 5, 6

Life expectancy 15-25 years

Astilbe (*Astilbe* cvs.)	3, 4, 5, 6
Bellflower (*Campanula* spp.)	3, 4, 5, 6
Coneflower (*Echinacea* spp.)	3, 4, 5, 6
Meadowsweet (*Filipendula* spp.)	3, 4, 5, 6
Cranesbill/true geranium (*Geranium* spp.)	3, 4, 5, 6
Gayfeather (*Liatris* spp.)	3, 4, 5, 6
Catmint (*Nepeta* spp.)	3, 4, 5, 6
Sundrops (*Oenothera* spp.)	4, 5, 6
Speedwell (*Veronica* spp.)	3, 4, 5, 6

Life expectancy 10-15 years

Yarrow (*Achillea* spp.)	3, 4, 5, 6
Aster (*Aster* spp.)	3, 4, 5, 6
Tickseed (*Coreopsis* spp.)	3, 4, 5, 6
Bleeding heart (*Dicentra* spp.)	3, 4, 5, 6
Spurge (*Euphorbia* spp.)	3, 4, 5, 6
Ox-eye (*Heliopsis* spp.)	3, 4, 5, 6
Phlox (*Phlox* spp.)	3, 4, 5, 6
Sage (*Salvia* spp.)	3/4, 5, 6

COME EARLY OR LATE: AN ALL-SEASON DAYLILY GARDEN

Lee and Diana Bristol have run Bloomingfields Farm, a twenty-five-acre daylily retail and mail-order nursery located in Gaylordsville, Connecticut, for more than three decades. They've never wavered in their enthusiasm for *Hemerocallis*—nor will you, if you visit the nursery or grow any of their cultivars. All of their plants—there are more than 300 to choose from—are grown organically and dug on demand.

To extend the daylily season in your garden, the Bristols recommend these cultivars: some flower early, some late. Three of them, 'Daily Bread', 'Little Wine Cup', and 'Stella de Oro', do both. All are hardy to Zone 3.

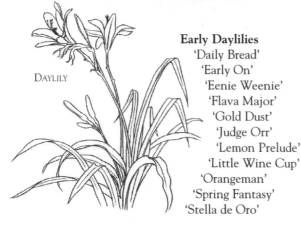

DAYLILY

Early Daylilies

'Daily Bread'	gold
'Early On'	raspberry-rose
'Eenie Weenie'	gold
'Flava Major'	yellow
'Gold Dust'	yellow
'Judge Orr'	yellow
'Lemon Prelude'	yellow
'Little Wine Cup'	wine
'Orangeman'	orange
'Spring Fantasy'	yellow and rose
'Stella de Oro'	gold

Late Daylilies

'Alice in Wonderland'	yellow
'August Pioneer'	apricot
'Autumn Accent'	red
'Autumn Daffodil'	yellow
'Autumn King'	gold
'Autumn Minaret'	peach
'Carol Sing'	red
'Challenger'	red
'Daily Bread'	gold
'Fall Fancy'	raspberry-rose
'Fall Festival'	apricot
'Late Cream'	white
'Letty Lately'	yellow
'Little Wine Cup'	wine
'Postlude'	salmon-peach
'Regal Finale'	black-violet
'Stella de Oro'	gold

PLANT 'EM AND FORGET 'EM: PERENNIALS FROM A MASSACHUSETTS EXPERT

Hilda Morrill, who lives south of Boston and maintains a half-acre, Zone 6 garden, is the publisher/editor of *www.bostongardens.com*, a gardening Website that focuses on the Boston area and Massachusetts in general. She's busy, so her favorite plants are those that "perform beautifully year after year with no work on my part. Pests don't bother them much, they don't droop if I don't water, and they don't have to be divided often. I've heard some of them described as boring; but I love them."

Allium (*Allium senescens*)	4, 5, 6
Garlic chives (*Allium tuberosum*)	3, 4, 5, 6
Japanese anemone (*Anemone hupenhensis* var. *japonica*)	4, 5, 6
Blue false indigo (*Baptisia australis*)	2/3, 4, 5, 6
Thread-leaf coreopsis (*Coreopsis verticillata*)	3, 4, 5, 6
'Sum and Substance' (*Hosta*)	3, 4, 5, 6
'Variegata' variegated blue lilyturf (*Liriope muscari*)	6
Russian sage (*Perovskia atriplicifolia*)	5, 6
Creeping phlox (*Phlox subulata*)	3, 4, 5, 6
Balloon flower (*Platycodon grandiflorus*)	3, 4, 5, 6
Sedum/stonecrop (*Sedum* spp.)	3, 4, 5, 6

"I like to have daffodils between my groupings of perennials for early spring color and spacing. I now always plant *Muscari*, grape hyacinths, in the planting hole at the same time, in between the daffodil bulbs. Not only do I get a flush of gorgeous blue color before the burst of yellows and creams, but in the fall I know exactly where the daffs are and don't dig them up inadvertently as I look for new spots to plant more perennials and bulbs. The *Muscari* always send up their leaves in the fall—providing perfect 'markers' in my perennial beds."
Hilda Morrill, editor and publisher, *www.bostongardens.com*, Boston, Massachusetts

A PLACE OUT OF THE SUN: MORE PERENNIALS FOR PARTIAL SHADE

Russ Bragg, the proprietor of Underwood Shade Nursery in North Attleboro, Massachusetts, is New England's guru of shade. His mail-order catalog is filled with perennials that thrive where the sun don't shine—or shines only part of the day. The nursery's inventory is impressive, everything from *Aconitum carmichaelii* 'Arendsii', a monkshood that Bragg describes as a "tall, stiff stemmed (no staking) variety with large, deep blue hoods," to *Zizia aurea*, or golden Alexanders, which is hardy to Zone 3. Bragg's catalog also includes a fine selection of ferns, shade-lovers of the first order. This list, which may contain some unfamiliar names, is a baker's dozen of his particular favorites.

Doll's eyes (*Actaea pachypoda*)	white flowers, white berries	3, 4, 5, 6
European ginger (*Asarum europaeum*)	purple to brown flowers	4, 5, 6
Heart-leafed aster (*Aster cordifolius*)	blue flowers	4, 5, 6
Yellow corydalis (*Corydalis lutea*)	yellow flowers	3/4, 5, 6
Dixie wood fern (*Dryopteris* x *australis*)	dark green fronds	5, 6
Bigroot cranesbill (*Geranium macrorrhizum*)	white, pink, or magenta flowers	3, 4, 5, 6
Lenten rose (*Helleborus orientalis*)	white, mauve to purple flowers	3, 4, 5, 6
Sharp-lobed hepatica (*Hepatica acutiloba*)	white or pink flowers	3, 4, 5, 6
Partridgeberry (*Mitchella repens*)	white flowers	3, 4, 5, 6
Solomon's seal (*Polygonatum pubescens*)	white flowers	3, 4, 5, 6
Christmas fern (*Polystichum acrostichoides*)	dark green fronds	3, 4, 5, 6
Celandine poppy (*Stylophorum diphyllum*)	yellow flowers	3/4, 5, 6
'Miyazaki' toad lily (*Tricyrtis hirta*)	white flowers	4, 5, 6

A FLOCK OF PHLOX

The popularity of garden phlox in New England has dropped off in the last fifty years, largely because of this perennial's susceptibility to powdery mildew, a fungus that leaves plant foliage splotched with white. Gardeners looking for tall bloomers for the back of the border, however, have kept their eyes out for cultivars of *Phlox paniculata* that are both beautiful and disease-resistant. These are some of their discoveries. All grow to 4 feet or taller.

Remember that *resistant* doesn't mean *immune*. Be sure to give your tall garden phlox full sun and elbow room.

'Bright Eyes'	pink with red eye	3, 4, 5, 6
'Brite Pink'	pink with white eye	3, 4, 5, 6
'David'	white	3, 4, 5, 6
'Franz Schubert'	lilac with dark eye	3, 4, 5, 6
'Graf Zeppelin'	white with pink eye	3, 4, 5, 6
'Katherine'	lavender with white eye	3, 4, 5, 6
'Prime Minister'	white with red eye	3, 4, 5, 6

A MAINE GARDENER'S FAVORITES FOR AN ORNAMENTAL BORDER

This complementary list of perennials for the ornamental border—several are just as popular in the herb garden—comes from Aurelia C. Scott, a garden writer and lecturer who has also lived and gardened in the West. She's a converted Yankee now and grows herbs, perennials, and vegetables within sight of Casco Bay in Portland, Maine. In addition to being a regular contributor to garden magazines (including *People, Places, Plants: The Gardening Magazine from Maine*), Scott keeps busy helping others as a Cooperative Extension Master Gardener.

'Johnson's Blue' geranium (*Geranium*)	light blue	3, 4, 5, 6
'Ballerina' geranium (*Geranium cinereum*)	rose-pink	4, 5, 6
Bloody cranesbill (*Geranium sanguineum*)	scarlet	3, 4, 5, 6
'Fire Opal' avens (*Geum*)	orange/scarlet	4/5, 6
'Mrs. Bradshaw' avens (*Geum*)	scarlet	4/5, 6
'Prinses Juliana' avens (*Geum*)	copper	4/5, 6
Common hyssop (*Hyssopus officinalis*)	dark blue	3, 4, 5, 6
Hyssop (*Hyssopus officinalis* f. *arbus*)	white	3, 4, 5, 6
Rock hyssop (*Hyssopus officinalis* subsp. *aristatus*)	blue	3, 4, 5, 6
'Hidcote' lavender (*Lavandula angustifolia*)	deep blue	4/5, 6
'Imperial Gem' lavender (*Lavandula angustifolia*)	soft purple	4/5, 6
'Twinkle Purple' lavender (*Lavandula angustifolia*)	medium purple	4/5, 6
'Six Hills Giant' catmint (*Nepeta*)	lavender-blue	4, 5, 6
Catmint (*Nepeta racemosa*)	lavender	4, 5, 6
'Blue Beauty' catmint (*Nepeta sibirica*)	blue	3, 4, 5, 6
'Prairie Fire' beardlip penstemon (*Penstemon barbatus*)	scarlet	3, 4, 5, 6
'Husker Red' penstemon (*Penstemon digitalis*)	pink-white	3, 4, 5, 6
Rocky Mountain penstemon (*Penstemon strictus*)	indigo blue	3, 4, 5, 6

THE BLUE NOTE: HOSTAS

Gardeners are forever looking for blue flowers and foliage to add to their gardens—and there are plenty of choices among hostas. These rugged perennials don't just provide different shades of blue—they also offer a range of different sized, shaped, and textured leaves. The blue color, which is a layer of "bloom," or wax, that covers the green leaf, fades quickly in sun, so plant blue hostas in a partially shaded location to preserve their color. Partial shade, and in organically rich soil, is also where they grow best.

Small leaves measure to 1 foot across; medium leaves to 2 feet; large leaves to 4 feet; and giant are greater than 4 feet across, big enough to to win a blue ribbon. All are hardy to Zone 3.

Small leaves
'Baby Bunting'
'Blue Danube'
'Blue Moon'

Medium leaves
'Blue Shadows'
'Blue Wedgwood'
'Pearl Lake'

Large leaves
'Big Daddy'
'Blue Heaven'
'Frances Williams'
'Elegans' (*H. sieboldiana*)

Giant
'Blue Angel'
'Blue Mammoth'
'Blue Umbrellas'

PERENNIALS THAT PUT UP WITH DAMP LOCATIONS

Well-known garden writer Sydney Eddison calls Martha McKeon her "neighbor and garden buddy, wonderfully knowledgeable and inventive enough to succeed on a difficult piece of wooded land." McKeon, who lives in Sandy Hook, Connecticut, gets her expertise from twenty-five years of working in the same garden, and from working in area nurseries and greenhouses. Her Zone 6 garden is "on the low side," so she's a reigning expert on plants that do well—or are forgiving—when their feet are damp. Her list contains a mix, species that want sun and those that prefer a bit of shade.

Lady's mantle (*Alchemilla mollis*)	sun	3, 4, 5, 6
Amsonia (*Amsonia hubrectii*)	sun	4, 5, 6
Astilbe (*Astilbe* cvs.)	sun/shade	3, 4, 5, 6
Siberian bugloss (*Brunnera macrophylla*)	shade	3, 4, 5, 6
Turtlehead (*Chelone glabra*)	sun	3, 4, 5, 6
Wild bleeding heart (*Dicentra eximia*)	shade	3/4, 5, 6
Yellow foxglove (*Digitalis grandiflora*)	shade	3, 4, 5, 6
'Bright Star' coneflower (*Echinacea purpurea*)	sun	3, 4, 5, 6
'White Swan' coneflower (*Echinacea purpurea*)	sun	3, 4, 5, 6
'Gateway' Joe-Pye weed (*Eupatorium fistulosum*)	sun	3/4, 5, 6
Daylily (*Hemerocallis* cvs.)	sun	3, 4, 5, 6
Hosta (*Hosta* cvs.)	shade	3, 4, 5, 6
'The Rocket' ligularia (*Ligularia stenocephala*)	shade	3, 4, 5, 6
'Variegata' variegated blue lilyturf (*Liriope muscari*)	sun	6
'Aurea' golden creeping Charley (*Lysimachia nummularia*)	shade	4, 5, 6
Ostrich fern (*Matteuccia struthiopteris*)	shade	2, 3, 4, 5, 6
Amur silver grass (*Miscanthus floridulus*)	sun	5, 6
Japanese silver grass (*Miscanthus sinensis* cvs.)	sun	4, 5, 6

Miscanthus (*Miscanthus yakushimensis*)	sun	5, 6
Cinnamon fern (*Osmunda cinnamomea*)	shade	3, 4, 5, 6
Royal fern (*Osmunda regalis*)	shade	2, 3, 4, 5, 6
Christmas fern (*Polystichum acrostichoides*)	shade	3, 4, 5, 6
Primrose (*Primula* spp.)	shade	3, 4, 5, 6
'Excalibur' pulmonaria (*Pulmonaria*)	shade	3/4, 5, 6
Blue lungwort (*Pulmonaria angustifolia*)	shade	3/4, 5, 6
Bethlehem sage/lungwort (*Pulmonaria saccharata*)	shade	3/4, 5, 6
'Goldsturm' rudbeckia (*Rudbeckia fulgida* var. *sullivantii*)	sun	3, 4, 5, 6
'Lavender Mist' meadow rue (*Thalictrum rochebruneanum*)	sun	4, 5, 6

"Choosing plants that are at home with plenty of moisture is the most sensible way to deal with a garden site that is wet. Raised beds are an alternative solution, especially if you want to grow plants that don't like wet conditions. Whatever you decide to grow, add plenty of organic matter to the soil to ensure it has an open structure."
Martha McKeon, former nurserywoman, Sandy Hook, Connecticut

RESTORING THE OLD ODOR: HEIRLOOM PERENNIALS

Rachel Kane began Perennial Pleasures Nursery in 1980 in East Hardwick, Vermont, a rugged Zone 3 location. Her purpose was to grow antique perennial plants and herbs, heirloom plants from the seventeenth, eighteenth, nineteenth, and early twentieth centuries. Over her twenty years in the retail and mail-order seed and plant business, Kane has collected nearly 1,000 different plants. Not all the perennials she sells are fragrant, but her favorites are the sweet-scented old-timers on this list. Kane grows nearly all her own plants, an indication of their hardiness, but she warns that "if you don't have the benefit of consistent snowcover, as I do, you should apply mulch after the ground freezes, and remove it early in spring." That's especially true of the regal lily, whose hardiness is iffy in Zone 3.

Sweet William (*Dianthus barbatus*)	3, 4, 5, 6
Cottage pink (*Dianthus plumarius*)	3, 4, 5, 6
Lemon lily (*Hemerocallis lilioasphodelus*)	3, 4, 5, 6
Dame's rocket (*Hesperis matronalis*)	3, 4, 5, 6
Regal lily (*Lilium regale*)	3/4, 5, 6
'Duchesse de Nemours' peony (*Paeonia*)	3, 4, 5, 6
'Edulis Superba' peony (*Paeonia*)	3, 4, 5, 6
'Old Cellarhole' tall garden phlox (*Phlox paniculata*)	3, 4, 5, 6
Soapwort (*Saponaria officinalis*)	3, 4, 5, 6
Garden heliotrope (*Valeriana officinalis*)	3, 4, 5, 6
Sweet violet (*Viola odorata*)	3, 4, 5, 6

PROBLEM-SOLVING PERENNIALS FOR DRY SHADE

Many gardeners agree that the toughest site in the garden is one that is both dry and shady. That's because the majority of plants that like shade like moist soil, and the majority of plants that tolerate drought are sun-lovers. Alice McGowan, who owns Blue Meadow Farm, a small, family-run retail and mail-order nursery located in rural western Massachusetts near Montague, has some solutions for plants to try in dry, shaded places. She specializes in unusual and tender perennials. If you'd like to

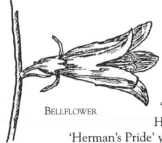

BELLFLOWER

inspect any of these plants before you plant, she recommends you visit her one-acre display garden any time from April through July.

Bellflower/campanula (*Campanula takesimana*)	4, 5, 6
Barrenwort (*Epimedium* spp.)	4, 5, 6
Bigroot cranesbill (*Geranium macrorrhizum*)	3, 4, 5, 6
'Garnet' coral flower (*Heuchera americana*)	3/4, 5, 6
Hosta (*Hosta lancifolia*)	3, 4, 5, 6
'Herman's Pride' yellow archangel (*Lamium galeobdolon*)	4, 5, 6
Spring vetchling (*Lathyrus vernus*)	4, 5, 6
Sedum/stonecrop (*Sedum ternatum*)	4, 5, 6
Vancouveria (*Vancouveria hexandra*)	4, 5, 6
Waldsteinia (*Waldsteinia ternata*)	3, 4, 5, 6

Most gardeners know that deadheading annuals is essential to keep them blooming but are unaware that deadheading perennials is also a smart thing to do. Not only does it keep them looking attractive, in many species it promotes branching lower on the plant, which will produce more flowers later in the season.

SIBERIAN IRIS

Jody Camille runs a retail and mail-order nursery, Mountain River Flower Farm, in West Dummer, New Hampshire, which is in western Coos County, the northern-most county in the state, bordering Quebec, Maine, and Vermont. Anyone living *that* far north has to like Siberian iris, *Iris sibirica*, and Camille does: "They're terrific landscape plants here in all seasons, virtually carefree and not particular about soil once they're established. Their blooms are among the earliest in our gardens, which is no small blessing after a long Coos County winter."

Technically, Siberian iris belong in the "Bulbs" chapter, but since most gardeners think of them as perennials, they appear here; all are hardy to Zone 3.

Favorite landscaping cultivars
'Halcyon Seas'
'Sparkling Rose'
'Sky Wings'
'White Swirl'

Favorite blue cultivars
'Appaloosa Blue'
'Dancing Shadows'
'Liberty Hills'
'Peg Edwards'
'Ruffled Velvet'

Favorite white cultivars
'Harpswell Happiness'
'White Swirl'

Favorite red cultivars
'Indy'
'Lady Vanessa'
'Temper Tantrum'

Favorite early blooming cultivars
'Illini Charm'
'My Love'

Favorite late blooming cultivars
'Chartreuse Bounty'
'Lilting Laura'
'Swirling Lavender'

THE EYES HAVE IT: BICOLOR DAYLILIES

Dorothy Pellett's Rock Crest Gardens is a small wholesale perennial nursery set about eight miles from Lake Champlain in Charlotte, Vermont. Pellett, who is also a writer, has gardened on this acreage for more than thirty years and is resigned to its rocky soil and the ravenous deer that live in the adjoining woods and fields. Despite those disadvantages, she is famous for knowing and growing top-notch daylilies. This list consists of her favorite daylilies with "eyes," a contrasting color that appears around the top of the flower's throat. A number of her choices also have ruffled edges, another quality that Pellett looks for in daylilies (a list of her favorite ruffled cultivars appears elsewhere in this chapter).

All are hardy to Zone 3. Two cultivars, 'Cherry-Eyed Pumpkin' and 'Rumble Seat Romance', are semi-evergreen.

'Black-Eyed Susan'	yellow with red-purple eye
'Cherry-Eyed Pumpkin'	ruffled orange pink with red eye
'Dark Eyed Magic'	ruffled cream with purple eye
'Don Stevens'	yellow with burgundy eye
'Made To Order'	ruffled pink with rose eye
'Rumble Seat Romance'	ruffled light yellow with cranberry eye
'Siloam Doodlebug'	ruffled icy yellow with black-purple eye
'Pink Cotton Candy'	ruffled pink with red eye
'Vanilla Candy'	ruffled creamy-white with red eye
'Tigerling'	ruffled light orange with red eye and picotee

TESTER'S CHOICE: MILDEW-RESISTANT BEE BALMS

If you like hummingbirds, bee balm is the garden plant for you. A North American native and perennial member of the mint family, *Monarda* cultivars have showy flowers and bracts and aromatic foliage. Plants are hardy to Zone 3, do well in sun or partial shade, stand up without help, and ask only for moist, organically rich soil to accommodate their shallow roots. Plant breeders have introduced cultivars that are resistant to powdery mildew, the only serious disease problem with bee balm. (Handpicking is the solution to the Japanese beetle problem).

Some of the most mildew-resistant cultivars, chosen in plant trials from throughout the country, are listed below. The list also indicates flower color, but for the best red, plant the nonresistant old-timer 'Cambridge Scarlet', give it full sun and plenty of room, and cross your fingers.

'Colrain Red'	purple-red
'Gardenview Scarlet'	red
'Marshall's Delight'	purple-pink
'Ohio Glow'	purple-red
'Raspberry Wine'	purple-red
'Rose Queen'	purple-red
'Rosy-Purple'	purple-red
'Squaw'	red
'Violet Queen'	purple

"Fertilizer is not a substitute for well-prepared soil with lots of organic matter incorporated before planting. We rarely fertilize our established beds and instead rely on a year-round, 3- to 4-inch thick mulch of soft wood bark as a slow and continuous source of nutrients and organic matter."
Don Avery, owner, Cady's Falls Nursery, Morrisville, Vermont

NORTH CREEK FARM FAVORITES

The owner of North Creek Farm, a retail and mail-order nursery, Suzy Verrier calls this list of hardy perennials her "core group." All these plants, she says, are "vigorous and dependable, things that I plant repeatedly. I think they deserve every square inch of space they occupy." Verrier's Maine garden, because of its coastal location, enjoys the luxury of Zone 6 conditions. Most of these plants, however, will thrive in far colder regions of New England.

Alpine columbine (*Aquilegia alpina*)	3, 4, 5, 6
Blue wood aster (*Aster cordifolius*)	3/4, 5, 6
'Esther' heath aster (*Aster ericoides*)	3, 4, 5, 6
'Blue Bird' smooth aster (*Aster laevis*)	3, 4, 5, 6
'Prince' calico aster (*Aster lateriflorus*)	3, 4, 5, 6
Yellow corydalis (*Corydalis lutea*)	3/4, 5, 6
'Emperor of China' hardy chrysanthemum (*Dendranthema*)	4, 5, 6
'Sheffield' hardy chrysanthemum (*Dendranthema*)	4, 5, 6
'Venus' hardy chrysanthemum (*Dendranthema*)	4, 5, 6
'Venusta' queen of the prairie (*Filipendula rubra*)	3, 4, 5, 6
'Splendens' geranium (*Geranium cinereum*)	4/5, 6
Bigroot cranesbill (*Geranium macrorrhizum*)	3, 4, 5, 6
Siberian catmint (*Nepeta sibirica*)	3, 4, 5, 6
'Purple Rain' lilac sage (*Salvia verticillata*)	5, 6
'Matrona' sedum/stonecrop (*Sedum*)	4, 5, 6
Caucasian daisy (*Tanacetum corymbosum*)	3/4, 5, 6
Ironweed (*Vernonia crinata*)	3, 4, 5, 6

DAYLILIES BY EDDISON: A HYBRID RAINBOW

All the wonderful daylilies (*Hemerocallis*) you see at nurseries and garden centers are hybrids and nearly all of them are terrific, which makes it impossibly hard to choose just a few. Why not begin with this list? It's from Sydney Eddison, a Newtown, Connecticut, garden writer—and active gardener (she grows more than 300 cultivars in her eight-acre garden)—who has written about daylilies: *A Passion for Daylilies* (1992). Classed by color, all of Eddison's favorites are hardy to Zone 3. Since most are relatively new, you're more likely to find them in mail-order catalogs than at a local garden center. While you're paging the catalogs, watch for 'Sydney Eddison', which is a creamy peach color.

Yellow
'Brocaded Gown'
'Prairie Moonlight'
'Renee'

Gold
'Bengaleer'
'Condilla'
'Pearl Lewis'

Red
'Cardinal Feathers'
'Chicago Ruby'
'Ed Murray'

Pink
'Barbara Mitchell'
'Lullaby Baby'
'Yesterday Memories'

Orange
'Green Eyes Wink'
'Paprika Velvet'
'Rocket City'

Purple
'Little Grapette'
'Malaysian Monarch'

Near White
'Iron Gate Glacier'
'Joan Senior'

LAST-MINUTE JOYS: PERENNIALS FOR LATE SUMMER AND FALL

It's not that spring flowers get too much attention but that autumn flowers get too little. Renée Beaulieu, who works for White Flower Farm in Litchfield, Connecticut, is a champion of perennials that bloom in late summer and fall. "They are plants to revive your garden and your spirits when you think the season's over," she says. "There are so many terrific flowers that bloom late in the season, and people just pass them over because the plants don't look like much in the spring when everyone's shopping. But they are such a joy later." Beaulieu gardens in Waterbury, Connecticut, a Zone 6 location where 'Autumn Sun' coneflower (*Rudbeckia*) flowers until November.

'Ozawa' allium (*Allium thunbergii*)	3/4, 5, 6
Japanese anemone (*Anemone hupenhensis* var. *japonica* cvs.)	4, 5, 6
White wood aster (*Aster divaricatus*)	3, 4, 5, 6
Big-leaf aster (*Aster macrophyllus*)	3, 4, 5, 6
New England aster (*Aster novae-angliae* cvs.)	3, 4, 5, 6
New York aster (*Aster novi-belgii* cvs.)	3, 4, 5, 6
'Sheffield Pink' chrysanthemum (*Chrysanthemum*)	4, 5, 6
'Venus' chrysanthemum (*Chrysanthemum*)	4, 5, 6
Woodland sunflower (*Helianthus divaricatus*)	3, 4, 5, 6
Daylily (*Hemerocallis* cvs.)	3, 4, 5, 6
'Autumn Sun' coneflower (*Rudbeckia*)	3, 4, 5, 6
'Autumn Joy' sedum/stonecrop (*Sedum*)	3, 4, 5, 6
'Amethystina' purple toad lily (*Tricyrtis formosana*)	4/5, 6
Yellow toad lily (*Tricyrtis macrantha*)	6

"If you plan to leave a daylily in the same place for ten years or more, it will need a planting space 2 feet in diameter. Be sure your plants get at least six hours of full sun daily. Mediocre soils can be improved by adding compost, rotted leaves or wood chips, old manure, or almost any other organic matter."
Lee and Diane Bristol, owners, Bloomingfields Farm, Gaylordsville, Connecticut

SPRING TONIC: PEONIES FROM A NEW HAMPSHIRE EXPERT

Herbaceous peonies (*Paeonia*) are famous for their longevity and hardiness. Marion Schafer, who lives in Dalton, New Hampshire ("USDA Zone 3 or 4, depending on whom you consult"), is an avid peony grower, who is also in the process of establishing a small peony nursery. She grows cultivars that are hardy in her garden and that have superior "stem strength and plant habit." These are her Top Ten, "all hardy to Zone 3, and with good winter cover, Zone 2. All of them make great cutting flowers, too."

PEONY

'Coral Charm'	deep coral double, fading to peach
'Do Tell'	orchid-pink and rose Japanese-like single
'Doris Cooper'	pink double, fragrant
'Festiva Maxima'	fragrant heirloom white double with red flecks
'Honey Gold'	fragrant cream and light yellow double

'Kansas'	watermelon-red double
'Krinkled White'	crepelike white single
'Miss America'	white semidouble
'Paula Fay'	vivid pink semidouble
'Red Charm'	dark red double

"Peonies are especially well suited for New England gardens because they thrive in clay soil, they require cold, and they usually escape late frosts that harm other perennials. Two things I've learned: First, plant the crown (the top part of the root that has the next year's buds growing from it) no more than 2 inches below the surface of the soil. Here in Zone 3, I plant crowns only an inch below the surface. If they're planted too deeply peonies won't flower. And second, remove all peony foliage after frost, and dispose of it in the trash. Don't put it in your compost bin where it might be returned to your peony bed. This prevents the only serious threat to peonies—botrytis fungus—from taking up residence in the peony garden."
Marion Schafer, peony breeder and nurserywoman, Dalton, New Hampshire

CHOICE PERENNIALS FROM A CONNECTICUT NURSERYWOMAN

Here are some choice perennials selected by nurserywoman and landscape designer Kathy Nelson. She and her husband run a small retail nursery, Kathleen Nelson Perennials in Gaylordsville, Connecticut, that is filled with nothing but choice perennials. Some plants, she says, "are missing from my plant catalog. Plants that don't do their job in the garden, that don't thrive or are disease prone, have been removed and relegated to the compost heap." In other words, Nelson has done the hard work for us! All we have to do is pick from the best.

Anise hyssop (*Agastache foeniculum*)	5, 6
Amsonia (*Amsonia hubrectii*)	4, 5, 6
Calamint (*Calamintha nepeta*)	4, 5, 6
Yellow corydalis (*Corydalis lutea*)	3/4, 5, 6
'Chameleon' spurge (*Euphorbia dulcis*)	4, 5, 6
Cranesbill (*Geranium psilostemon*)	3/4, 5, 6
Kalimeris (*Kalimeris integrifolia*)	5, 6
'Six Hills Giant' catmint (*Nepeta*)	4, 5, 6
'Herbstonne' black-eyed Susan (*Rudbeckia nitida*)	3, 4, 5, 6
'Helene Von Stein' lamb's ears (*Stachys byzantina*)	3, 4, 5, 6
Meadow rue (*Thalictrum pubescens*)	3, 4, 5, 6

PEONY HEAVEN: FLOWERING TREES FOR THE PERENNIAL GARDEN

Chinese tree peonies (*Paeonia*) have been garden favorites for nearly 1,500 years, and no wonder: dozens of large fragrant blooms carried on handsome shrublike plants. Cricket Hill Garden, a retail and mail-order nursery located in Thomaston, Connecticut, is the premier tree peony nursery in the country. Owners Kasha and David Furman suggest visiting during the height of flowering, mid May to early June.

Fall planting is imperative (September in Zone 4, October to early November in Zones 5 and 6), and the Furmans recommend a site that gets afternoon shade, which will extend the life of the flowers. Plants *are* pricey—they are difficult to propagate and Cricket Hill sells only three-year-old plants—but these fragrant perennials will be around for decades. After all, most need twenty years to reach their full height! All are hardy to Zone 4.

To 4 feet

'Jade Plate White'	white light semidouble

6–8 feet

'Coral Terrace'	pink-coral ruffled ball
'Grand Duke Dressed in Blue and Purple'	pink-purple ruffled ball

To 8 feet

'Better Than Jade with Triple Magic'	variable chartreuse green to pink-white ruffled ball
'Black Dragon Holds a Splendid Flower'	magenta-red ruffled ball
'Elegant Fragrance in White'	white heavy semidouble
'Green Dragon Lying on a Chinese Ink Stone'	maroon double
'Luoyang Red'	magenta-red heavy semidouble
'Multi-Colored Butterfly'	pink with maroon veining heavy semidouble
'Phoenix White'	white single

"Chinese peonies need to be sited in a well-drained location with semi-shade or dappled shade, away from trees where roots will compete. They prefer soil with a pH of 6.5 to 7.0. Allow a space no less than 5 feet square for each plant. In the fall, remove dead leaves; this sanitary procedure will help keep your plants free of botrytis. Mulch plants after the ground freezes with 6 inches of leaves or straw during the first winter to prevent the earth from heaving."

Kasha and David Furman, owners, Cricket Hill Garden, Thomaston, Connecticut

CITY DWELLERS

Sally Williams is the publisher-editor of *Garden Literature*, a comprehensive index of horticulture publications. She also maintains a 20- by 40-foot fenced garden in Boston. When she began tending her small space two decades ago, it was a sunny plot that now is mostly shady. "I've mixed these well-behaved perennials with ferns and shrubs around a moss lawn, all shaded by a huge old pink dogwood. The colors are predominately restful green and white with pink accents to complement the old brick of house, patio, and curving walkway." Here's what works in her garden.

'Kristall' Rocky Mountain columbine (*Aquilegia caerulea*)	3, 4, 5, 6
Dwarf goatsbeard (*Aruncus aethusifolius*)	2, 3, 4, 5, 6
Goatsbeard (*Aruncus dioicus*)	3, 4, 5, 6
'Bumalda' false spirea (*Astilbe*)	3, 4, 5, 6
'Queen of Holland' false spirea (*Astilbe*)	3, 4, 5, 6
'Sprite' false spirea (*Astilbe*)	3, 4, 5, 6
'Washington' false spirea (*Astilbe*)	3, 4, 5, 6
'Snowline' sedge (*Carex conica*)	5, 6

Alpine strawberry (*Fragaria vesca*)	4, 5, 6
'Karmina' geranium (*Geranium cantabrigiense*)	3/4, 5, 6
'Pewter Veil' coral flower (*Heuchera americana*)	3/4, 5, 6
'Palace Purple' coral flower (*Heuchera micrantha*)	3, 4, 5, 6
Yellow wax-bells (*Kirengeshoma palmata*)	5, 6
Foamflower (*Tiarella wherryi*)	5, 6

PATH PARTNERS: LOW-GROWING PERENNIALS

Paths and walkways are softened by plantings, especially informal borders and edgings. This list of low-growing perennials is a place to start when looking for plants to edge and front. Most have pretty flowers, and all have interesting, attractive foliage that stays fresh throughout the garden season. Several herbs are part of this list; you may want to add more, as brushing against fragrant plants always makes a walk more fun.

Lady's mantle (*Alchemilla* spp.)	3, 4, 5, 6
Thrift (*Armeria maritima*)	3, 4, 5, 6
'Powis Castle' artemisia (*Artemisia*)	5, 6
Silvermound (*Artemisia schmidtiana*)	4, 5, 6
Astilbe (*Astilbe* spp.)	3, 4, 5, 6
Heartleaf bergenia (*Bergenia cordifolia*)	3, 4, 5, 6
Maiden pink (*Dianthus deltoides*)	2, 3, 4, 5, 6
Cottage pink (*Dianthus plumarius*)	3, 4, 5, 6
Blue fescue (*Festuca glauca*)	3, 4, 5, 6
Sweet woodruff (*Galium odoratum*)	3, 4, 5, 6
Bloody cranesbill (*Geranium sanguineum*)	3, 4, 5, 6
Lavender (*Lavandula* spp.)	4, 5, 6
Lilyturf (*Liriope muscari*)	6
Catmint (*Nepeta faassenii*)	4, 5, 6
Moss phlox (*Phlox subulata*)	3, 4, 5, 6
Lamb's ears (*Stachys byzantina*)	3, 4, 5, 6
Thyme (*Thymus* spp.)	3/4, 5, 6

RUFFLES AND FLOURISHES: DAYLILIES FROM A VERMONT NURSERY

Dorothy Pellett's small wholesale nursery is perched between Zones 4 and 5 in Charlotte, Vermont. It's aptly named Rock Crest Gardens, as her display garden is set on a steep slope punctuated with granite boulders. (In fact, deer are a greater menace than the stones, she says.) Daylilies (*Hemerocallis*) are one of the nursery's specialties, and this list of Pellett's favorites reflects her fondness for ruffled daylilies. Each cultivar, she says, was chosen because it has "sturdy stems, abundance of bloom, beauty of flower and good branching on the flower scapes." All cultivars are dormant in winter except for 'Porcelain Ruffles', which is semi-evergreen in all but the coldest parts of New England. All of these *Hemerocallis* are hardy to Zone 3.

'Finlandia Gold'	ruffled gold
'Frosted Pink Ice'	ruffled pink
'Jerusalem'	ruffled gold
'In Depth'	ruffled double creamy yellow

'Indy Rhapsody'	ruffled dark rose-red
'Margaret Seawright'	ruffled yellow and orange
'Porcelain Ruffles'	ruffled ivory
'Siloam Spizz'	ruffled yellow
'Smuggler's Treasure'	ruffled deep coral-rose
'Tahitian Dancer'	ruffled cream with rose edge

"Once daylilies have settled in, they require very little to produce colorful blooms year after year. We recommend you spread a balanced dry organic fertilizer, compost, or well-rotted manure around the plants each spring, as foliage growth is beginning. Clean out old foliage after plants go dormant in late fall. Daylilies may be divided every few years, or left for decades as long as they continue to flower well."
Wendy Forest, owner, Seaside Daylily Farm, West Tisbury, Massachusetts

GROUND COVERS, GRASSES, AND FERNS

A lawn is the preeminent American ground cover—and a ten-billion-dollar industry in North America. Interestingly, the tidy, short-cropped lawn that we know is a new kid on the horticultural block. Colonial New England had its village greens, but they were created for livestock grazing not for ornament or recreation. The small front yards of New England houses, set close to the road, were filled with flowers not turf grasses.

There had been lawns well before the nineteenth century, of course. George Washington had a huge lawn, but Mount Vernon was an exception. Lawns were available only to the wealthy; it took the mechanical lawnmower to make the lawn accessible to the middle-class. Invented by Englishman Edwin Budding in 1830, the lawnmower replaced servants, sheep, and scythes. It and the natural landscape movement led by Frederick Law Olmsted revolutionized the look of home landscapes. Moreover, in an unlikely conjugation of sport and horticulture, the growing popularity of golf and other lawn games further popularized the grass lawn.

A lawn is one way to cover the ground, but in an era when gardeners are increasingly conscious of the liabilities of lawn chemicals and are protective of their time, the pastoral ideal of acres of mown grass is less appealing than it once was. Enter alternative ground covers, including ornamental grasses and ferns, which have lives of their own but also make first-rate ground covers.

One theory behind using a ground cover—any plant that creeps, crawls, clumps, mats, or spreads horizontally in some other way—is that Mother Nature doesn't like a vacuum. Leave your soil bare, open to sun, rain, and wind and it will not only erode, it will lure every weed seed released within 50 miles. While turf grasses are cheaper to plant, ground covers save time, labor, and money in the long run.

Ground covers, as many others have written, are landscape problem-solvers. Not only do they blanket and protect the soil, they soften sharp edges and angles; they unify and integrate unlike elements, such as a house and patio; they provide transitions and mark boundaries; they relieve monotony by introducing contrasting colors, shapes, and textures.

Evergreen or deciduous, any plant that tends to grow more out than up can serve as a ground cover, but you'll probably want to look for perennial plants that don't require pampering and that stay green throughout the garden season, and through the winter, if your garden is one of the few in New England that isn't covered with 2 feet of snow. There are lots of choices, so consider your location before you choose your plant or plants: Hens and chickens, *Sempervivum tectorum*, will smother a small sunny spot, but it's not appropriate for a huge expanse. As a rule, you'll want to use tidy, small-leafed species, such as mountain rock cress (*Arabis alpina*) in small areas and save rambunctious plants, such as crown vetch (*Coronilla varia*) or ostrich fern (*Matteuccia struthiopteris*) for covering big areas.

This chapter focuses primarily on low-growing plants, but don't forget that daylilies, hostas, and many other taller perennials can be used as ground covers.

Many ornamental grasses and ferns are superb used as ground covers. In addition to their interesting foliage, most spread with ease and are of no interest to hungry deer. Some, such as Japanese sweetflag (*Acorus gramineus*) and New York fern (*Thelypteris noveboracensis*) may spread with too much ease to plant in a small area or garden, so read the fine print before you purchase.

The usual advice—actually it's good advice—is to use only one species when planting a ground cover. Combing several different plants often makes the area look cluttered. But it's your garden. Make a thyme checkerboard—creeping red and lemon—if that's what you've always wanted.

LOOKING GOOD: LAWN GRASSES

A lawn, according to one wit, is anything that looks good from the house across the street. According to the experts, a good lawn is likely to be a mix of 50 percent fine fescue, 30 percent Kentucky bluegrass, and 20 percent perennial ryegrass. This mix will look good from across the street and will provide a quality lawn for sun or partial shade. You can grab a prepackaged mix of grass seeds at your local hardware store, but be sure to read the fine print so that you don't end up with a lawn that contains a high percent of annual grasses. If you decide to do your own mixing, here are some names to look for; all are hardy throughout New England. (For endophytic grass cultivars, which resist garden pests, see the next list.)

Fine Fescues (*Festuca*)	Perennial Ryegrasses (*Lolium perenne*)	Kentucky Bluegrasses (*Poa pratensis*)
'Aurora'	'All Star'	'America'
'Banner'	'Omega'	'Adelphi'
'Flyer'	'Manhattan II'	'Glade'
'Fortress'	'Pennant'	'Ram I'
'Jamestown II'	'Regal'	'Nugget'
'Longfellow'	'Prelude'	'Mystic'
'Spartan'		'Rugby'
'Walinda'		'Princeton'

According to Vermonter Warren Schultz, former editor of *National Gardening* magazine and author of *A Man's Turf: The Perfect Lawn* (1999), the best time to seed a lawn in New England is when the summer heat breaks in late August or early September. "Weed seeds won't germinate then, but grass seeds will as long as they miss the heat and drought of midsummer. A young lawn can handle cool fall weather as long as the plants are six to eight weeks old before the first hard frost."

LAWNS THAT DISCOURAGE GARDEN PESTS

Lawns are a multimillion-household concern and a multibillion-dollar industry, so it's no wonder that lawn scientists keep busy developing new and better grasses. One of the latest achievements is breeding endophytes into grass cultivars. Endophytes, which are microscopic fungi that repel insects, occur naturally in some grasses. By using these endophytic grasses, which discourage aphids, armyworms, billbugs, cutworms, greenbugs, and other pests, gardeners can eliminate the use of lawn insecticides. In addition to being insect-resistant, endophytic grasses show good ability to weather drought and other stresses.

The perennial ryegrasses are hardy to Zone 3; the fescues are hardy to Zone 2.

Endophytic Perennial Ryegrasses (*Lolium perenne*)	Endophytic Fine Fescues (*Festuca*)	Endophytic Tall Fescues (*Festuca arundinacea*)
'Advent'	'Reliant'	'Mustang'
'Citation II'	'SR 5000'	'Rebel'
'Express'	'Warwick'	'Shenandoah'
'Palmer II'		'Titan'
'Repell II'		
'Yorktown II'		

Government turf scientists discovered that cutting grass at a height of 2 and one-half inches, rather than 1 inch, produces a healthier lawn: The grass has deeper roots and lateral shoots, and it requires less fertilizer because it has more mass for photosynthesis. Don't wait too long to mow, however. If you cut more than four-tenths of the height of the grass, you will damage your lawn.

Researchers at the University of Connecticut Agricultural Experiment Station have demonstrated conclusively that grass clippings don't cause thatch, so let them fertilize your lawn when you mow. The data show that one season's worth of clippings from a 1,000-square-foot plot contains 1.8 pounds of nitrogen. The exceptions to the no-bag rule are the first time you mow in the spring and the last time you mow in autumn: Removing the clippings after those mowings will help prevent lawn diseases.

BEST LITTLE BULBS IN THE LAWN

Naturalizing spring bulbs in lawns is an English garden icon; in fact, they are typically naturalized not in the lawn but rough grass, areas that will be mowed only once or twice a year. However, if you're a full-blooded Anglophile, take a look at this list from Renée Beaulieu. She gardens on weekends in Waterbury and on weekdays at White Flower Farm in Litchfield, Connecticut. Hers is a Zone 6 lawn, and it waits to be mowed until the bulb foliage has died back.

Glory of the snow (*Chionodoxa luciliae*)	3, 4, 5, 6
Snow crocus (*Crocus chrysanthus*)	3, 4, 5, 6
Crocus (*Crocus tommasinianus*)	3, 4, 5, 6
Dutch crocus (*Crocus vernus* cvs.)	3, 4, 5, 6
Spring starflower (*Ipheion uniflorum*)	5, 6
Spring snowflake (*Leucojum vernum*)	4, 5, 6
Siberian squill (*Scilla siberica*)	2, 3, 4, 5, 6

CROCUS

CONIFER COVERS

One of the best and most permanent solutions to covering ground, especially covering slopes and banks, is to plant conifers. The exposure—sun or shade—will dictate what species you plant, but there are plenty of evergreens to choose from. If you're perusing a nursery catalog, look for terms such as *horizontalis*, *procumbens*, and *prostrata*, words that indicate the growth is more out than up. Many dwarf weeping conifers also make good ground covers (see the list in the "Trees" chapter). Be sure to mulch around your conifers with a coarse organic material, such as shredded bark, to discourage weeds.

'Prostrata' balsam fir (*Abies balsamea*)	3, 4, 5, 6
'Prostrata Beauty' Korean dwarf fir (*Abies koreana*)	5, 6
'Prostrata Glauca' Lawson false cypress (*Chamaecyparis lawsoniana*)	5, 6
'Blue Cloud' Chinese juniper (*Juniperus chinensis*)	4, 5, 6
'Gold Star' Chinese juniper (*Juniperus chinensis*)	3, 4, 5, 6
'Gold Beach' common juniper (*Juniperus communis*)	3, 4, 5, 6
'Mother Lode' juniper (*Juniperus horizontalis*)	4, 5, 6
'Golden' Japanese juniper (*Juniperus procumbens*)	5, 6
'Kiyomi' Japanese juniper (*Juniperus procumbens*)	5, 6
'Grey Owl' eastern red cedar (*Juniperus virginiana*)	3, 4, 5, 6
'Prostrata' eastern red cedar (*Juniperus virginiana*)	4, 5, 6
'Nidiformis' Norway spruce (*Picea abies*)	3, 4, 5, 6
'Procumbens' Norway spruce (*Picea abies*)	3, 4, 5, 6
'Gotelli Prostrata' Colorado spruce (*Picea pungens*)	3, 4, 5, 6
'Prostrata' Korean pine (*Pinus koraiensis*)	3, 4, 5, 6
'Spaan's Pygmy' Korean pine (*Pinus koraiensis*)	3, 4, 5, 6
'Aurea' mugo pine (*Pinus mugo*)	3, 4, 5, 6
'Albyn's Prostrata' Scotch pine (*Pinus sylvestris*)	3, 4, 5, 6
'Globosa Nana' Scotch pine (*Pinus sylvestris*)	3, 4, 5, 6
'Hillside Creeper' Scotch pine (*Pinus sylvestris*)	3, 4, 5, 6
'Beaujean' Canadian hemlock (*Tsuga canadensis*)	3, 4, 5, 6
'Prostrata' Canadian hemlock (*Tsuga canadensis*)	3, 4, 5, 6
'West Coast Creeper' Canadian hemlock (*Tsuga canadensis*)	3, 4, 5, 6

GROUND COVERS THAT BLOOM

The plants most often used as ground covers, such as ivy and pachysandra, are notable for their uniform foliage not for producing flowers. If you want blossoms as well as coverage, consider some of the plants on this list. All have a fairly long bloom time, which you can extend by planting different cultivars or by mixing species. Most of these low-growing plants are especially good for blanketing smaller spaces and for covering hillsides. Shearing back plants will encourage plants to produce new shoots and flowers.

Woolly yarrow (*Achillea tomentosa*)	3, 4, 5, 6
Alpine rock cress (*Arabis alpina*)	3, 4, 5, 6
Rock cress (*Arabis caucasica*)	3, 4, 5, 6
Thrift (*Armeria maritima*)	3, 4, 5, 6
Astilbe (*Astilbe* cvs.)	3, 4, 5, 6
Purple rock cress (*Aubrieta deltoidea*)	4, 5, 6
Poppy mallow/winecups (*Callirhoe involucrata*)	4, 5, 6
Bellflower (*Campanula* spp.)	3, 4, 5, 6
Dwarf plumbago (*Ceratostigma plumbaginoides*)	5, 6
Sun rose (*Helianthemum nummularium*)	5, 6
Daylily (*Hemerocallis* cvs.)	3, 4, 5, 6
Coralbells (*Heuchera sanguinea*)	3, 4, 5, 6
Lavender (*Lavandula angustifolia*)	4/5, 6
Lilyturf (*Liriope spicata*)	4, 5, 6
Catmint (*Nepeta racemosa*)	4, 5, 6
Moss pink (*Phlox subulata*)	3, 4, 5, 6
Japanese primrose (*Primula japonica*)	3, 4, 5, 6
European pasque flower (*Pulsatilla vulgaris*)	4/5, 6

Feverfew (*Tanacetum parthenium*)	3/4, 5, 6
'Spicata' woolly speedwell (*Veronica incana*)	3, 4, 5, 6

EASY GROUND COVERS

Too many gardeners turn up their noses at familiar plants. The truth is that commonly used plants are common because they are good. The tried-and-true ground covers on this list tend to be vigorous, self-reliant, easy to grow, and able to cover good-sized areas. They are real success stories. No one wants English ivy covering every shady glen in New England, but it has a place, especially in parts of our region where it doesn't have to be subdued. Here's a list of old friends, ground covers that have earned their keep.

Woolly yarrow (*Achillea tomentosa*)	3, 4, 5, 6
Lily-of-the-valley (*Convallaria majalis*)	2, 3, 4, 5, 6
'Nana' cranberry cotoneaster (*Cotoneaster apiculatus*)	4/5, 6
Rock spray cotoneaster (*Cotoneaster horizontalis*)	4/5, 6
Sweet woodruff (*Galium odoratum*)	3, 4, 5, 6
English ivy (*Hedera helix*)	4/5, 6
Canadian juniper (*Juniperus communis* var. *depressa*)	2, 3, 4, 5, 6
Creeping juniper (*Juniperus horizontalis* cvs.)	2, 3, 4, 5, 6
Japanese spurge/pachysandra (*Pachysandra terminalis*)	4, 5, 6
Creeping phlox (*Phlox stolonifera*)	3, 4, 5, 6
Moss pink (*Phlox subulata*)	3, 4, 5, 6
Lamb's ears (*Stachys byzantina*)	3/4, 5, 6
Periwinkle (*Vinca minor*)	3/4, 5, 6

 The most important step in planting a ground cover is to prepare the site properly. That means removing all weeds, then enriching the soil with organic matter, such as compost or shredded leaves. Closely spaced but staggered planting usually provides the best effect; mulch after you plant to retain soil moisture and retard weed seeds from germinating. This is a garden that you want to take care of itself—it will if you start it off right.

GROUND COVERS FOR SLOPES

A perennial ground cover is one solution for a bank or slope that needs to be presentable but is so steep that it requires your taking out life insurance before you attempt to mow it. The choices for these big jobs are enormous—conifers, vines, herbaceous perennials. Some are more tidy and uniform than others, some evergreen and others dying back in winter, some flowering and some not. All will help stabilize your slope as well as make it more attractive. Whatever you choose—and you can combine several plants—make sure you mulch heavily with shredded bark or some other organic material to prevent erosion while your plants are getting established.

CREEPING JUNIPER

Woolly yarrow (*Achillea tomentosa*)	3, 4, 5, 6
Creeping bugleweed (*Ajuga reptans*)	3, 4, 5, 6
Five-leaf akebia/chocolate vine (*Akebia quinata*)	5, 6
Heartleaf bergenia (*Bergenia cordifolia*)	3, 4, 5, 6

Heather (*Calluna vulgaris*)	4, 5, 6
Snow-in-summer (*Cerastium tomentosum*)	3, 4, 5, 6
Lily-of-the-valley (*Convallaria majalis*)	2, 3, 4, 5, 6
Crown vetch (*Coronilla varia*)	4, 5, 6
Rock spray cotoneaster (*Cotoneaster horizontalis*)	4/5, 6
'Aurea' winter heath (*Erica carnea*)	4, 5, 6
Silky-leaf woodwaxen (*Genista pilosa*)	6
English ivy (*Hedera helix*)	4/5, 6
Daylily (*Hemerocallis* cvs.)	3, 4, 5, 6
Hosta (*Hosta* cvs.)	3, 4, 5, 6
Creeping St. John's wort (*Hypericum calycaium*)	6
Juniper (*Juniperus* spp.)	2, 3, 4, 5, 6
Lilyturf (*Liriope spicata*)	5, 6
Honeysuckle (*Lonicera* spp.)	4, 5, 6
Bird's-foot trefoil (*Lotus corniculatus*)	5, 6
Ostrich fern (*Matteuccia struthiopteris*)	2, 3, 4, 5, 6
Woodbine/Virginia creeper (*Parthenocissus quinquefolia*)	3, 4, 5, 6

DOWNSCALE GROUND COVERS FOR SMALL SPACES

Small-leafed plants make the best ground covers when the scale is also small. Because they are proportional to the space, they look at home; at the same time, they create a sense of spaciousness. Use them in corners and crevices, any limited area where they can work their magic. Just because these species have small leaves doesn't mean they're timid: Dwarf plumbago spreads quickly and may need reining in.

Redspine (*Acaena microphylla*)	6
Thrift (*Armeria maritima*)	3, 4, 5, 6
Poppy mallow/winecups (*Callirhoe involucrata*)	4, 5, 6
Dwarf plumbago (*Ceratostigma plumbaginoides*)	5, 6
Goldthread (*Coptis groenlandica*)	2, 3, 4, 5, 6
Fringed bleeding heart (*Dicentra eximia*)	3/4, 5, 6
Creeping gold wallflower (*Erysimum kotschyanum*)	6
Sweet woodruff (*Galium odoratum*)	3, 4, 5, 6
Dwarf crested iris (*Iris cristata*)	3, 4, 5, 6
Corsican mint (*Mentha requienii*)	6
Forget-me-not (*Myosotis scorpioides*)	4/5, 6
Blue-eyed Mary (*Omphalodes verna*)	6
'Mrs. Moon' pulmonaria (*Pulmonaria saccharata*)	3, 4, 5, 6
Bearberry (*Arctostaphylos uva-ursi*)	2, 3, 4, 5, 6
Ellacombe's stonecrop (*Sedum ellacombianum*)	3, 4, 5, 6
Houseleeks (*Sempervivum* spp.)	3/4, 5, 6
Large-flowered comfrey (*Symphytum grandiflorum*)	4, 5, 6
Ground germander (*Teucrium chamaedrys* var. *prostratum*)	4, 5, 6
Thyme (*Thymus* spp.)	3/4, 5, 6
Labrador violet (*Viola labradorica*)	2/3, 4, 5, 6

GROUND COVERS THAT TAKE FOOT TRAFFIC

A number of plants are willing to put up with foot traffic. Their tolerance varies, but for most that's *modest* foot traffic, not every-afternoon baseball games, or garden parties every Sunday. If the ban against constant trodding is the disadvantage, the advantage is that these alternatives to lawn grasses don't require mowing (plant heights range from a couple of inches to a foot). In many cases—chamomile and thyme are two—there is the bonus of flowers. Turning your entire yard over to one of these species may be too limiting, but planting on a smaller scale can be both labor-saving and ornamental. A few species, such as bishop's weed, are invasive, so plant with care. Finally, creeping bugleweed (*Ajuga repans*) is one exception to the modest foot traffic rule: Walk on!

'Blue Haze' bidi-bidi (*Acaena*)	sun/partial shade	6
Woolly yarrow (*Achillea tomentosa*)	sun	3, 4, 5, 6
Bishop's weed/goutweed (*Aegopodium podagraria*)	sun/shade	3, 4, 5, 6
Creeping bugleweed (*Ajuga reptans*)	sun/partial shade	3, 4, 5, 6
Pussy toes (*Antennaria dioica*)	sun/partial shade	3, 4, 5, 6
Alpine rock cress (*Arabis alpina*)	sun	3, 4, 5, 6
Snow-in-summer (*Cerastium tomentosum*)	sun	3, 4, 5, 6
Roman chamomile (*Chamaemelum nobile*)	sun/partial shade	4, 5, 6
Mock strawberry (*Duchesnea india*)	sun/partial shade	4, 5, 6
Creeping gold wallflower (*Erysimum kotschyanum*)	sun	5/6
'Kewensis' wintercreeper (*Euonymus fortunei*)	sun/partial shade	4/5, 6
Rupturewort (*Herniaria glabra*)	sun/partial shade	5, 6
Japanese loosestrife (*Lysimachia japonica*)	partial shade	5, 6
'Aurea' golden creeping Charley (*Lysimachia nummularia*)	partial sun	4, 5, 6
Corsican mint (*Mentha requienii*)	partial sun/shade	6
Moss pink (*Phlox subulata*)	sun	3, 4, 5, 6
Goldmoss stonecrop (*Sedum acre*)	sun	3, 4, 5, 6
Woolly thyme (*Thymus pseudolanuginosus*)	sun	5/6
Creeping thyme (*Thymus serpyllum*)	sun	4, 5, 6
Periwinkle (*Vinca minor*)	sun/shade	3/4, 5, 6

PAINTED WITH DELIGHT: MEADOW GARDENS

If you don't have a seed packet of the "cuckoo-buds of yellow hue" that painted Shakespeare's "meadows with delight," try creating an herbal landscape. Connecticut garden writer Rita Buchanan suggests these herbs, all sun-loving perennials, for combining with native grasses, such as sweet vernal grass (*Anthoxanthum odoratum*) and sweet grass (*Hierochloe odorata*) and other meadow species as a replacement for lawn grasses. You may want to consult her *Making a Garden* (1999) for other ideas about covering the ground with herbs.

Yarrow (*Achillea millefolium*)	3, 4, 5, 6
Giant hyssop (*Agastache foeniculum*)	3, 4, 5, 6
Pearly everlasting (*Anaphalis margaritacea*)	3, 4, 5, 6
Dyer's chamomile (*Anthemis tinctoria*)	3/4, 5, 6
Butterflyweed (*Asclepias tuberosa*)	4, 5, 6
Purple coneflower (*Echinacea purpurea*)	3, 4, 5, 6
Joe Pye weed (*Eupatorium purpureum*)	3, 4, 5, 6
Meadowsweet (*Filipendula ulmaria*)	3, 4, 5, 6
Lady's bedstraw (*Galium verum*)	3, 4, 5, 6
St. John's wort (*Hypericum perforatum*)	4, 5, 6
Motherwort (*Leonurus cardiaca*)	3, 4, 5, 6
Great blue lobelia (*Lobelia siphilitica*)	3/4, 5, 6
Horehound (*Marrubium vulgare*)	4, 5, 6
Bee balm (*Monarda didyma*)	3, 4, 5, 6

Wild bergamot (*Monarda fistulosa*)	4, 5, 6
Mountain mint (*Pycnanthemum muticum*)	5, 6
Soapwort (*Saponaria officinalis*)	2, 3, 4, 5, 6
Tansy (*Tanacetum vulgare*)	3, 4, 5, 6
Mother-of-thyme (*Thymus pulegioides*)	4, 5, 6
American blue vervain (*Verbena hastata*)	3, 4, 5, 6

THE HERBAL TREATMENT

Although creeping thyme is a standard recommendation for planting between pavers, we don't often think of herbs as ground covers. Some species handle that role nicely, however. In addition to being attractive and providing different textures and hues, they are fragrant, largely problem-free, and easy to grow. And if some become a little too tall or a little ragged, get out your shears and cut away, then reap the benefits in the kitchen or in a potpourri. Mints have the ability to cover too much ground, so plant them with caution.

CALAMINT

'Nana' wooly yarrow (*Achillea tomentosa*)	3, 4, 5, 6
Pussy toes (*Antennaria dioica*)	3, 4, 5, 6
Western mugwort (*Artemisia ludoviciana* cvs.)	4, 5, 6
Artemisia (*Artemisia stelleriana* cvs.)	2/3, 4, 5, 6
Calamint (*Calamintha nepeta*)	4, 5, 6
Roman chamomile (*Chamaemelum nobile*)	3, 4, 5, 6
Sweet woodruff (*Galium odoratum*)	3, 4, 5, 6
Mint (*Mentha* spp.)	3, 4, 5, 6
Catmint (*Nepeta faassenii*, *N. racemosa*)	4, 5, 6
Common sage (*Salvia officinalis*)	4, 5, 6
Thyme (*Thymus* spp.)	3/4, 5, 6
Speedwell (*Veronica officinalis*)	3, 4, 5, 6
Violet (*Viola* spp.)	3, 4, 5, 6

UNDER THE BLACK WALNUT

If you have a black walnut tree (*Juglans nigra*) and the naked area that usually lies beneath it, here are some ideas for covering the ground. The toxin juglone, which is present in the roots, leaves, and bark of black walnuts—and to lesser degrees in English walnuts, shagbark hickories, and pecans—is responsible for that bare earth. The plants on this list, however, are immune to juglone.

Creeping bugleweed (*Ajuga reptans*)	3, 4, 5, 6
Astilbe (*Astilbe* spp. and cvs.)	3, 4, 5, 6
Sweet woodruff (*Galium odoratum*)	3, 4, 5, 6
Daylily (*Hemerocallis fulva*)	3, 4, 5, 6
Hosta (*Hosta fortunei*)	3, 4, 5, 6
Narrow-leaf hosta (*Hosta lancifolia*)	3, 4, 5, 6
'Variegata' wavy-leaf hosta (*Hosta undulata*)	3, 4, 5, 6
Sundrops (*Oenothera fruticosa*)	3/4, 5, 6
Cinnamon fern (*Osmunda cinnamomea*)	3, 4, 5, 6
Showy stonecrop (*Sedum spectabile*)	3, 4, 5, 6

"Using native mosses is one solution for underplanting trees, especially where the soil is acidic. Mosses are evergreen, and many are cold hardy as far north as Zones 2 and 3. They may go dormant and turn brown in dry, hot summers, but they revive with the first autumn rains."
Rita Buchanan, garden author, Winsted, Connecticut

GOOD MANNERS: NONINVASIVE GROUND COVERS

New Englanders who have been invaded by English ivy, ajuga, or another aggressive ground cover are always on the prowl for plants that spread easily but don't take over the garden ten days after being planted. Here is a list of candidates to cloak those parts of your yard that you want to plant and forget.

Remember to remove *all* weeds before you establish a ground cover, for any weed seeds or bits of root that remain in the soil will plague you for years to come. Solarizing—which involves laying clear plastic over the area for a period of several months—is a safe and effective weed-removal treatment. After planting the area, mulch generously with compost or other organic matter.

'Wood's Red' bearberry (*Arctostaphylos*)	5, 6
Alpine bearberry (*Arctostaphylos alpina*)	2, 3, 4, 5, 6
Red bearberry (*Arctostaphylos rubra*)	2, 3, 4, 5, 6
Bearberry (*Arctostaphylos uva-ursi*)	2, 3, 4, 5, 6
Bellflower (*Campanula* spp.)	3, 4, 5, 6
Goldenstar/green and gold (*Chrysogonum virginianum*)	5, 6
Bunchberry (*Cornus canadensis*)	2, 3, 4, 5, 6
Wintercreeper (*Euonymus fortunei*)	1, 5, 6
Alpine strawberry (*Fragaria vesca*)	5, 6
Sweet woodruff (*Galium odoratum*)	3, 4, 5, 6
Christmas rose (*Helleborus niger*)	3, 4, 5, 6
Lenten rose (*Helleborus orientalis*)	4/5, 6
'Aurea' golden creeping Charley (*Lysimachia nummularia*)	4, 5, 6
Lungwort/Bethlehem sage (*Pulmonaria saccharata*)	3, 4, 5, 6
Thyme (*Thymus* spp.)	3/4, 5, 6
Foamflower (*Tiarella cordifolia*)	3, 4, 5, 6
Cowberry/lintonberry (*Vaccinium vitis-idaea*)	3, 4, 5, 6
Lingberry (*Vaccinium vitis-idaea* var. *minus*)	2, 3, 4, 5, 6

ORNAMENTAL GRASSES AS GROUND COVERS

Ornamental grasses are typically used as accent plants in the home landscape. Another fine use is as ground covers. In fact, untroubled by diseases and insect pests, these grasses are among the most carefree ground covers you can plant. Species with running roots spread especially quickly and are ideal for controlling erosion.

These grasses offer a variety of heights—many tall enough to sway in the wind—and foliage forms. There is a range of stem and leaf colors (green, brown, yellow, red, purple, and more), and all of the grasses in this list bear handsome flowers which persist into winter. The heart-shaped flowers of quaking grass, for example, are iridescent green in spring, then turn golden yellow. The flowers of tufted hair grass are produced in loose panicles that also start out green, then change to yellow, bronze, and finally near-purple.

Sand reed (*Ammophila breviligulata*)	1-3 feet	1, 5, 6
Quaking grass (*Briza media*)	12-18 inches	4/5, 6

Sand reed grass (*Calamovilfa longifolia*)	2-5 feet	3, 4, 5, 6
Tufted hair grass (*Deschampsia caespitosa*)	1-3 feet	3, 4, 5, 6
'Elijah Blue' blue fescue (*Festuca glauca*)	8 inches	3, 4, 5, 6
Blue oat grass (*Helictotrichon sempervirens*)	12-18 inches	3, 4, 5, 6
'Glaucus' blue lyme grass (*Elymus arenarius*)	3-4 feet	3, 4, 5, 6
Japanese silver grass (*Miscanthus sinensis* cvs.)	height varies	4/5, 6
Switch grass (*Panicum virgatum* cvs.)	height varies	5, 6
Fountain grass (*Pennisetum alopecuroides*)	2-3 feet	5, 6
White-flowering fountain grass (*Pennisetum caudatum*)	3-4 feet	6
Ribbon grass (*Phalaris arundinacea* var. *picta*)	6-8 inches	4, 5, 6

ORNAMENTAL GRASSES FOR ARCTIC CONDITIONS

The last decade's romance with ornamental grasses fell largely on deaf ears in northern New England, for many of the choice species and cultivars are hardy only to Zones 5 and 6, Zone 4 at best. Although plant encyclopedias may not agree, according to Don Avery, the owner of Cady's Falls Nursery in Morrisville, Vermont, and other Zone 3 gardeners, these grasses can survive *real* cold. While they're unusually cold-tolerant, they also depend on excellent drainage and good snowcover to make it through the winter. Some are not as spectacular or refined as their warmer-blooded cousins, but they still are fine additions to any home landscape.

Broomsedge (*Andropogon virginicus*)	3, 4, 5, 6
'Variegatum' bulbous oat grass (*Arrhenatherum elatius* var. *bulbosum*)	3, 4, 5, 6
Mosquito grass/blue gramma (*Bouteloua gracilis*)	3, 4, 5, 6
'Skinner's Golden' smooth brome (*Bromus inermis*)	2, 3, 4, 5, 6
'Karl Foester', 'Overdam' feather reed grass (*Calamagrostis acutiflora*)	3, 4, 5, 6
Fall-blooming reed grass (*Calamagrostis brachytricha*)	3, 4, 5, 6
Mountain sedge (*Carex montanensis*)	3, 4, 5, 6
'Variegated' (*Carex siderosticha*)	3, 4, 5, 6
'Goldgehaenge' tufted hair grass (*Deschampsia caespitosa*)	3/4, 5, 6
'Glaucus' blue lyme grass (*Elymus arenarius*)	3, 4, 5, 6
Canada wild rye (*Elymus canadensis*)	3, 4, 5, 6
'Elijah Blue' blue fescue (*Festuca glauca*)	3, 4, 5, 6
Blue oat grass (*Helictotrichon sempervirens*)	3, 4, 5, 6
Sweet grass (*Hierochola odorata*)	2, 3, 4, 5, 6
Soft rush (*Juncus effusus*)	3, 4, 5, 6
Common reed (*Phragmites australis*)	3/4, 5, 6
Little bluestem (*Schizachyrium scoparium*)	2/3, 4, 5, 6
'Aureomarginata' variegated cord grass (*Spartina pectinata*)	3/4, 5, 6
Eastern feather grass (*Stipa extremorientalis*)	3, 4, 5, 6

SOFT RUSH

ORNAMENTAL GRASSES FOR WARMER ZONES

These ornamental grasses—all appropriate for planting *en masse* as ground covers or singly as accent plants—aren't quite as hardy as the plants in the "Ornamental Grasses for Arctic Conditions" list, but they are able to survive even in gardens where the mercury regularly falls well below zero. Lucky New England gardeners in balmy Zone 6 can grow all of these cultivars, plus many others.

Yellow foxtail grass (*Alopecurus pratensis* var. *aureus*)	5, 6
'Sentinel' big bluestem (*Andropogon gerardii*)	5, 6

'Green Fountain' arundo (*Arundo formosana*)	5, 6
Side oats gramma (*Bouteloua curtipendula*)	4, 5, 6
Quaking grass (*Briza media*)	4/5, 6
Feather reed grass (*Calamagrostis acutiflora*)	4, 5, 6
'Old Gold', 'Variegata' Japanese sedge (*Carex morrowii*)	5, 6
Black-flowering sedge (*Carex nigra*)	5, 6
Ravenna grass (*Erianthus ravennae*)	4, 5, 6
Large blue fescue (*Festuca amethystina*)	5, 6
Snowy woodrush (*Luzula nivea*)	4, 5, 6
Wood rush (*Luzula sylvatica*)	4, 5, 6
'Arabesque', 'Cabaret', 'Graziella', 'Morning Light', 'Silver Feather', 'Strictus' Japanese silver grass (*Miscanthus sinensis*)	5, 6
'Purpurescens', 'Gracilimus', 'Malepartus' Japanese silver grass (*Miscanthus sinensis*)	4, 5, 6
'Skyracer', 'Windspell' purple moor grass (*Molinia caerulea*)	5, 6
'Variegata' variegated purple moor grass (*Molinia caerulea*)	4, 5, 6
'Squaw', 'Heavy Metal', 'Cloud Nine' switch grass (*Panicum virgatum*)	5, 6
'Bunny' dwarf fountain grass (*Pennisetum alopecuroides*)	5, 6
'Hamelin', 'Little Honey' fountain grass (*Pennisetum alopecuroides*)	5, 6
Ribbon grass (*Phalaris arundinacea* var. *picta*)	4, 5, 6
Green moor grass (*Sesleria caerulea*)	4, 5, 6
Gray moor grass (*Sesleria heufleriana*)	4, 5, 6
Prairie dropseed (*Sporobolus heterolepsis*)	4, 5, 6

"Ornamental grasses are great low-maintenance plants. Mine have not been troubled by insects or diseases. Or by deer, which are real pests in my part of Connecticut. *Miscanthus* species are especially easy and do fine in ordinary, well-drained soil. Their purple flower plumes turn silver in the fall, and the foliage fades to pale gold and lasts all winter. You should cut plants to the ground by April, or before the new shoots appear. Narrow-leafed cultivars, such as 'Gracillimus', are the best types for windy sites."
Kathy Nelson, owner, Kathleen Nelson Perennials, Gaylordsville, Connecticut

FAVORITE GRASSES FROM A CONNECTICUT CONNOISSEUR

Ornamental grasses are superb low-maintenance plants, wonderfully ornamental, and rarely bothered by deer, which are a concern for most New England gardeners. Rather than grabbing the usual suspects, landscape designer and retail nurserywoman Kathy Nelson suggests these choice cultivars. Nelson's nursery, Kathleen Nelson Perennials, is located in Gaylordsville, Connecticut, which is Zone 5 on a hardiness map. Hers is largely a dry, rocky property, ideal for ornamental grasses, most of which hate having wet feet. Tall moor grass is an exception and prefers a wet site.

Wild oats/northern sea oats (*Chasmanthium latifolium*)	4/5, 6
'Sapphire' blue oat grass (*Helictotrichon sempervirens*)	4, 5, 6
Giant Chinese silver grass (*Miscanthus floridulus*)	4/5, 6
'Gracillimus' Japanese silver grass (*Miscanthus sinensis*)	5, 6
'Skyracer' tall moor grass (*Molinia caerulea* subsp. *arudinacea*)	5, 6
'Hamelin' fountain grass (*Pennisetum alopecuroides*)	5/6
'The Blues' little bluestem (*Schizachyrium scoparium*)	3/4, 5, 6

GOLDEN GRASSES FOR SHADE

Gardeners are always looking for attractive plants to lighten shaded corners and crannies. One interesting solution is to plant any of the yellow/gold ornamental grasses and sedges that do well in partly shaded locations. Not deep shade, mind you, but dappled light. One warning: Variegated cord grass is very invasive—to be safe, grow it in a container sunk in the ground.

'Aureovariegatus' yellow foxtail grass (*Alopecurus pratensis*)	5, 6
'Snowline' sedge (*Carex conica*)	5, 6
'Kaga-nishiki' gold fountain sedge (*Carex dolichostachya*)	6
Bowles' golden sedge (*Carex elata* 'Aurea')	5, 6
'Evergold' sedge (*Carex hachijoensis*)	6
'Goldgehaenge' tufted hair grass (*Deschampsia caespitosa*)	3/4, 5, 6
'Aureola' Japanese forest grass (*Hakonechloa macra*)	5, 6
'Aureum' Bowles' golden grass (*Milium effusum*)	6
'Aureomarginata' variegated cord grass (*Spartina pectinata*)	3/4, 5, 6

HEATHER ON THE HILL

You'll be humming the music from *Brigadoon* while you plant these heathers (*Calluna vulgaris*) recommended by Kate Herrick. For the last twenty years, she's been running Rock Spray Nursery in Truro, Massachusetts, a retail and mail-order nursery that specializes in hardy heaths and heathers. For New England gardens, Herrick recommends cultivars of *Calluna vulgaris*. They are hardy to Zone 4 or, as Herrick points out, "maybe to Zone 3 with good winter protection." Like all heathers, this species requires acid soil and superb drainage. Sir Walter Scott wrote that "there are worse things in life than a tumble on the heather." In fact, there may be few better things.

'Allegro'	crimson flowers on dark green foliage	4, 5, 6
'County Wicklow'	double shell pink flowers on dark green foliage	4, 5, 6
'Darts Hedge Hog'	mauve flowers on lime green foliage that turns orange	4, 5, 6
'E. F. Brown'	lavender flowers on light green foliage	4, 5, 6
'J. H. Hamilton'	double dark pink flowers on dark geen foliage	4, 5, 6
'Mrs. R. H. Grey'	pale purple flowers on dark green foliage	4, 5, 6
'Multicolor'	pale mauve flowers on gold foliage that turns orange-red	4, 5, 6
'Sister Anne'	pink flowers on downy grey foliage	4, 5, 6
'White Lawn'	white flowers on bright green foliage	4, 5, 6

"Heather needs full sun and good air circulation. The ideal soil is slightly acid with generous amounts of peat moss or compost mixed. Heather won't survive in soil that is too fertile—the plants will produce lush growth that is too fragile to withstand cold—so never fertilize with a high-nitrogen fertilizer. Plants also need excellent drainage, so a sloping site is ideal as it drains naturally. Mulch heather with a 3-inch layer of pine bark or pine needles to keep the soil surface cool and retain moisture in summer, and to prevent heaving in winter. Prune heathers in early spring to promote multiple branching."
Kate Herrick, owner, Rock Spray Nursery, Truro, Massachusetts

SEDGE WHO?

Sedges, members of the Cyperaceae family, are just beginning to come into their own in New England gardens. While not true grasses (remember the botany class jingle: "Sedges have edges and rushes are round. / Grasses are hollow and rush all around"), they are grasslike and wonderfully ornamental. Most names on this list are species that thrive in organically rich, moist garden soil. The sedges that prefer having their feet soppy wet are marked with an asterisk (*).

Lesser marsh sedge (*Carex acutiformis*)*	4, 5, 6
Blonde sedge (*Carex albula*)	5, 6
Leatherleaf sedge (*Carex buchananii*)	4/5, 6
"Bronze' New Zealand hairy sedge (*Carex comans*)	5, 6
'Snowline' sedge (*Carex conica*)	5, 6
Fringed sedge (*Carex crinita*)*	5, 6
Bowles' golden sedge (*Carex elata* 'Aurea')*	5, 6
Grey's sedge (*Carex grayi*)	3, 4, 5, 6
'Ice Dance' variegated Japanese sedge (*Carex morrowii*)	5, 6
'Wachtposten' palm branch sedge (*Carex muskingumensis*)*	3/4, 5, 6
'Evergold' sedge (*Carex oshimensis*)	6
Drooping sedge (*Carex pendula*)*	3, 4, 5, 6
Plantain sedge (*Carex plantaginea*)	5, 6
'Variegated' sedge (*Carex siderosticha*)	3, 4, 5, 6
Northeastern tussock sedge (*Carex stricta*)*	4, 5, 6
Forest sedge (*Carex sylvatica*)	3, 4, 5, 6

"The statuesque miscanthus grasses (*Miscanthus* spp.) look wonderful in summer, fall, and winter, their arching forms nodding gracefully in the back of the border. But the space seems very bare after they receive their annual haircut in early spring. I take advantage of the wide swath of earth around the plant's crown by planting daffodils or tulips thickly in the available space between grasses. The bulbs bloom in spring before the grasses sprout much, and then the burgeoning miscanthus distract me from the fading bulb foliage. A perfect match.

"If deer are a problem in your garden, use daffodils for a relatively carefree and very pest-resistant display."

Renée Beaulieu, editor and horticulturist, White Flower Farm, Litchfield, Connecticut

HEATHCLIFF'S HAVEN: WINTER HEATHS IN NEW ENGLAND GARDENS

Heaths are tough plants but far better known to English than to New English gardeners, except those who have read *Wuthering Heights* more than a half-dozen times. Kate Herrick, who runs a retail and mail-order heath and heather nursery, Rock Spray Nursery in Truro, Massachusetts, wants to make heaths better known on this side of the Atlantic. For Yankee gardeners she recommends cultivars of winter heath, *Erica carnea*, which have shiny, needlelike foliage and bell-shaped flowers. Heaths are "fast growing," Herrick warns, "spreading in habit, they form dense, weed-smothering mats." Even if you don't like Emily Brontë, you have to like the weed-smothering part.

'Aurea'	lilac-pink flowers on gold foliage	4, 5, 6
'Loughrigg'	deep rose-pink flowers on dark green foliage	4, 5, 6

| 'Pirbright Rose' | lilac-pink flowers on greyish green foliage | 4, 5, 6 |
| 'Springwood White' | white flowers on light green foliage | 4, 5, 6 |

BAMBOO JUNGLE

Well, maybe not a jungle, but definitely bamboo. That's the planting suggestion from Albert Adelman, co-owner of Burt Associates Bamboo, a retail nursery in Westford, Massachusetts (Zone 5). You can visit his display gardens or shop by mail, or both. Adelman recommends these cultivars. All have rhizomes that are hardy to Zone 5, "maybe even Zone 4 with protection," Adelman says. He recommends a thick organic mulch during the plant's first winter to protect the rhizomes, the modified underground stems that run just beneath the soil surface. The cane, or culm, hardiness of each cultivar is indicated below.

Most bamboos take three to five years to establish themselves, but species that spread by runners are potentially invasive in the warmest parts of New England. Three of the bamboos in this list—*Fargesia murielae*, *Fargesia nitida*, and *Indocalamus tessellatus*—are clumping, or non-running, species.

Fargesia murielae	5, 6
Fargesia nitida	5, 6
Indocalamus tessellatus	5, 6
Phyllostachys aureosulcata, yellow-groove bamboo	5, 6
Phyllostachys aureosulcata var. *aureocaulis*	5, 6
Phyllostachys aureosulcata var. *spectabilis*	5, 6
Phyllostachys bissetii, David Bisset's bamboo	5, 6
Phyllostachys nuda	5, 6
Phyllostachys rubromarginata	6
Pleioblastus chino var. *murakamianus*	6
Pleioblastus humilis	6
Pleioblastus shibuyanus 'Tsuboi'	6
Pleioblastus variegatus, dwarf white-stripe bamboo	6
Pleioblastus viridistriatus, golden-haired bamboo	6
Sasa tsuboiana	5, 6
Sasa veitchii	5, 6
Sasaella masamuniana var. *albostriata*	6

"Bamboos do best in well-drained fertile soil. They're tolerant of a broad variety of conditions, but don't plant them in soil that is constantly wet. Mulch plants during their first year, and give them protection from the wind during their first winter. They become increasingly tough as they mature. Pruning isn't necessary, but it will improve the appearance of your bamboos. Cut some of the lower branches to expose the culms, or canes."
Albert Adelman, owner, Burt Associates Bamboo, Westford, Massachusetts

FERNS FOR BEGINNERS

Most ferns are easy to grow—the majority want humus-rich soil, even moisture, and partial shade. Be aware that a few species, such as ostrich fern, can be invasive if given these ideal conditions. The half-dozen ferns listed below are especially undemanding and trouble-free, a good place to begin when establishing a fernery. For a shady but dry location, try Christmas fern, *Polystichum acrostichoides*.

| Lady fern (*Athyrium filix-femina*) | 2, 3, 4, 5, 6 |
| Fragile fern (*Cystopteris fragilis*) | 2, 3, 4, 5, 6 |

Male fern (*Dryopteris filix-mas*)	3, 4, 5, 6
Marginal wood fern (*Dryopteris marginalis*)	2, 3, 4, 5, 6
Ostrich fern (*Matteuccia struthiopteris*)	2, 3, 4, 5, 6
Christmas fern (*Polystichum acrostichoides*)	3, 4, 5, 6
Soft-shield fern (*Polystichum setiferum*)	5, 6

"All ferns have shallow roots. Rather than use a hoe or garden rake to work around plants, weed by hand to avoid damaging the roots and the croziers, or fiddleheads. Mulch plants to discourage weeds and to conserve soil moisture."
Jake Chapline, Durham, New Hampshire

YANKEE FAVORITES: FERNS AS GROUND COVERS

Despite their lack of flowers—or perhaps because of it—ferns make superb garden and landscape plants. Their value as accent plants in woodland and rock gardens, along pools, waterways, and paths is inestimable. They are also superb ground cover plants. Many are evergreen in warmer parts of New England, and there are species for both sun and shade.

The species listed below spread easily and evenly, and they are North American natives. All are able to put up with temperatures as low as -40 degrees F—a few even tolerate -50 degrees F. (For more fern lists, see the "Native Plants" chapter.)

Maidenhair fern (*Adiantum pedatum*)	shade	2, 3, 4, 5, 6
Lady fern (*Athyrium filix-femina*)	shade	2, 3, 4, 5, 6
Deer fern (*Blechnum spicant*)	partial shade	2, 3, 4, 5, 6
Spinulose wood fern, (*Dryopteris carthusiana*)	partial shade	2, 3, 4, 5, 6
Male fern (*Dryopteris filix-mas*)	sun/shade	3, 4, 5, 6
Marginal wood fern (*Dryopteris marginalis*)	shade	2, 3, 4, 5, 6
Oak fern (*Gymnocarpium dryopteris*)	shade	2, 3, 4, 5, 6
Ostrich fern (*Matteuccia struthiopteris*)	sun/partial shade	2, 3, 4, 5, 6
Cinnamon fern (*Osmunda cinnamomea*)	shade/partial sun	3, 4, 5, 6
Royal fern (*Osmunda regalis*)	shade/partial sun	2, 3, 4, 5, 6
Northern beech fern (*Phegopteris connectilis*)	shade	3, 4, 5, 6
Christmas fern (*Polystichum acrostichoides*)	shade	3, 4, 5, 6

Native ferns are among the plants that are ripped from the New England landscape by unscrupulous sellers. When you purchase native ferns, ask for an assurance that the plants were nursery propagated and not dug from the wild.

FERNS FOR BRIGHT LIGHT

Say the word "fern" and most people, even many gardeners, think "shade." In fact, a fair number of ferns do fine in a sunny location, and even more thrive in partial sun, especially where summers are cool. Most ferns growing in sun also require organically rich, evenly moist soil, but there are a few, such as male fern and hay-scented fern, that are willing to put up with sun *and* dry soil.

Hairy lip fern (*Cheilanthes tomentosa*)	4/5, 6
Hay-scented fern (*Dennstaedtia punctilobula*)	4, 5, 6
Male fern (*Dryopteris filix-mas*)	3, 4, 5, 6

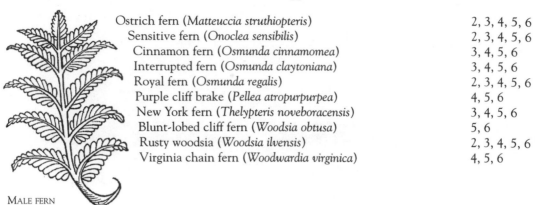

MALE FERN

Ostrich fern (*Matteuccia struthiopteris*)	2, 3, 4, 5, 6
Sensitive fern (*Onoclea sensibilis*)	2, 3, 4, 5, 6
Cinnamon fern (*Osmunda cinnamomea*)	3, 4, 5, 6
Interrupted fern (*Osmunda claytoniana*)	3, 4, 5, 6
Royal fern (*Osmunda regalis*)	2, 3, 4, 5, 6
Purple cliff brake (*Pellea atropurpurea*)	4, 5, 6
New York fern (*Thelypteris noveboracensis*)	3, 4, 5, 6
Blunt-lobed cliff fern (*Woodsia obtusa*)	5, 6
Rusty woodsia (*Woodsia ilvensis*)	2, 3, 4, 5, 6
Virginia chain fern (*Woodwardia virginica*)	4, 5, 6

ROSES

In England, as we all know, a garden isn't a garden without roses. *Real* roses with pedigreed names, such as 'Duchesse d'Angoulême' and 'Königin von Dänemark.' It's no wonder that the first New England colonists turned their noses up at the few native roses they encountered in their new land. News of this *Rosa* paucity obviously got back home, for one English nurseryman wrote John Winthrop Jr. and offered to send him "some damaske, red and white, and province rose plants," if Winthrop had no roses for his garden.

New England wasn't England, however, and many of the swank roses that immigrated to Massachusetts Bay didn't survive the harsh climate. One rose that did was the common sweetbrier, *Rosa eglanteria*, which was as familiar a resident of English hedgerows as the sparrow and hedgehog. John Josselyn, in his *Account of Two Voyages to New England* (1673), reported that the sweetbrier was among the plants "as do prosper," noting that it "is best sown with Juniper berries, two or three to one Eglantine-berry put into a hole made with a stick." In a year, the plants should be separated and in three years, he wrote, the roses "will make a hedge so high as a man, which you may keep thick and handsome with cutting." There must have been something to Josselyn's technique: Pink sweetbrier roses have colonized throughout our region. The wayside rose, one American poet called it.

We twenty-first-century New Englanders have the same problems with roses that our ancestors did: Many choice cultivars can't survive the climate. In particular, hybrid teas have found many New England gardens inhospitable. First imported in the 1860s, tea roses soon surpassed all other rose types in popularity. They remain this country's most popular rose form, the essence of roseness.

Tea roses thrive only in Zones 6 and higher, although many can be grown in Zone 5 if given ample winter protection and you're prepared for ample winter dieback. In addition to this lack of hardiness the majority of hybrid teas are heir to every pest and disease the genus can attract. The result was a horticultural line in the sand. On one side was the rose-growing brother- and sisterhood made up of gardeners who were willing to spend hours indulging and pampering their roses. On the other side were gardeners who decided roses weren't worth the trouble, donated their leather gauntlets to Good Will, and planted something else.

It's not easy to turn your back on the garden plant that has been cultivated for thousands of years, is a symbol in nearly every culture and religion, and has been immortalized by every important poet. The good news is that the disaffected have a new opportunity. A growing interest in more informal landscapes, in old-fashioned, or heirloom, plants, and in gardens that require less tending and no spraying with toxic chemicals has renewed enthusiasm for and the availability of species roses, old garden roses, large ramblers and shrubs, and all their cultivars. These roses—especially the rugosas, *Rosa rugosa*—are hardy, vigorous, and largely pest- and disease-free. They are roses that are at home in New England.

Not even all of these roses are created equal, however, so as you page through rose catalogs, bedazzled by the color photographs, keep these terms in mind:

- *fully hardy:* the unprotected rose should survive with only limited cane dieback.
- *hardy:* the rose canes will have some dieback.
- *crown hardy:* all of the canes are likely to die back to the ground, but the plant will resprout and bloom in the new season.
- *tender:* the rose will die unless given winter protection, and may die even with it.

Look, too, for cultivars that are disease-resistant, and watch for the word "fragrant." If you don't see it, the rose probably is scentless. Think of the line from Robert Browning—"Any nose / May ravage with impunity the rose"—and don't settle for a cultivar without fragrance.

I'm a fan of roses with *hips* (the vitamin C-fortified fruits of the rose plant), which last far longer than the flowers do, and of *remontant* roses—plants that are either *recurring* or *repeating*. Recurring means that the plant blooms periodically throughout the garden season; a repeating rose flowers twice, usually in spring and again in autumn. Some rose fanciers insist on *own-root roses*, plants that are growing on their own roots, but grafted roses that are planted properly (with the union below the soil surface) appear to do just as well as nongrafted plants. Similarly, bare-root roses are every bit as good as those sold in containers.

Rosarians in your neighborhood are your best source of information about which rose to buy, and how to plant and care for it. If you can't find a rose-grower near you, take advantage of the "consulting rosarians" on the American Rose Society website (www.ars.org). They are listed by state and town and are ready to answer your questions and give advice.

Most experts agree that New England gardeners should plant roses in spring. The site should be sunny and drain well, the soil slightly acid and amended with plenty of organic matter. Compost and well-rotted manure are the usual choices, but some rosarians have been more creative. The story goes that one English vicar, famous for growing fabulous roses, was bullied by other gardeners until he revealed the secret of his success: "I bury a cat under each bush."

Garden books and nursery catalogs aren't always consistent in describing types of roses, but these are some of the terms you'll encounter.

- **Species Roses:** roses that grow naturally in the wild. They tend to have single flowers (with five petals), to bloom only once, and to be vigorous; they are especially appropriate for informal gardens.
- **Old Garden Roses:** roses popular before the first hybrid tea (1867); the group is divided into many classes, and includes albas, Bourbons, damasks, gallicas, mosses, teas, and more. Old garden roses tend to be quite large plants, to flower only once, and to be fragrant.
- **Climbing Roses:** roses that have long canes that can be trained to trellises and arbors.
- **Rambler Roses:** roses that grow vigorously, have long canes, and can be used to cover trellises; they tend to be more hardy than climbing roses.
- **Shrub Roses:** a catch-all category for roses that don't fit easily in other classes. Many of the most hardy roses, including the hybrid rugosas and the Canadian Explorer roses, fall in this category; shrub roses are usually larger than hybrid teas.
- **Miniature Roses:** extremely small plants with proportionally small blossoms; miniature climbers, however, can grow to 10 feet in Zone 6 gardens.
- **Hybrid Tea Roses:** remontant roses that tend to have long stems and large blooms; many are unscented and most are reliably hardy only in Zone 6.
- **Grandiflora Roses:** upright, remontant medium-sized shrubs with either single blooms or clusters of flowers.
- **Polyantha Roses:** compact, remontant roses with clusters of small flowers; most are unscented.
- **Floribunda Roses:** everblooming, medium-sized (up to 3 or 4 feet), upright shrub roses bearing clusters of smaller flowers rather than single blooms.

BRACE'S BEST MAINE ROSES

Lloyd Brace, who runs The Roseraie at Bayfields in Waldoboro, Maine, subtitles his mail-order cat-alog "Practical Roses for Hard Places." That means his specialty is "old garden, modern shrub and climbing, unique and hardy roses" that thrive in New England. Brace emphasizes the importance of planting bare-root roses in early spring (by April 6 in Zone 6, April 20 in Zone 5, May 4 in Zone 4, and May 18 in Zone 3) and in keeping the canes from drying out by mulching them as far up as prac-ticable. "When you see the leaf buds breaking open, remove the mulch in stages of one-third at a time over a week." With more than 300 cultivars to choose from, picking his favorites, rosarian Brace says, "is a joy and an agony."

'Apart'	crimson-mauve rugosa	3, 4, 5, 6
'Astrid Lindgren'	slight pink shrub	5, 6
'Celestial'	pink alba	4, 5, 6
'Celsiana'	pink damask	5/6
'Delicata'	pink rugosa	3, 4, 5, 6
'Henry Kelsey'	red Canadian Explorer shrub	4, 5, 6
'Jacques Cartier'	pink Portland damask	6
'La Belle Sultane'	dark red gallica	5, 6
'Mary Queen of Scots'	rose-purple scotchbrier	4, 5, 6
'Morden Fireglow'	red-orange shrub	3, 4, 5, 6
'Nozomi'	light pink climbing miniature	5, 6
'Rosanna'	light pink climbing miniature	5, 6
Scotch brier rose (R. spinosissima)	white species	3, 4, 5, 6
'Sydonie'	pink hybrid perpetual	5, 6

 Many roses available for sale are not grown on their own roots, so be sure to remove any suck-ers, or shoots, that come from the rootstock. If your rose starts having flowers that aren't what you expect—pink instead of red, for example, or singles instead of doubles—look carefully and determine where the cane originates. If it's coming from below the bud union, cut it off. If it's coming from above the union, someone's made a mistake. Ask for a refund.

PRETTY IN PINK

Pink roses are among the prettiest, but don't think that pink is for sissies—some of the names on this list, including 'Prairie Joy', a shrub rose, are hardy to Zone 2 (-50 to -40 degrees F). Gertrude Jekyll, the color maven of English horticulture, liked to combine pink blossoms with grey-leaved plants, such as artemisias, santolina, lamb's ears, and the annual *Euphorbia marginata*, known both as snow-on-the-mountain and ghost weed. Add a few purple blooms (perhaps 'Johnson's Blue' geranium and 'Purpurascens' salvia) for contrast, and the picture is perfect.

'Belle Poitevine'	hybrid rugosa	3, 4, 5, 6
'Bonica'	shrub	4, 5, 6
'Celestial'	alba	4, 5, 6
'Celsiana'	damask	5, 6
'Clair Matin'	climber	5, 6
'Constance Spry'	shrub	6
'Dainty Bess'	hybrid tea	5, 6

'Fashion'	floribunda	5, 6
'Frau Dagmar Hastrup'	rugosa	3, 4, 5, 6
'Gertrude Jekyll'	shrub	5/6
'Heritage'	shrub	5, 6
'Ispahan'	damask	4, 5, 6
'Jeanne Lajoie'	miniature	6
'John Davis'	Canadian Explorer shrub	3, 4, 5, 6
'Königin von Dänemark'	alba	3, 4, 5, 6
'Lady Curzon'	hybrid rugosa	3/4, 5, 6
'Playgirl'	floribunda	5, 6
'Prairie Joy'	shrub	2/3, 4, 5, 6
'Queen Elizabeth'	grandiflora	5, 6
'Redouté'	shrub	5, 6
'The Fairy'	polyantha	4, 5, 6
'Tournament of Roses'	hybrid tea	5, 6
Sweetbrier rose (R. eglanteria)	species	4, 5, 6

HYBRID RUGOSA ROSES

Rugosas—also known as Japanese roses, beach roses, hedgehog roses, and the sea tomato—should be known as New England roses, for they are ideally suited to our region. Tolerant of poor soil, drought, cold, wind, and saltspray, they resist nearly every disease and insect known to plague roses; Japanese beetles are a notable exception. In addition to clusters of lovely blooms, rugosas are fragrant, have interesting wrinkled, or rugose, leaves (the source of the species name), and most produce large red or orange hips in autumn. Although the species are enough to make even a fussy gardener happy, you'll want to investigate some of the hybrid rugosas listed below. *Rosa Rugosa* (1999), the definitive book about these roses, was written by Suzanne Verrier, who runs North Creek Farm, a mail-order nursery in Phippsburg, Maine.

'Agnes'	yellow double	3, 4, 5, 6
'Amelie Gravereaux'	purple-crimson double	3, 4, 5, 6
'Belle Poitevine'	pink semidouble	3, 4, 5, 6
'Blanc Double de Coubert'	white double	2/3, 4, 5, 6
'Charles Albanel'	red double	3, 4, 5, 6
'Conrad Ferdinand Meyer'	pink double	4, 5, 6
'Dart's Dash'	purple-crimson semidouble	3, 4, 5, 6
'David Thompson'	red semidouble	3, 4, 5, 6
'Delicata'	pink semidouble	3, 4, 5, 6
'Frau Dagmar Hastrup'	pink single	3, 4, 5, 6
'Hansa'	red-magenta double	3, 4, 5, 6
'Henry Hudson'	white semidouble	2/3, 4, 5, 6
'Jens Munk'	pink semidouble	2/3, 4, 5, 6
'Martin Frobisher'	pink double	3, 4, 5, 6
'Robusta'	scarlet single	4, 5, 6
'Sarah Van Fleet'	pink semidouble	4, 5, 6
'Schneezwerg'	white semidouble	3, 4, 5, 6
'Souvenir de Philemon Cochet'	white double	3, 4, 5, 6
'Superba'	pink single	3, 4, 5, 6

According to nurseryman Dave King, who runs Royall River Roses in North Yarmouth, Maine, location is a key to outstanding growth and bloom. "Pick a sunny, well-protected site with good air circulation and rich, well-drained soil. If you don't have an ideal site, choose roses that tolerate less-than-ideal conditions, such as species, older roses of simple heritage, or rugosa hybrids."

ROSES FOR STOPPING AND BLOCKING

Looking for something to discourage your neighbor's golden retriever? Something to provide a bit of privacy? Something that will add more to your landscape than a tidy hedge of yew or privet? A hedge of roses may be the answer, prickly enough to discourage trespassers, tall enough to hide garbage cans and the neighbor's rusting swing set, pretty enough to brag about, and fragrant to boot. Be sure to offset the plants when you set them out, and prune cautiously—allow these roses to take their natural form.

'Alba'	white rugosa	3, 4, 5, 6
'Alba Maxima'	white alba	4, 5, 6
'Belle Poitevine'	pink rugosa	3, 4, 5, 6
'Celestial'	pink alba	4, 5, 6
'Conrad Ferdinand Meyer'	pink rugosa	3, 4, 5, 6
'Constance Spry'	rose-pink shrub	6
'David Thompson'	crimson rugosa	3, 4, 5, 6
'Dortmund'	red Kordesii	4/5, 6
'Hansa'	red-magenta rugosa	3, 4, 5, 6
'Jens Munk'	mid-pink rugosa	2/3, 4, 5, 6
'John Cabot'	red Canadian Explorer shrub	3, 4, 5, 6
'Louise Odier'	dark pink Bourbon	6
'Mme. Hardy'	white damask	4, 5, 6
R. rugosa	mauve rugosa	2/3, 4, 5, 6
'Roseraie de l'Hay'	purple-crimson rugosa	3, 4, 5, 6
'Rubra'	red rugosa	3, 4, 5, 6
'Superba'	deep pink rugosa	3, 4, 5, 6
'Wassagaming'	mid-pink rugosa	3, 4, 5, 6
'William Baffin'	deep pink Canadian Explorer shrub	2/3, 4, 5, 6

"Rope is a simple material for trellising roses on walls. Set screw eyes in a row at the expected upper limits of the rose, and set another row near the base of the plant (the number of eyes in the row depends on the vigor of the rose, but in most cases three or four eyes are enough). Then string rope—ropes made of soft fibers work best—between the bottom and top eyes, pulling it taut. As the rose grows, twine the long canes around the rope, letting the thorns catch and hold."
Suzanne Verrier, owner, North Creek Farm, Phippsburg, Maine

LOOK AT THOSE HIPS!

Gardeners choose roses for their blooms, not their foliage. But flowers aren't the only source of color and beauty in this genus—many roses also have gorgeous hips. (No bad jokes, please.) Hips, which are the fruits produced by rose plants, are a good source of vitamin C, but you may choose to forgo picking them in order to enjoy their ornamental virtues. Variously shaped—round or elongated—they can be as small as a pea or as large as a crabapple. The roses on this list have brilliant orange or red hips. One warning: Rugosa roses are justly famous for their large, brightly colored fruits, but some cultivars are hipless.

'Alika'	medium red gallica	4, 5, 6
'Carefree Beauty'	rose-pink shrub	4, 5, 6
'Complicata'	rose-pink gallica	3, 4, 5, 6
'Delicata'	pink rugosa	3, 4, 5, 6
'Frau Dagmar Hastrup'	pink rugosa	3, 4, 5, 6
'Hansa'	red-magenta rugosa	3, 4, 5, 6
'Rubra'	red rugosa	3, 4, 5, 6
'Scabrosa'	mauve rugosa	3, 4, 5, 6
R. alba 'Semi-plena'	white alba	3, 4, 5, 6
R. glauca	medium pink species	3, 4, 5, 6
R. rugosa	mauve rugosa	3, 4, 5, 6
R. rugosa 'Alba'	white rugosa	3, 4, 5, 6
Sweetbrier rose (R. eglanteria)	light pink species	4, 5, 6

SCENTED CHAMPIONS

Modern roses aren't known for fragrance, which is one reason the American Rose Society's James Alexander Gamble Fragrance Medal has been awarded to only ten cultivars since it was established in 1953. All of the medal winners, modern cultivars that are listed below, score high in general desirable characteristics in addition to having pronounced fragrance. (The date within the parentheses is the year in which the cultivar received its award.) If you are looking for an exceptionally fragrant rose, the American Rose Society suggests you choose one of these, or 'Mister Lincoln', which is gloriously scented but was never awarded the Gamble Medal.

The roses in this list are hardy only to Zone 5 or 6. Fragrance-seeking gardeners in colder regions should look into planting some of the rugged rugosa roses that appear in other lists in this chapter and are showcased in the list called "Hybrid Rugosa Roses." Practically all rugosas have scent.

'Chrysler Imperial' (1965)	dark red hybrid tea	6
'Crimson Glory' (1961)	dark red hybrid tea	6
'Double Delight' (1986)	red blend hybrid tea	5/6
'Fragrant Cloud' (1970)	orange-red hybrid tea	6
'Fragrant Hour' (1997)	orange-pink hybrid tea	6
'Granada' (1968)	red blend hybrid tea	6
'Papa Meilland' (1974)	dark red hybrid tea	6
'Sunsprite' (1979)	dark yellow floribunda	5, 6
'Sutter's Gold' (1966)	orange blend hybrid tea	6
'Tiffany' (1962)	pink blend hybrid tea	6

FLORIBUNDA FOLLIES

Most floribunda roses, the second largest rose class after hybrid teas, are grafted, so it's important to remove any shoots that may sprout from the roots. Floribundas don't flower throughout the garden season, but they are good repeaters, which is one reason for their popularity. Another reason is fragrance—most are at least slightly perfumed. Like all roses, they want full sun and rich soil that both drains well and retains moisture. Interestingly, orange and yellow cultivars are most susceptible to black spot, so you may want to forgo those hues. This list includes some of the more hardy cultivars, but all floribundas should be given ample protection in winter, even in Zone 5.

'Apricot Nectar'	apricot blend	5, 6
'Betty Prior'	pink	4, 5, 6
'Charles Dickens'	salmon-pink	4, 5, 6
'Chuckles'	pink	4, 5, 6
'Cordula'	orange-red	4, 5, 6
'Fragrant Delight'	salmon-coral	5, 6
'Hans Christian Andersen'	red	4, 5, 6
'Iceberg'	white	4/5, 6
'Margaret Merril'	white	5, 6
'Margo Koster'	salmon	4, 5, 6
'Nearly Wild'	pink	5, 6
'Spirit of Canada'	scarlet	4, 5, 6
'Sun Flare'	yellow	5, 6
'Sunsprite'	yellow	5, 6

 If you know your roses are likely to become infected with black spot, a fungal disease that gets its name from the black spots that appear on the leaves in early summer, mix a preventative baking-soda spray: To a gallon of water, add 1 tablespoon of baking soda and a few drops of dishwashing soap. Spray your plants every five days. Your life will be easier, though, if you choose disease-resistant roses. Rugosas and the Canadian Explorer series cultivars bred by Felicitas Svejdalf are among the roses most resistant to black spot.

COLD COMFORT: ROSES FOR THE FAR NORTH

Gardeners in the most-northern parts of New England have fewer choices when it comes to roses. But fewer doesn't mean none. There are roses that flourish in Zone 3, where the mercury falls as low as -40 degrees F. This list of arctic survivors comes from the small but superb Cady's Falls Nursery in Morrisville, Vermont. (The nursery has a catalog but does not do mail-order). The roses on this list are able to handle cold weather, and they have good disease-resistance. To encourage new growth, nursery owner Don Avery recommends spring pruning to remove dead wood and old stems. Most of these roses bloom in late spring or early summer, then rebloom lightly throughout the summer.

If you are looking for a fragrant rose, try 'Harison's Yellow', 'Tuscany Superb', or any of the rugosas. All of the roses in this list are hardy to Zone 3. 'Blanc Double de Coubert' and 'Henry Hudson' have been known to survive in Zone 2.

'Agnes'	rugosa	yellow
'Belle Poitevine'	rugosa	pink
'Blanc Double de Coubert'	rugosa	white
'Champlain'	Canadian Explorer shrub	red

'Charles Albanel'	rugosa	red-magenta
'Complicata'	gallica	rose-pink
'David Thompson'	rugosa	red
'Delicata'	rugosa	pink
'Grootendorst Supreme'	rugosa	red
'Hansa'	rugosa	red-magenta
'Harison's Yellow'	foetida	yellow
'Henry Hudson'	rugosa	white
'John Franklin'	Canadian Explorer shrub	red
'Martin Frobisher'	rugosa	pink
'Topaz Jewel'	rugosa	yellow
'Tuscany Superb'/'Superb Tuscan'	gallica	mauve

"The most common mistake people make with roses," nurserywoman and garden writer Suzanne Verrier says, **"is not planting them deep enough. Grafted plants should be set with the graft at least 3 inches below the soil surface; own-root plants should be set equally deep. Roses do best if their roots grow deep enough that they aren't subjected to extremes of heat and cold, or wet and dry."**

ROSES FOR XERISCAPING

Many roses—the luxuriant hybrid teas come to mind—need mild winters and plenty of moisture during their growing season. But not all roses are cold-susceptible water hogs. Many *Rosa* cultivars do well where there are sub-zero temperatures in winter and precious little rain in summer. This list comes from Jennifer Bennett, who is the author of *Dry-Land Gardening: A Xeriscaping Guide for Dry-Summer, Cold-Winter Climates* (1998). The term *xeriscape* comes from the Greek word *xeros*, meaning "dry."

'Belle Poitevine'	pink rugosa	3, 4, 5, 6
'Blanc Double de Coubert'	white rugosa	2/3, 4, 5, 6
'Frau Dagmar Hastrup'	pink rugosa	3, 4, 5, 6
'Hansa'	red-magenta rugosa	3, 4, 5, 6
'Harison's Yellow'	yellow foetida	3, 4, 5, 6
'Hazeldean'	yellow spinosissima	3, 4, 5, 6
Hudson's Bay rose (*R. blanda*)	pink	3, 4, 5, 6
Persian yellow rose (*R. foetida persiana*)	yellow	3, 4, 5, 6
R. acicularis	dark pink	3, 4, 5, 6
'Thérèse Bugnet'	pink rugosa	3, 4, 5, 6

LOW-MAINTENANCE ROSES

Gardening is never entirely carefree, but there are plants that require so little help to flourish that they come close to being entirely carefree. These cultivars, all recommended by David King, who runs Royall River Roses nursery in Yarmouth, Maine, are notable for their vigor and disease-resistance. Ideal for gardeners without the desire—or time—to prune, water, spray, and fertilize, these roses, as King puts it, "thrive on neglect." These also are perfect roses for King, who not only runs a rose nursery but moonlights as an American Rose Society certified consulting rosarian, a licensed real estate broker, an experienced sailor, and an instrument-rated pilot.

'Betty Prior'	pink floribunda	4, 5, 6
'Carefree Beauty'	rose-pink shrub	4, 5, 6
'Carefree Delight'	rose-pink shrub	4, 5, 6
'Frontenac'	pink shrub	4, 5, 6
'Jens Munk'	pink rugosa	2/3, 4, 5, 6
'Magnifica'	purple-crimson double rugosa	3, 4, 5, 6
Scotch brier rose (*R. spinosissima*)	white species	3, 4, 5, 6
'William Baffin'	deep pink Canadian Explorer climber	2/3, 4, 5, 6

> Preventive measures can discourage many rose diseases. Give your plants full sun and space them generously so they have good air circulation. Don't stress roses by overfertilizing them, or underfeeding them. Remove infected and dead foliage so that diseases, such as black spot and rust, don't spread or overwinter in your garden. Planting roses throughout your landscape, rather than in one bed, will make them more difficult for insect pests to target.

A LILLIPUTIAN GARDEN: MINIATURE ROSES

Miniature roses are an especially fine choice for New England gardeners with patios and decks. All the cultivars listed below, recommended by John Saville, who owns Nor'East Miniature Roses, a mail-order nursery in Rowley, Massachusetts, do well when grown in containers. Saville says that they also can hold their own when planted in the garden. Locate them where they will receive at least six hours of sun daily and protection from heavy rains and wind. These roses may be small, but they're hardy to Zone 3, according to Saville. He recommends overwintering them, in the pot, outdoors. Bury the pot in the garden in late fall, and mulch heavily with soil, hay, or leaves—cover the entire plant. Pull out the pot in spring, once the ground has thawed.

'Absolutely'	cream and yellow	3, 4, 5, 6
'Child's Play	white and pink double	3, 4, 5, 6
'Cupcake'	pink double	3, 4, 5, 6
'Denver's Dream'	copper-orange	3, 4, 5, 6
'Glory Be'	yellow	3, 4, 5, 6
'Minnie Pearl'	pink blend	3, 4, 5, 6
'Overnight Scentsation'	fragrant medium pink	3, 4, 5, 6
'Pacific Serenade'	yellow	3, 4, 5, 6
'Rainbow's End'	yellow and scarlet	3, 4, 5, 6
'Scentsational'	fragrant mauve and pink	3, 4, 5, 6
'Sorcerer'	medium red	3, 4, 5, 6
'Teddy Bear'	terra cotta	3, 4, 5, 6

A WHITE BOUQUET

It may be entirely true that "luve is like a red, red rose," but for many gardeners, white roses, which also are "newly sprung in June," create the ultimate pleasure. Every rose group—Bourbons, albas, rugosas, teas, and more—contains white cultivars. White roses are sometimes less vigorous than their red, pink, and yellow cousins, but many, such as the hybrid rugosa 'Blanc Double de Coubert', are about as hardy as roses come. In the language of flowers, the white rose represents clarity of thought and intentions, an appropriately cool contrast to the red rose, which represents passion.

'Blanc Double de Coubert'	rugosa	2/3, 4, 5, 6
'Bobbie James'	multiflora	5, 6
'Boule de Neige'	Bourbon	6
'Cecile Brunner White'	polyantha	5, 6
'Cinderella'	miniature	5, 6
'City of York'	climber	5, 6
'Class Act'	floribunda	5, 6
'Comtesse de Murinais'	moss	5, 6
'Dupontii'	old garden	4, 5, 6
'Francine Austin'	shrub	5, 6
'Henry Hudson'	rugosa	2/3, 4, 5, 6
'Iceberg'	floribunda	4/5, 6
'Margaret Merril'	floribunda	5, 6
'Mme. Hardy'	damask	4, 5, 6
'Mme. Legras de St. Germain'	alba	3, 4, 5, 6
'Mme. Plantier'	alba	3, 4, 5, 6
'Paloma Blanca'	grandiflora	4, 5, 6
'Pascali'	hybrid tea	4, 5, 6
'Polar Star'	hybrid tea	5, 6
R. alba 'Semi-plena'	alba	3, 4, 5, 6
'Sally Holmes'	shrub	5, 6
'Schneezwerg'	rugosa	3, 4, 5, 6
'Sir Thomas Lipton'	rugosa	3, 4, 5, 6
'Stanwell Perpetual'	spinosissima	3, 4, 5, 6
'White Dawn'	climber	5, 6
'White Lightnin''	grandiflora	5, 6
'White Meidiland'	shrub	5, 6
'White Pet'	polyantha	5, 6
Scotch brier rose (R. spinosissima)	species	3, 4, 5, 6

BEST-OF-THE-BEST ROSES

No one keeps closer track of what's best in new roses than the people at All-America Rose Selections, a national organization that has been judging roses since 1938. New cultivars are tested at official trial gardens located throughout the United States. The sites—usually botanic or university gardens—span a wide range of climates; each site follows standards specified by AARS to ensure that the roses undergoing testing receive the care normally provided by an average home gardener. And the best of the best? According to AARS, five cultivars qualify as all-time favorites with home gardeners. Rated hardy to Zone 5, they can be grown successfully in slightly colder regions if given extra protection in winter. (The date within the parentheses is the year that the cultivar was an AARS winner.)

'Double Delight' (1977)	white with red hybrid tea	5/6
'Mr. Lincoln' (1965)	dark red hybrid tea	5, 6
'Peace' (1946)	yellow and pink hybrid tea	5, 6
'Queen Elizabeth' (1955)	pink grandiflora	5, 6
'Tropicana/Super Star' (1963)	coral-orange hybrid tea	5, 6

AARS TRIAL GARDENS
Want to see the very latest in rose breeding? The All-America Rose Selections public gardens are where to go. They're filled with past award winners, new introductions, and much more.

Connecticut: Norwich Memorial Rose Garden, Norwich; Boothe Park Wedding Rose Garden, Stratford; Elizabeth Park Rose Garden, West Hartford.
Maine: City of Portland Rose Circle at Deering Oaks Park, Portland.
Massachusetts: James P. Kelleher Rose Garden, Boston; Stanley Park, Westfield.
New Hampshire: Fuller Gardens Rose Garden, North Hampton.

FRAGRANT HEIRLOOM ROSES

A rose by any other name may still be a rose, but a rose without fragrance is, well, incomplete. While some modern breeders, such as David Austin, have ensured that their creations smell as good as they look, the best rose perfumes still belong to heirloom cultivars. Gallicas, damasks, and rugosas are famous for their perfume. David King, who specializes in "old-fashioned, uncommon, and hardy roses" (more than 200 species and cultivars) at Royall River Roses, his nursery in Yarmouth, Maine, recommends these old-timers for gardeners who like to sniff as well as see. (For prize-winning modern roses with fragrance, see "Scented Champions.")

Apothecary's rose (*R. gallica officinalis*)	pink gallica	4, 5, 6
'Blanc Double de Coubert'	white rugosa	3, 4, 5, 6
'Charles de Mills'	mauve gallica	4, 5, 6
'Comte de Chambord'	pink blend Portland damask	5, 6
'Hansa'	red-magenta rugosa	3, 4, 5, 6
'La Reine Victoria'	lilac-rose Bourbon	6
'Louise Odier'	dark pink Bourbon	6
'Mme. Hardy'	white damask	4, 5, 6
'Thérèse Bugnet'	pink rugosa	3, 4, 5, 6
'Tuscany Superb'/'Superb Tuscan'	mauve gallica	3, 4, 5, 6

RISE AND SHINE: CLIMBING ROSES

Climbing roses are a challenge to grow in the coldest parts of New England, but even gardeners in Zone 3 can find roses to ascend—not to the top of a 20-foot arbor but well upward. Unlike true vines, which hoist themselves upward by twining and other means, most climbing roses are rambling culti-

vars that produce long shoots that must be tied to a vertical support. Despite the hardiness ratings of some of these cultivars, gardeners in the colder zones of our region should expect extensive dieback in winter, especially on roses located on sites unprotected from winter sun and wind. This list contains both true climbers, such as 'Awakening' and 'New Dawn', and representatives from other rose groups that have long canes that Yankee gardeners can substitute for true climbing cultivars.

'Aïcha'	yellow spinosissima	3, 4, 5, 6
'American Pillar'	pink rambler	5/6
'Awakening'	pink climber	6
'Blaze Improved'	red climber	5, 6
'City of York'	white climber	5, 6
'Don Juan'	red climber	6

'Dortmund'	red Kordesii	4/5, 6
Eglantine rose (*R. rubiginosa*)	pink species	3, 4, 5, 6
'Golden Showers'	yellow climber	5/6
'Henry Kelsey'	red Canadian Explorer shrub	4, 5, 6
'John Cabot'	red Canadian Explorer shrub	3, 4, 5, 6
'Leverkusen'	yellow Kordesii	4/5, 6
'Mrs. John McNab'	white shrub	3, 4, 5, 6
'New Dawn'	pink climber	6
'Paul's Scarlet Climber'	red climber	5, 6
'Polsjärnam'/'Polestar'	white rambler	3, 4, 5, 6
'Prairie Dawn'	salmon-pink Canadian Explorer shrub	3, 4, 5, 6
'William Baffin'	deep pink Canadian Explorer shrub	2/3, 4, 5, 6

"My definition of a hardy rose is one that has the tenacity to grow back from ground level after a severe snowless winter. In places like England and the Brooklyn Botanic Garden, climbing roses persist high about the ground for many years. Here in Zone 3, after a mild winter our climbers may have live buds at 6 feet, but the next year they may die back to knee high 'snow level.' Like many of our favorite plants, climbing roses are often grown for the sake of nostalgia in northern New England."
Don Avery, owner, Cady's Falls Nursery, Morrisville, Vermont

TEN OF CANADA'S BEST ROSES

Eric and Jennifer Welzel, who live in Freeport, Maine, proudly say that their Fox Hill Nursery is "a real nursery, not a 'rose company.' We don't grow any grafted or hybrid tea roses. Our roses are field grown and trial tested in our nursery, not trucked in and sold as 'Maine Grown.'" The Welzels look for hardiness as well as beauty in roses, which is why they're so enthusiastic about the Canadian Explorer Series. Canadians also know something about the cold, and these roses are the best export from our neighbor to the north since hockey. They are often mistakenly designated by the American Rose Society and others as "Kordesii" roses, after the German breeder Wilhelm Kordes, who also is famous for producing hardy cultivars.

'Alexander MacKenzie'	red shrub	3, 4, 5, 6
'Captain Samuel Holland'	red climber	3, 4, 5, 6
'Champlain'	red shrub	3, 4, 5, 6
'Charles Albanel'	red-magenta shrub	3, 4, 5, 6
'George Vancouver'	red shrub	3, 4, 5, 6
'Henry Hudson'	white shrub	2/3, 4, 5, 6
'Jens Munk'	pink shrub	2/3, 4, 5, 6
'John Cabot'	red climber	3, 4, 5, 6
'Louis Jolliet'	medium pink climber	3, 4, 5, 6
'William Baffin'	deep pink climber	2/3, 4, 5, 6

TIME FOR TEAS

The name Jackson & Perkins is synonymous with roses in this country. New hybrids, especially hybrid teas, are its stock-in-trade. While not nearly as hardy as many other classes, hybrid teas can be grown in cold regions if they are given extra protection during winter. Jason Cheeseman, J&P's man in New England, recommends these hybrid teas, all of which are hardy to Zone 6. They should be planted with their graft union below the soil surface, Cheeseman warns, and should be mulched once the ground freezes. With heavy mulching and a good snowcover, they may survive in even more frigid hardiness zones.

'Fragrant Cloud'	coral red
'French Perfume'	rose-pink
'Garden Party'	ivory and cream
'Legend'	red
'Olympiad'	red
'Pristine'	pink and white

If your climate says "no" to hybrid tea roses but your heart says "yes," try this trenching technique for protecting your plants in winter:

- Remove all mulch and cut the rose back to knee height.
- Water thoroughly and apply a dormant spray.
- Tie the canes together.
- Dig an 8-inch-deep trench up to the base of the rose. The trench should be as long as the canes are tall. Use a shovel to dig the trench, but when working around the rose, use a spading fork to avoid damaging the roots.
- Loosen the ground at the base of the rose on the side opposite the trench, then dig under the rose and tip it into the trench.
- Cover the canes with soil. After the ground freezes, mulch with at least 6 inches of organic matter.

ROSES AS GROUND COVER

Roses as a deciduous ground cover? Yes, indeed. Although New Englanders have fewer choices than gardeners in warmer regions, there are still many handsome roses that will blanket both flat and sloped land. Be sure to mulch your plants generously in order to suppress weeds. Most of the cultivars on this list grow 4 feet tall, even a little taller; timely pruning will keep them lower and encourage dense growth.

'Alba Meidiland'	white shrub	4/5, 6
'Bonica'	pink shrub	4, 5, 6
'Champlain'	red Canadian Explorer shrub	3, 4, 5, 6
'Charles Albanel'	red rugosa	3, 4, 5, 6
'Francine Austin'	white shrub	5, 6
'Frau Dagmar Hastrup'	pink rugosa	3, 4, 5, 6
'Henry Hudson'	white rugosa	2/3, 4, 5, 6
'John Franklin'	medium red Canadian Explorer shrub	3, 4, 5, 6

'Maiden's Blush Small'	pink hybrid alba	4, 5, 6
'Max Graf'	pink rugosa	4, 5, 6
'Morden Amorette'	carmine miniature	3, 4, 5, 6
'Morden Ruby'	pink shrub	3, 4, 5, 6
'Nearly Wild'	pink floribunda	5, 6
'Orange Triumph'	red-orange polyantha	5, 6
'Petite Pink Scotch'	pink shrub	3, 4, 5, 6
'Red Meidiland'	red miniature	5, 6
R. paulii	white species	2/3, 4, 5, 6
'Rose de Meaux'	pink centifolia	4, 5, 6
'Rote Apart'	crimson ground cover	3, 4, 5, 6
'Scarlet Meidiland'	scarlet shrub	5, 6
'Schneekoppe'	white rugosa	3, 4, 5, 6
'Sea Foam'	creamy white shrub	4/5, 6
'Stanwell Perpetual'	pink spinosissima	3, 4, 5, 6
'The Fairy'	pink polyantha	4, 5, 6
Scotch brier rose (R. spinosissima)	white species	3, 4, 5, 6

DAVID AUSTIN ROSES

No roses have received more publicity in the last few years than the hybrids produced by English rosarian David Austin. They've been promoted as combining the form and fragrance of old roses and the repeat blooming trait of modern roses. Lloyd Brace, owner of The Roseraie at Bayfields, which is located about fifty miles north of Portland, Maine, in Waldoboro, admires Austin's skills as a breeder and enjoys many of the blooms that have come out of Shropshire. But Shropshire is not the northern U.S., to whom Brace caters with roses that winter without protection. That narrows down the choices considerably. Of the Austin roses that are happy in midcoast Maine, Brace recommends these cultivars as worth trying.

'Ambridge Rose'	apricot-pink double	5, 6
'Heritage'	soft pink cupped	5, 6
'L. D. Braithwaite'	crimson double	5, 6
'Lucetta'	pink semidouble	5, 6
'Peach Blossom'	peach-pink semidouble	5, 6
'Perdita'	pink rosette	5, 6
'Winchester Cathedral'	white cupped	5, 6
'Windrush'	yellow-white semidouble	5, 6

"The cane hardiness of a rose is not affected by the roots it's growing on. As long as the graft union is set 3 inches below the soil surface and gets 6 to 8 inches of mulch after it goes dormant in late fall, it will behave exactly as an own-root rose. Even if there is a cataclysmic freeze that kills the canes to the ground, the plant will have 10 or so inches of buried cane of the scion from which to regenerate."
Lloyd Brace, owner, The Roseraie at Bayfields, Waldoboro, Maine

SHRUB ROSES

Shrub roses are a popular modern type and often are described as roses that don't belong in any of the traditional categories, such as floribundas, gallicas, or rugosas. Where they do belong is in New England gardens, as most are remontant, blooming twice in the growing season, once in summer and again in autumn. Many cultivars on this list produce their flowers in clusters. Height varies, anywhere from 3 to 7 feet, and plants typically grow as wide as they are tall, making them a fine choice for a hedge. Most have good disease-resistance, and nearly all have some scent; a few, including 'Graham Thomas', 'Penelope', and 'Golden Celebration', are strongly fragrant. All need good protection in winter.

'Abraham Darby'	apricot-pink	5, 6
'Alexander MacKenzie'	red	3, 4, 5, 6
'Assiniboine'	pink	4, 5, 6
'Carefree Delight'	rose-pink	4, 5, 6
'Champlain'	red	3, 4, 5, 6
'Country Dancer'	dark pink	4, 5, 6
'Dr. Merkely'	pink	4, 5, 6
'Golden Celebration'	yellow	6
'Graham Thomas'	yellow	5/6
'Henry Kelsey'	red	4, 5, 6
'Lillian Gibson'	pink	4, 5, 6
'Mary Rose'	rose-pink	5, 6
'Morden Blush'	pink	3, 4, 5, 6
'Morden Centennial'	pink	3, 4, 5, 6
'Morden Fireglow'	red-orange	3, 4, 5, 6
'Prairie Dawn'	salmon-pink	3, 4, 5, 6
'Prairie Youth'	salmon	3, 4, 5, 6
'Redouté'	pale pink	5, 6
'Royal Bonica'	pink	4, 5, 6
'Sea Foam'	white	4/5, 6
'Striped Mary Rose'	pink and white	5, 6
'Wildenfels Gelb'	yellow	4, 5, 6
'William Baffin'	deep pink	2/3, 4, 5, 6
Persian Yellow (*R. foetida persiana*)	yellow	3, 4, 5, 6

SHRUBS AND VINES

My ninety-five-year-old mother still likes to tell the story of sending her family into panic when she was four—by disappearing. After searching for several hours, they found her sleeping under the white arching branches of a huge bridalwreath spirea, *Spiraea prunifolia*. The species comes from China, where its common name means "smile-laugh flowers." Certainly I smile-laugh every time she repeats the tale.

Shrubs should be an important element in our gardens, for they can create a framework for all other plants. Yet shrubs are plants that most of us buy on a whim. We visit a nursery, are seduced by a butterfly bush in flower, take it home, and plant it wherever we can find room. In the best designed, most striking gardens, though, shrubs are used thoughtfully and always to advantage. Strategically placed, they serve as a background to other plants, as eye-catching accents, things worth growing in their own right, or both.

Loosely defined, shrubs are woody plants that have several stems rather than a single trunk and grow to 10 or 20 feet. They give us interesting shapes, colors, textures, flowers, fruits, and fragrances. You can mix them in flower borders (turning them into "mixed borders"), use them to disguise foundations, screen eyesores, and create privacy. They can serve as ground covers and be grown in containers on patios and decks. They attract and shelter wildlife (and little girls). There isn't much a shrub can't do.

And can't do on its own. A shrub requires little from the gardener after it's established. Or *they're* established, for shrubs are even nicer when planted in the plural. If you have the room, consider creating a shubbery, or border of shrubs. Do a little homework and you can have flowers from spring until frost, colorful fall foliage, and bright fruits and interesting forms to cheer you in winter.

Vines are an underused group of plants in this country, especially compared with England, where gardeners are likely to plant a clematis at the foot of anything that remains still for more than thirty minutes. While all vines have the urge to ascend, they don't all have the same climbing equipment. Some, such as wisteria, twine. Some adhere to surfaces ("cleaveth wonderfull hard," one sixteenth-century writer put it) as Boston ivy and climbing hydrangea do. Some clasp with tendrils or petioles (sweet peas), and some hook with thorns (roses). The gardener's job is to make sure each has an appropriate support: A clematis can't scale a bare wall although Boston ivy can, and English ivy can't climb strings although a morning glory can.

With the right home and a little guidance, most vines grow quickly and without assistance. "Plant it and stand back," a friend once cautioned when she gave me a wisteria cutting. Even edible vines can be aggressive. The first time I planted an heirloom cucumber named 'True Lemon', the vine swarmed over the beans and tomatoes, through the lawn, and mounted the raspberries. There wasn't a second time. If your space is small or your trellis flimsy, choose your species carefully.

Like shrubs, vines can enclose and frame, and camouflage; they offer flowers, berries, and varied foliage. They come little and big, and their verticality makes them ideal for small gardens, their vigor for large settings. You'll want to avoid our native poison ivy ("Leaflets three / Let it be"), and woe is you if bindweed gets started in your garden. But don't avoid vines. A third-rank poet once wrote that "on heaven's wall a golden vine clambers bright." Smart gardeners up there.

One practical item: Plant scientists now recommend the same tough-love treatment for planting woody vines and shrubs as they do for trees. Unless your soil is extremely poor, don't amend the planting hole with fertilizer or organic matter. Research indicates that enriching the soil can discourage roots from expanding beyond the planting hole.

BEYOND FORSYTHIA: OVERLOOKED FLOWERING SHRUBS

Flowering shrubs are an asset to any garden, large or small, but most gardeners know only the ubiquitous plants, such as forsythia, potentilla, lilacs, and rhododendrons. So none of those appear on this list, which includes many shrubs with fragrant flowers (Carolina allspice, sweetspire, and mock orange are three) as well as species that have ornamental fruits and colorful foliage in autumn. You may have to search a little to find some of these plants, but they're worth the extra trouble.

'Royal Red', 'Black Knight' butterfly bush (*Buddleia davidii*)	5, 6
Carolina allspice/sweetshrub (*Calycanthus floridus*)	4, 5, 6
'Scarff's Red' flowering quince (*Chaenomeles speciosa*)	4/5, 6
'Ruby Spice', 'Rosea' summersweet (*Clethra alnifolia*)	3, 4, 5, 6
'Winterthur' winter hazel (*Corylopsis*)	5, 6
Spiked winter hazel (*Corylopsis spicata*)	5, 6
'Carol Mackie' daphne (*Daphne burkwoodii*)	3, 4, 5, 6
'Carminea' deutzia (*Deutzia rosea*)	5, 6
'Copper' copper bush honeysuckle (*Diervilla lonicera*)	4, 5, 6
'Annabelle' hills of snow (*Hydrangea arborescens*)	3, 4, 5, 6
Smooth hydrangea (*Hydrangea arborescens*)	3, 4, 5, 6
Panicled hydrangea (*Hydrangea paniculata*)	4, 5, 6
Oakleaf hydrangea (*Hydrangea quercifolia*)	5, 6
'Henry's Garnet' sweetspire (*Itea virginica*)	5, 6
Mountain laurel (*Kalmia latifolia*)	4/5, 6
'Shannon' single kerria (*Kerria japonica*)	4/5, 6
Fragrant/winter honeysuckle (*Lonicera fragrantissima*)	4, 5, 6
'Avalanche', 'Innocence' mock orange (*Philadelphus coronarius*)	4, 5, 6
'Mountain Fire' Japanese andromeda (*Pieris japonica*)	5, 6
Nanking cherry (*Prunus tomentosa*)	2, 3, 4, 5, 6
Japanese white spirea (*Spiraea japonica* var. *albiflora*)	4, 5, 6
'Fairy Queen' spirea (*Spiraea trilobata*)	3, 4, 5, 6
Mapleleaf viburnum (*Viburnum acerifolium*)	4, 5, 6
Koreanspice viburnum (*Viburnum carlesii*)	4, 5, 6
'Susquehanna' Sargent viburnum (*Viburnum sargentii*)	4, 5, 6
'Compactum' American cranberry bush (*Viburnum trilobum*)	2/3, 4, 5, 6
'Polka', 'Samba', 'Tango' weigela (*Weigela*)	4, 5, 6

CAROLINA
ALLSPICE

ARCTIC SHRUBS

Don't believe what some garden books say. Lewis and Nancy Hill *know* that these shrubs can take the cold—they grow them all in their Zone 3 garden. In addition to running a retail daylily nursery at their Greensboro, Vermont, homestead, the Hills keep busy writing garden articles and books. If you need advice about keeping any of these hardy plants tidy, look at of their *Pruning Simplified*

(1986). For more about gardening in the frigid parts of New England, they've written *Cold-Climate Gardening* (1987). Both books are published by Storey Communications, located in Pownal, Vermont.

EUROPEAN
CRANBERRY
BUSH

'Carol Mackie' daphne (*Daphne burkwoodii*)	3, 4, 5, 6
'Annabelle' hills of snow (*Hydrangea arborescens*)	3, 4, 5, 6
'Grandiflora Compacta' PeeGee hydrangea (*Hydrangea paniculata*)	4, 5, 6
Mock orange (*Philadelphus coronarius*)	3/4, 5, 6
'Goldfinger' bush cinquefoil (*Potentilla fruticosa*)	3, 4, 5, 6
'Belle Poitevine' rose (*Rosa*)	3, 4, 5, 6
'Grootendorst Red' rose (*Rosa*)	3, 4, 5, 6
'Harison's Yellow' rose (*Rosa*)	3, 4, 5, 6
'Sir Thomas Lipton' rose (*Rosa*)	3, 4, 5, 6
'Fairy Queen' spirea (*Spiraea trilobata*)	3, 4, 5, 6
Van Houtte spirea (*Spiraea vanhouttei*)	3, 4, 5, 6
'Agnes Smith' lilac (*Syringa prestoniae*)	3, 4, 5, 6
'James Macfarlane' lilac (*Syringa vulgaris*)	3, 4, 5, 6
'Monge' lilac (*Syringa vulgaris*)	3, 4, 5, 6
'Compactum' European cranberry bush (*Viburnum opulus*)	3, 4, 5, 6

ZONING IN: RHODODENDRONS FOR NEW ENGLAND

There are enormous numbers of rhododendron cultivars available, but most home gardeners grab whatever local nurseries offer in spring—usually run-of-the-mill varieties that often are only marginally suited for New England's climate. Rather than be disappointed, shop from these lists provided by Dick Brooks, a Massachusetts gardener and former president of the American Rhododendron Society. Brooks grows more than 800 different rhododendrons on his wooded lot in Concord. Many of the cultivars he lists are new and available only from specialty nurseries (see "The Mail-Order Garden," in this book).

Zone 3
'Helsinki University'
'Mikkeli'
'Orchid Lights'
'Peter Tigerstedt'
'PJM'
'Rosy Lights'
'White Lights'

Zone 4
'Anna H. Hall'
'April Rose'
'April White'
'Connecticut Yankee'
'Cornell Pink'
'Henry's Red'
'Vernus'
Rhododendron maximum
Rhododendron minus

Zone 5
'Bali'
'Calsap'
'Capistrano'
'Firestorm'
'Janet Blair'
'Jonathan Shaw'
'Mist Maiden'

Zone 6
'Dexter's Champagne'
'Fantastica'
'Ginny Gee'
'Hachmann's Polaris'
'Morgenrot'
'Parker's Pink'
'Patty Bee'
'Percy Wiseman'
'Scintillation'

Richard Brooks, a Concord, Massachusetts, gardener and former president of the American Rhododendron Society, advises that the following are the most important ingredients for growing rhododendrons and azaleas in New England:

1. **Acid soil.** Rhododendrons do best in soil (pH 5.0 to 6.0) that is loose, open, well-drained, and has a high percentage of large, coarse organic particles.
2. **Shallow planting.** The roots of these plants seldom penetrate more than half a foot deep, unless the soil below that point is also open, organic, and well-drained. The top of the root ball should be somewhat above the level of the surrounding ground and should not be covered with soil.
3. **Mulch.** A year-round mulch of coarse organic material such as pine needles, chopped oak leaves, or bark will insulate the shallow roots against extremes of heat and cold, conserve soil moisture, and suppress weeds.
4. **Moisture.** Especially during the first year or two, newly planted azaleas and rhododendrons should not be allowed to suffer from lack of water.

SHRUBS FOR DRY SPOTS

If you have a place in your landscape that needs a shrub but dries out oh-so-quickly, do two things. First, add organic matter to your soil. *Lots* of organic matter. Second, pick a shrub from this list of species and cultivars that are willing to put up with dry conditions. Dry conditions, remember, does not mean arid. Even these plants will need watering if there is an extended drought—and they will need ample water when planted in order to get established.

Bearberry (*Arctostaphylos uva-ursi*)	2, 3, 4, 5, 6
Siberian peashrub (*Caragana arborescens*)	2, 3, 4, 5, 6
Russian peashrub (*Caragana frutex*)	2, 3, 4, 5, 6
Flowering quince (*Chaenomeles speciosa*)	4/5, 6
Smokebush (*Cotinus coggygria*)	4, 5, 6
Autumn olive (*Elaeagnus umbellata*)	3, 4, 5, 6
'Happy Centennial' forsythia (*Forsythia*)	4, 5, 6
Common witch hazel (*Hamamelis virginiana*)	3, 4, 5, 6
Kerria (*Kerria japonica*)	4/5, 6
Shrub bush clover (*Lespedeza bicolor*)	5, 6
Privet (*Ligustrum* spp.)	4, 5, 6
Northern bayberry (*Myrica pensylvanica*)	3, 4, 5, 6
Bush cinquefoil (*Potentilla fruticosa*)	2/3, 4, 5, 6
Beach plum (*Prunus maritima*)	4, 5, 6
Mountain currant (*Ribes alpinum*)	3, 4, 5, 6
Rugosa rose (*Rosa rugosa*)	3, 4, 5, 6
Ural false spirea (*Sorbaria sorbifolia*)	2/3, 4, 5, 6
Snowberry (*Symphoricarpos albus*)	3, 4, 5, 6
Common lilac (*Syringa vulgaris*)	3, 4, 5, 6
Nannyberry (*Viburnum lentago*)	2/3, 4, 5, 6

WITCH
HAZEL

WATERPROOF SHRUBS

For the last twenty-two years, Martha McKeon has gardened in a wet spot in Sandy Hook, Connecticut. Years of working in greenhouses and nurseries honed her knowledge of plants, and she has stocked her yard with "bullet-proof roses and all kinds of perennials," as well as shrubs that don't mind having wet feet. McKeon's garden is located in Zone 6, but many of her favorites will do well in far colder regions of New England. All her choices thrive with a minimum of care.

Eastern redbud (*Cercis canadensis*)	4, 5, 6
Summersweet (*Clethra alnifolia*)	3, 4, 5, 6
'Elegantissima' variegated redtwig dogwood (*Cornus alba*)	2, 3, 4, 5, 6
'Grandiflora Compacta' PeeGee hydrangea (*Hydrangea paniculata*)	4, 5, 6
Winterberry (*Ilex verticillata*)	3, 4, 5, 6
Swamp azalea (*Rhododendron viscosum*)	4, 5, 6
'Wentworth' American cranberry bush (*Viburnum trilobum*)	2/3, 4, 5, 6

MAY THE FORCE BE WITH YOU

The best shrubs for *forcing*—manipulating light and temperature to make a plant bloom prematurely—are familiar names, hardy species that also are proven performers in the garden. Here they are again, in case you've forgotten, plus a few names that may be new to you. Make cuttings at the end of January, place the stems in water, and move to a bright location (but not in direct sun) where the nighttime temperature is between 55 and 60 degrees F. Mist the stems daily to keep the humidity high. The number of days until the flower buds open varies by species, anywhere from twenty to seventy-five.

White forsythia (*Abeliophyllum distichum*)	4, 5, 6
Eastern redbud (*Cercis canadensis*)	4, 5, 6
Flowering quince (*Chaenomeles* spp.)	4/5, 6
February daphne (*Daphne mezereum*)	5, 6
Forsythia (*Forsythia* hyb.)	4, 5, 6
Common witch hazel (*Hamamelis virginiana*)	3, 4, 5, 6
Mountain laurel (*Kalmia latifolia*)	4/5, 6
Star magnolia (*Magnolia stellata*)	4, 5, 6
Japanese andromeda (*Pieris japonica*)	5, 6
Korean azalea (*Rhododendron mucronulatum*)	4, 5, 6
Pussy willow (*Salix discolor*)	2, 3, 4, 5, 6
Bridalwreath (*Spiraea prunifolia*)	4, 5, 6
Sargent viburnum (*Viburnum sargentii*)	4, 5, 6

VERTICALLY CHALLENGED: SHRUBS FOR SUNNY SLOPES

While all but the most wind- or sun-sensitive shrubs will succeed, some species seem more at home than others when planted on a hillside. Every slope is different, but the deciduous shrubs on this list will tolerate the conditions of a sunny slope, including drying winds and less-than-perfect soil. In addition to their sturdy constitutions, many bear exceptionally beautiful blossoms. The blooms of a few—lilac, mock orange, and witch hazel for example—are wonderfully fragrant.

'Texas Scarlet' flowering quince (*Chaenomeles superba*)	4/5, 6
'Golden Twig' red osier dogwood (*Cornus stolonifera*)	3, 4, 5, 6
Red osier dogwood (*Cornus stolonifera*)	2, 3, 4, 5, 6
'Albus' Warminster broom (*Cytisus praecox*)	5, 6
Weeping forsythia (*Forsythia suspensa*)	5/6
Common witch hazel (*Hamamelis virginiana*)	3, 4, 5, 6
'Avalanche' mock orange (*Philadelphus coronarius*)	4, 5, 6

Bush cinquefoil (*Potentilla fruticosa*)	2/3, 4, 5, 6
'Rutgers' firethorn (*Pyracantha*)	4/5, 6
'Dissecta' staghorn sumac (*Rhus typhina*)	3, 4, 5, 6
Rugosa rose (*Rosa rugosa*)	3, 4, 5, 6
'Alpina' spirea (*Spiraea japonica*)	4, 5, 6
Lilac (*Syringa* spp.)	3, 4, 5, 6
Koreanspice viburnum (*Viburnum carlesii*)	4, 5, 6

THE TEN DWARFS: A RHODE ISLAND EXPERT'S FAVORITE SMALL CONIFERS

Mort White lives in Cranston, Rhode Island, a Zone 6 location where he can grow a wide range plants. A former nurseryman and landscaper, he began Rhode Island's first radio call-in gardening program in 1982. The show—*The Magic Garden*—is now carried by more than 100 stations, including fourteen in New England. You can also find him on the Web at www.themagicgarden.com. Dwarf conifers are a special interest of White's, since he has scaled back the size of his garden in order to save time, he confesses, for playing golf.

Korean small-leaved boxwood (*Buxus microphylla* var. *koreana*)	5, 6
'Nana Gracilis' dwarf Hinoki cypress (*Chamaecyparis obtusa*)	4/5, 6
Garland flower/bush daphne (*Daphne cneorum*)	5, 6
'Emerald 'n Gold' wintercreeper (*Euonymus fortunei*)	5, 6
'Wiltonii' blue rug juniper (*Juniperus horizontalis*)	3, 4, 5, 6
'Compacta' compact dwarf blue spruce (*Picea pungens* f. *glauca*)	3, 4, 5, 6
Dwarf mugo pine (*Pinus mugo* var. *mugo*)	3, 4, 5, 6
'Densa' dwarf Japanese yew (*Taxus cuspidata* f. *nana*)	4, 5, 6
'Aurea Nana' oriental arborvitae (*Thuja orientalis*)	6
'Bennett', 'Gracilis' dwarf hemlock (*Tsuga canadensis*)	3, 4, 5, 6

"At some time, most gardeners need or want to move shrubs that grow in their yards. Flowering shrubs should be transplanted when they are leafless, either in early spring or late fall. Small, young shrubs, two or three years old, can be transplanted without a root ball. And if you break the root ball on older, larger shrubs, don't panic. As long as you get them back into the ground quickly, they should survive. Don't add chemical fertilizer or fresh manure to the planting hole, which can burn the roots, and be sure not to overwater. Add a bucket or two of water to the planting hole and then let Mother Nature do the rest (help out only if there is prolonged drought). Last, don't expect miracles from transplanted flowering shrubs. The first year will be one of reestablishing strong roots, rather than producing many flowers."
Mort White, radio call-in garden show host (*The Magic Garden*) and former commercial nurseryman and landscaper, Cranston, Rhode Island

SHRUBS FOR SHADED SPOTS

A good number of sun-demanding ornamentals won't suceed if your garden is filled with shadows, but that doesn't mean you're without resources. There is a healthy supply of shrubs that thrive in light to moderate shade. Set in deep shade, however, and these species are likely to as be pale and wan as the fond lover in the old poem. If trees are casting the shadows in your yard, remember that their roots are thirsty and hungry: Don't plant shrubs where they will have to compete. One more bit of advice from the experts: Shrubs with light flowers and bark and variegated leaves will brighten shaded spots.

Moderate Shade

Red chokeberry (*Aronia arbutifolia*)	4, 5, 6
Carolina allspice/sweetshrub (*Calycanthus floridus*)	4, 5, 6
Gray dogwood (*Cornus racemosa*)	3/4, 5, 6
Red osier dogwood (*Cornus stolonifera*)	2, 3, 4, 5, 6
'Variegatus' variegated five-leaf aralia (*Eleutherococcus sieboldianus*)	4, 5, 6
Redvein enkianthus (*Enkianthus campanulatus*)	4, 5, 6
Burning bush (*Euonymus alata*)	3/4, 5, 6
Witch hazel (*Hamamelis intermedia*)	5, 6
Common witch hazel (*Hamamelis virginiana*)	3, 4, 5, 6
Sweetspire (*Itea virginica*)	5, 6
Kerria (*Kerria japonica*)	4/5, 6
Coast leucothoe (*Leucothoe axillaris*)	5, 6
Drooping leucothoe (*Leucothoe fontanesiana*)	4, 5, 6
Russian arborvitae/Siberian carpet cypress (*Microbiota decussata*)	3, 4, 5, 6
Mountain currant (*Ribes alpinum*)	3, 4, 5, 6
Snowberry (*Symphoricarpos albus*)	3, 4, 5, 6
Yew (*Taxus* spp.)	3, 4, 5, 6

Light Shade

AZALEA

Glossy abelia (*Abelia grandiflora*)	6
Purple beautyberry (*Callicarpa dichotoma*)	5/6
Summersweet (*Clethra alnifolia*)	3, 4, 5, 6
Fragrant winter hazel (*Corylopsis glabrescens*)	5, 6
Smokebush (*Cotinus coggygria*)	4, 5, 6
Dwarf fothergilla (*Fothergilla gardenii*)	4, 5, 6
Bigleaf hydrangea (*Hydrangea macrophylla*)	6
Oakleaf hydrangea (*Hydrangea quercifolia*)	5, 6
Winterberry (*Ilex verticillata*)	3, 4, 5, 6
Mountain laurel (*Kalmia latifolia*)	4/5, 6
Honeysuckle (*Lonicera* spp.)	4, 5, 6
Oregon grape holly (*Mahonia aquifolium*)	4, 5, 6
Northern bayberry (*Myrica pensylvanica*)	3, 4, 5, 6
Nandina (*Nandina domestica*)	6
Japanese andromeda (*Pieris japonica*)	5, 6
Firethorn (*Pyracantha* spp.)	5, 6
Rhododendron and azalea (*Rhododendron* spp.)	3, 4, 5, 6
Highbush blueberry (*Vaccinium corymbosum*)	3, 4, 5, 6
Viburnum (*Viburnum* spp.)	3, 4, 5, 6

Showy bigleaf hydrangea (*Hydrangea macrophylla*) is a clue to your soil's pH reading. If its flowers are blue, the soil is acidic; pink flowers indicate alkaline soil.

GONE TO POT: SHRUBS FOR CONTAINERS

Gardeners with limited space and those with patios, decks, balconies, or rooftops are always looking for plants that do well in containers. Annual flowers are the usual suspects, but many shrubs also make first-class container plants. One advantage to pot culture is that you can grow species, such as flowering maples and camellias, that wouldn't survive in a New England garden. This list, however, is limited to plants that will survive outdoors twelve months a year, provided you sink the pot in the ground during the winter. Don't forget that potted shrubs need regular watering and feeding—and occasional repotting when they outgrow their container.

'Sibirica' tartarian dogwood (*Cornus alba*)	2, 3, 4, 5, 6
Harry Lauder's walking stick (*Corylus avellana* 'Contorta')	3/4, 5, 6
Burkwood daphne (*Daphne burkwoodii*)	3, 4, 5, 6
Redvein enkianthus (*Enkianthus campanulatus*)	4, 5, 6
Dwarf fothergilla (*Fothergilla gardenii*)	4, 5, 6
Rose of Sharon (*Hibiscus syriacus*)	4/5, 6
Oakleaf hydrangea (*Hydrangea quercifolia*)	5, 6
Mountain laurel (*Kalmia latifolia*)	4/5, 6
Nandina (*Nandina domestica*)	6
'Miniature Snowflake' dwarf mock orange (*Philadelphus*)	4, 5, 6
Japanese andromeda (*Pieris japonica*)	5, 6
Doublefile viburnum (*Viburnum plicatum* f. *tomentosum*)	4/5, 6
'Variegata' weigela (*Weigela florida*)	5, 6

A RHODODENDRON TOP TEN

Pinning down Richard Brooks, the former president of the American Rhododendron Society, to list ten of the best rhododendrons for New England gardens is no easy task. "There are so many good ones," he insists—a natural reaction from a man who grows more than 800 different species and cultivars on one and a half wooded acres in Concord, Massachusetts. That said, here are the ten cultivars that Brooks recommends for our region. 'White Lights' and 'Cornell Pink' are deciduous.

'April White'	double white	early	4, 5, 6
'Calsap'	white with deep purple flare	midseason	5, 6
'Capistrano'	light yellow	midseason	5, 6
'Cornell Pink'	bright pink	very early	4, 5, 6
'Firestorm'	bright red	late midseason	5, 6
'Ginny Gee'	pink to white	early midseason	6
'Janet Blair'	ruffled pale pink	late midseason	5, 6
'Mikkeli'	white tinged pink	midseason	3, 4, 5, 6
'Mist Maiden'	pink to white	midseason	5, 6
'White Lights'	fragrant white	midseason	3, 4, 5, 6

DECK THE HALLS: HOLLIES FOR NEW ENGLAND

Since English holly, *Ilex aquifolium*, is hardy only in the downright tropical parts of New England, Yankee gardeners have to substitute. Many holly species and cultivars are now available, however, but check for cold hardiness before you leave the nursery with a new shrub. Winterberry, *Ilex verticillata*, is especially hardy.

Some hollies require both male and female plants to produce berries—check with your plant seller. American holly, *Ilex opaca*, is usually classed as a small tree, but careful pruning can tame it to shrub status. Don't forget that hollies prefer a well-drained, acid soil that has been enriched with organic matter.

AMERICAN
HOLLY

'Spavy', 'Spriber', 'Winter Red' winterberry (*Ilex*)	4, 5, 6
'Angustifolia' English holly (*Ilex aquifolium*)	6
'Slack' Chinese holly (*Ilex cornuta*)	5, 6
'Angyo', 'Beehive', 'Glory', 'Jersey Pinnacle' Japanese holly (*Ilex crenata*)	5, 6
'Densa' inkberry (*Ilex glabra*)	5, 6
'Shamrock' holly (*Ilex glabra* var. *compacta*)	4, 5, 6
'Argentine', 'Ashumet', 'Bivens', 'Canary', 'Hume's Choice', 'Old Heavy Berry' American holly (*Ilex opaca*)	5, 6
Longstalk holly (*Ilex pendunclosa*)	5, 6
Prostrate holly (*Ilex rugosa*)	3, 4, 5, 6
'Aurantiaca' orange winterberry (*Ilex verticillata*)	4, 5, 6
'Red Sprite' dwarf winterberry (*Ilex verticillata*)	3, 4, 5, 6
'Winter Gold' golden winterberry (*Ilex verticillata*)	4, 5, 6

> Some shrub species, such as holly and winterberry, are *dioecious*, which means they produce male and female flowers on separate plants. In order to produce berries on the female plant, you also must have a male plant growing nearby.

WINTER JOYS FROM SHRUBS

This list of shrubs and a few small trees for winter interest comes from Winsted, Connecticut, garden writer Rita Buchanan and is a godsend for gardeners in New England, where winter extends longer than some of us would like. Buchanan calls them plants "you'll enjoy looking at while you wait for spring." When you're not looking out the window, you'll enjoy reading any of Buchanan's garden books, including *Making a Garden* (1999). Her latest is *Taylor's Master Guide to Landscaping* (2000). Both are published by Houghton Mifflin Company.

Broadleaf Evergreen Shrubs

Common boxwood (*Buxus sempervirens*)	5, 6
Inkberry holly (*Ilex glabra*)	4, 5, 6
Mountain laurel (*Kalmia latifolia*)	4/5, 6
Mountain andromeda (*Pieris floribunda*)	4, 5, 6
Japanese andromeda (*Pieris japonica*)	5, 6
Cranberry (*Vaccinium macrocarpon*)	3, 4, 5, 6
Lingonberry (*Vaccinium vitis-idaea*)	4, 5, 6

Handsome Bark

Paperbark maple (*Acer griseum*)	5, 6
'Whitespire' birch (*Betula platyphylla*)	4, 5, 6
Kousa dogwood (*Cornus kousa*)	5, 6
Amur chokecherry (*Prunus maackii*)	2, 3, 4, 5, 6
Lacebark elm (*Ulmus parvifolia*)	4, 5, 6

Interesting Structure

Harry Lauder's walking stick (*Corylus avellana* 'Contorta')	3/4, 5, 6

'Snow Fountain' white weeping cherry (*Prunus subhirtella*)	4, 5, 6
'Scarlet Curls', 'Golden Curls' corkscrew willow (*Salix matsudana*)	4, 5, 6

Winter Berries

Cranberry cotoneaster (*Cotoneaster apiculatus*)	4, 5, 6
Rock spray cotoneaster (*Cotoneaster horizontalis*)	4, 5, 6
Many-flowered cotoneaster (*Cotoneaster multiflorus*)	3/4, 5, 6
Washington hawthorn (*Crataegus phaenopyrum*)	3, 4, 5, 6
Possumhaw (*Ilex decidua*)	5, 6
Winterberry (*Ilex verticillata*)	3, 4, 5, 6
'Donald Wyman' crabapple (*Malus*)	4, 5, 6
Rugosa rose (*Rosa rugosa*)	3, 4, 5, 6

BORDER BACKBONES: SHRUBS FOR FLOWER GARDENS

Suzy Verrier, who runs North Creek Farm nursery in Phippsburg, Maine, calls these shrubs the "backbones of the border," essential plants for giving a garden form. In addition to handsome shapes and foliage, many of these plants, such as kerria, also bear lovely flowers. Although Verrier keeps current with the best new cultivars, she confesses that she still makes plant lists in longhand and that both her rose books, *Rosa Rugosa* (1999) and *Rosa Gallica* (1999), were written in pencil.

'Crimson Velvet' Japanese barberry (*Berberis thunbergii* f. *atropurpurea*)	4, 5, 6
Butterfly bush (*Buddleia alternifolia*)	5, 6
Kerria (*Kerria japonica*)	4/5, 6
'Pleniflora' kerria (*Kerria japonica*)	4/5, 6
'Clavey's Dwarf' fly honeysuckle (*Lonicera xylosteum*)	4, 5, 6
'Benenden' bramble (*Rubus*)	5, 6
Crimson bramble (*Rubus arcticus*)	2, 3, 4, 5, 6
Flowering raspberry (*Rubus odoratus*)	4, 5, 6
'Goldmound', 'Magic Carpet' Japanese spirea (*Spiraea japonica*)	4, 5, 6
Sargent viburnum (*Viburnum sargentii*)	4, 5, 6

Connecticut gardener Sydney Eddison, author of *The Self-Taught Gardener* (1997), is famous for the extensive perennial borders in her one-and-a-half-acre garden. All perennial borders, she says, "should include evergreen shrubs for geometry and deciduous shrubs for linear structure and bulk."

UNDERSTORY COLOR: SHRUBS TO BRIGHTEN FALL

When we think of brilliant fall foliage, we normally think of New England's deciduous trees, especially its sugar and red maples. Shrubs, however, are another first-rate source of color in autumn, and especially useful to gardeners who don't have room for 90-foot maples. This sampler of deciduous shrubs can add yellows, oranges, and reds to your landscape.

	Foliage color	
Barberry (*Berberis aggregata*)	red	6
Korean barberry (*Berberis koreana*)	red	3, 4, 5, 6

Summersweet (*Clethra alnifolia*)	yellow	3, 4, 5, 6
Redtwig dogwood (*Cornus alba*)	red	2, 3, 4, 5, 6
Redvein enkianthus (*Enkianthus campanulatus*)	yellow, orange, red	4, 5, 6
Dwarf fothergilla (*Fothergilla gardenii*)	yellow, orange, red	4, 5, 6
Japanese witch hazel (*Hamamelis japonica*)	yellow, orange, red	5, 6
Chinese witch hazel (*Hamamelis mollis*)	yellow, orange	5, 6
Vernal witch hazel (*Hamamelis vernalis*)	yellow	4, 5, 6
Common witch hazel (*Hamamelis virginiana*)	yellow	3, 4, 5, 6
Oakleaf hydrangea (*Hydrangea quercifolia*)	red	5, 6
'Henry's Garnet' sweetspire (*Itea virginica*)	red-purple	5, 6
Japanese spirea (*Spiraea japonica* cvs.)	yellow, red	4, 5, 6
Bridalwreath (*Spiraea prunifolia*)	orange, red	4, 5, 6
Highbush cranberry (*Vaccinium corymbosum*)	red	3, 4, 5, 6
Blackhaw viburnum (*Viburnum prunifolium*)	red	3/4, 5, 6
Rusty blackhaw viburnum (*Viburnum rufidulum*)	red	5, 6
Yellowroot (*Xanthorhiza simplicissima*)	yellow, orange	3, 4, 5, 6

NOSE CANDY: FRAGRANT LILACS FOR NEW ENGLAND

As with many species that started off with wonderful fragrance, such as roses, the number of lilac (*Syringa*) cultivars that have little or no scent is far too large. Many, such as 'Sensation', have spectacular flowers—pure "eye candy," as the under-thirty crowd likes to say—but offer almost nothing for the nose. The lilacs on this list are a treat for both eyes and nose, although not all of them (the hardy Preston hybrids, bred by Isabella Preston in Canada, are a good example) have the traditional fragrance of the common lilac, *Syringa vulgaris*. Many lilacs not on this list also have good fragrance—sniff before you buy.

	Flower color	
'Assessippi' (*Syringa hyacinthiflora*)	pale blue	3, 4, 5, 6
'Excel' (*Syringa hyacinthiflora*)	pink	3, 4, 5, 6
'Sister Justina' (*Syringa hyacinthiflora*)	white	3, 4, 5, 6
'Donald Wyman' (*Syringa prestoniae*)	wine red	3, 4, 5, 6
'Miss Canada' (*Syringa prestoniae*)	red-pink	2, 3, 4, 5, 6
'Superba' littleleaf (*Syringa pubescens* subsp. *microphylla*)	pink	4/5, 6
'Miss Kim' (*Syringa pubescens* subsp. *patula*)	light purple	3, 4, 5, 6
'Frank Klager' (*Syringa vulgaris*)	dark purple	3, 4, 5, 6
'Marie Frances' (*Syringa vulgaris*)	pink	3, 4, 5, 6
'Mieczta' (*Syringa vulgaris*)	violet	3, 4, 5, 6
'Rochester' (*Syringa vulgaris*)	white	3, 4, 5, 6
'Ruhm von Horstenstein' (*Syringa vulgaris*)	magenta	3, 4, 5, 6
'Wonder Blue' (*Syringa vulgaris*)	blue	3, 4, 5, 6
'Yankee Doodle' (*Syringa vulgaris*)	dark purple	3, 4, 5, 6
Common lilac (*Syringa vulgaris*)	lilac	3, 4, 5, 6

BOTANICAL BONDAGE: THE ART OF ESPALIER

Shrubs and small trees can be trained to grow flat against a wall or trellis. It's called *espalier*, which is from the Italian word *spalla*, meaning "to shoulder" or "lean on." Espaliers, which are wonderfully ornamental, can be formal or informal in design. They are a disguised method of giving marginally hardy plants extra protection from the cold—on a south-facing, heat-retaining wall, for example.

Originally, espalier was used mainly for fruit shrubs and trees, but today any plant is fair game. The attractiveness of a well-espaliered plant is enough to give the word "bondage" new meaning.

Flowering quince (*Chaenomeles* spp. and cvs.)	4/5, 6
Dogwood (*Cornus* spp.)	3, 4, 5, 6
Rose of Sharon (*Hibiscus syriacus*)	4/5, 6
Oakleaf hydrangea (*Hydrangea quercifolia*)	5, 6
Winter jasmine (*Jasminum nudiflorum*)	6
Magnolia (*Magnolia* spp. and cvs.)	3/4, 5, 6
Cherry (*Prunus avium*)	4/5, 6
Peach (*Prunus persica* cvs.)	5, 6
Firethorn (*Pyracantha* cvs.)	5, 6
Pear (*Pyrus communis* cvs.)	4, 5, 6

GARDEN COMPACTS: A MIX OF SMALL SHRUBS

In *The Self-Taught Gardener* (1997), Sydney Eddison shares what she's learned from working in her Newtown, Connecticut, garden during the last forty years. She says that her "gut feeling is that gardeners really do not need another book or computer program. They need a gardening friend who is a step or two ahead of them." A superb plantswoman with a wonderful eye for design, Eddison is a step or two ahead of almost everyone, and in the spirit of friendship she has provided this list of compact evergreen shrubs.

Korean small-leaved boxwood (*Buxus microphylla* var. *koreana*)	5, 6
'Wintergreen' Korean small-leaved boxwood (*Buxus microphylla* var. *koreana*)	5, 6
'Graham Blandy' common boxwood (*Buxus sempervirens*)	5, 6
'Emerald Gaiety' variegated euonymus (*Euonymus fortunei*)	5, 6
Japanese holly (*Ilex crenata*)	5, 6
'Pencil Point' juniper (*Juniperus communis*)	4, 5, 6
Miniature mountain laurel (*Kalmia latifolia* f. *myritolia*)	4/5, 6
'Conica' dwarf Alberta spruce (*Picea glauca*)	3, 4, 5, 6
'Compacta' compact dwarf blue spruce (*Picea pungens* f. *glauca*)	3, 4, 5, 6
American arborvitae (*Thuja occidentalis*)	3, 4, 5, 6
'Degroot's Emerald Spire' American arborvitae (*Thuja occidentalis*)	3, 4, 5, 6

LENGTHENING THE LILAC SEASON

Truth be told, lilacs grow as well in New England as any place in the world. That means that we have the cream of the crop to pick from, a huge array of colors, sizes, habits, and fragrances. Lilac specialists Eric and Jennifer Welzel, who run Fox Hill Nursery in Freeport, Maine, suggest these ten cultivars, each chosen to keep lilacs blooming in your dooryard in several colors for as long as possible. All of Fox Hill's plants, which are available by mail order, are grown on their own roots, not grafted.

Early

'Assessippi' (*Syringa hyacinthiflora*)	lavender	2, 3, 4, 5, 6
'Maiden's Blush' (*Syringa hyacinthiflora*)	pink	2, 3, 4, 5, 6
'Pocahontas' (*Syringa hyacinthiflora*)	purple	2, 3, 4, 5, 6

Midseason

'Lucie Baltet' (*Syringa vulgaris*)	pink	2, 3, 4, 5, 6
'Président Grévy' (*Syringa vulgaris*)	blue	2, 3, 4, 5, 6
'Sarah Sands' (*Syringa vulgaris*)	purple	2, 3, 4, 5, 6

Late

'Miss Kim' (*Syringa patula*)	ice blue	3, 4, 5, 6
'Donald Wyman' (*Syringa prestoniae*)	purple	2, 3, 4, 5, 6
'James Macfarlane' (*Syringa prestoniae*)	pink	2, 3, 4, 5, 6
'Ivory Silk' tree lilac (*Syringa reticulata*)	creamy white	4, 5, 6

For better lilacs, Eric Welzel, owner of Fox Hill Nursery in Freeport, Maine, recommends:

- Grow lilacs in full sun in organically rich soil that drains well and has a neutral pH.
- Make the planting hole at least three times as wide as the root ball.
- Mulch lilacs with a 2- or 3-inch layer of pine bark.
- Prune lilacs soon after flowering stops.
- Feed plants with a balanced fertilizer in spring and again after pruning.
- Water lilacs during extended dry weather.

HANG IN THERE: SHRUBS THAT KEEP ON BLOOMING

The problem with flowers is that they don't last forever. Nothing is more lovely than a lilac in full bloom, but it's a short-lived picture, usually no longer than a couple of weeks. The shrubs on this list do better, and unless temperatures soar or a drought strikes, you can usually plan on a month of flowers.

Glossy abelia (*Abelia grandiflora*)	6
Butterfly bush (*Buddleia davidii*)	5, 6
Summersweet (*Clethra alnifolia* cvs.)	3, 4, 5, 6
Rose of Sharon (*Hibiscus syriacus*)	4/5, 6
'Grandiflora Compacta' PeeGee hydrangea (*Hydrangea paniculata*)	4, 5, 6
Oakleaf hydrangea (*Hydrangea quercifolia*)	5, 6
Mock orange (*Philadelphus coronarius*)	3/4, 5, 6
Japanese spirea (*Spiraea japonica*)	4, 5, 6
Weigela (*Weigela florida* cvs.)	4, 5, 6

IT'S THE BERRIES: SHRUBS WITH ORNAMENTAL FRUIT

The late Fr. John Fiala, an authority on and breeder of flowering crabs, always argued that flowers were nice, but berries were better—fruits could be just as bright as blossoms and they last three and four times as long. Vividly colored ornamental fruits, especially those that hang on into winter, are a bright spot in the garden landscape, and a lure to birds and other wildlife. Many rugosa roses produce brightly colored hips, or fruits; a list appears in the chapter on roses.

When planting shrubs for their fruits, don't forget that some species, such as winterberry and holly, require both a male and female plant in order to produce berries. Check a garden encyclopedia or with a nursery to be sure you won't be disappointed.

Bearberry (*Arctostaphylos uva-ursi*)	2, 3, 4, 5, 6
Red chokeberry (*Aronia arbutifolia*)	4, 5, 6
Korean barberry (*Berberis koreana*)	3, 4, 5, 6
'Crimson Pygmy' Japanese barberry (*Berberis thunbergii*)	3/4, 5, 6
Purple beautyberry (*Callicarpa dichotoma*)	5, 6

White beautyberry (*Callicarpa dichotoma* var. *albatructus*)	5, 6
Redtwig dogwood (*Cornus alba*)	2, 3, 4, 5, 6
Cornelian cherry (*Cornus mas*)	4, 5, 6
Cranberry cotoneaster (*Cotoneaster apiculatus*)	4, 5, 6
'Red Glory' wintergreen cotoneaster (*Cotoneaster conspicuus*)	6
Bearberry cotonester (*Cotoneaster dammeri*)	5, 6
Rock spray (*Cotoneaster horizontalis*)	4, 5, 6
Many-flowered cotoneaster (*Cotoneaster multiflorus*)	3/4, 5, 6
'Beehive' Japanese holly (*Ilex crenata*)	5, 6
'Blue Princess' blue holly (*Ilex meserveae*)	4, 5, 6
'Berry Nice', 'Berry Heavy', 'Sparkleberry', 'Winter Red' winterberry (*Ilex verticillata*)	4, 5, 6
'Red Sprite' dwarf winterberry (*Ilex verticillata*)	3, 4, 5, 6
'Winter Gold' golden winterberry (*Ilex verticillata*)	4, 5, 6
Tatarian honeysuckle (*Lonicera tatarica*)	3, 4, 5, 6
Oregon grape holly (*Mahonia aquifolium*)	4, 5, 6
Northern bayberry (*Myrica pensylvanica*)	3, 4, 5, 6
Nandina (*Nandina domestica*)	6
Hardy orange (*Poncirus trifoliata*)	5, 6
Nanking cherry (*Prunus tomentosa*)	2, 3, 4, 5, 6
'Mohave', 'Rutgers', 'Teuton' firethorn (*Pyracantha*)	5/6
Silver buffaloberry (*Shepherdia argentea*)	3, 4, 5, 6
Japanese skimmia (*Skimmia japonica*)	6/7
Ural false spirea (*Sorbaria sorbifolia*)	2/3, 4, 5, 6
Snowberry (*Symphoricarpos albus*)	3, 4, 5, 6
Mapleleaf virburnum (*Viburnum acerifolium*)	4, 5, 6
'Erie', 'Iroquois' linden viburnum (*Viburnum dilatatum*)	5, 6
Nannyberry (*Viburnum lentago*)	2/3, 4, 5, 6
European cranberry bush (*Viburnum opulus*)	3, 4, 5, 6
Sargent viburnum (*Viburnum sargentii*)	4, 5, 6
American cranberry bush (*Viburnum trilobum*)	2/3, 4, 5, 6

SHRUBS FROM THE MAGIC GARDEN

Mort White, who lives in balmy Zone 6 Cranston, Rhode Island, is a former nurseryman, garden center owner, greenhouse grower, and landscaper. He now keeps busy writing a newspaper garden column and hosting *The Magic Garden*, a weekly radio program carried by more than 100 stations throughout the country. He admits he no longer maintains a large garden of his own but still has definite ideas, based on years of experience in the garden, about which flowering shrubs do well in New England. Here are ten of his favorites.

Red osier dogwood (*Cornus stolonifera*)	2, 3, 4, 5, 6
Rose of Sharon (*Hibiscus syriacus*)	4/5, 6
Mock orange (*Philadelphus coronarius*)	3/4, 5, 6
Korean azalea (*Rhododendron mucronulatum* cvs.)	4, 5, 6
Korean azalea (*Rhododendron yedoensis* var. *poukhanense*)	5, 6
'Hansa' rugosa rose (*Rosa rugosa*)	3, 4, 5, 6
Van Houtte spirea (*Spiraea vanhouttei*)	3, 4, 5, 6
Koreanspice viburnum (*Viburnum carlesii*)	4, 5, 6
Doublefile viburnum (*Viburnum plicatum* f. *tomentosum*)	4/5, 6
'Red Prince' weigela (*Weigela florida*)	5, 6

HARDY FLOWERING CLIMBERS

There isn't an over abundance of perennial vines that are both ornamental and can survive winter in New England, so most of the names on this list will be familiar to you. But don't let familiarity breed contempt—these are superb plants. Moreover, good nurseries are continually offering new and interesting cultivars that may be new to you. Beautiful in their own right, perennial vines also are useful. As Frank Lloyd Wright observed, "A physician may bury his mistakes, but an architect can only plant a vine."

One warning: In the warmer parts of New England, some of the plants on this list grow quickly enough or spread rampantly enough to deserve the adjective "aggressive." Look out for five-leaf akebia, porcelain berry, trumpet creeper, woodbine, silver lace vine, and wisteria.

DUTCHMAN'S PIPE

Hardy kiwi (*Actinidia arguta*)	3, 4, 5, 6
Silver vine (*Actinidia polygama*)	3/4, 5, 6
Five-leaf akebia/chocolate vine (*Akebia quinata*)	5, 6
Porcelain berry (*Ampelopsis brevipedunculata*)	3/4, 5, 6
Dutchman's pipe (*Aristolochia macrophylla*)	3/4, 5, 6
Cross vine (*Bignonia capreolata*)	6
Trumpet creeper (*Campsis radicans*)	4/5, 6
'Mme. Galen' trumpet creeper (*Campsis tagliabuana*)	4/5, 6
American bittersweet (*Celastrus scandens*)	2, 3, 4, 5, 6
Climbing bleeding heart (*Dicentra scandens*)	6
Climbing hydrangea (*Hydrangea petiolaris*)	3/4, 5, 6
Perennial pea (*Lathyrus latifolia*)	3/4, 5, 6
Scarlet trumpet honeysuckle (*Lonicera brownii*)	3, 4, 5, 6
Goldflame honeysuckle (*Lonicera heckrottii*)	5, 6
Woodbine/common honeysuckle (*Lonicera periclymenum*)	4, 5, 6
Trumpet honeysuckle (*Lonicera sempervirens*)	3, 4, 5, 6
Silver lace vine/fleece vine (*Polygonum aubertii*)	4, 5, 6
Magnolia vine (*Schisandra chinensis*)	5, 6
Japanese hydrangea vine (*Schizophragma hydrangeoides*)	6
Japanese wisteria (*Wisteria floribunda*)	4, 5, 6

LARGE-FLOWERED CLEMATIS

Clematis (*Clematis*) deserves its designation as "the queen of vines." Although New England is too cold for growing some species, many clematis can be grown successfully as far north as Zone 3. Several of those hardy types are included in this list of cultivars.

The experts divide clematis into three groups, based on whether they bloom on "old wood" (stems produced in previous seasons) or "new wood" (stems produced in the current season). Since large-flowered clematis in Groups II and III should be pruned severely, winter dieback isn't fatal.

Group II: late spring/midseason flowers

'Bees Jubilee'	pink	4, 5, 6
'Elsa Späth'	mauve-blue	4, 5, 6
'General Sikorski'	lavender-blue	3, 4, 5, 6
'Henryi'	white	3, 4, 5, 6
'Marie Boisselot'	white	3, 4, 5, 6
'Mrs. Cholmondeley'	lavender-blue	3, 4, 5, 6
'Nelly Moser'	pink with rose band	4, 5, 6
'Niobe'	red	3, 4, 5, 6

'Proteus'	mauve double	4, 5, 6
'Richard Pennell'	purple-blue	4, 5, 6
'Vyvyan Pennell'	lilac double	4, 5, 6

Group III: late summer/autumn flowers

'Comtesse de Couchard'	rose-lilac	3, 4, 5, 6
'Ernest Markham'	magenta	3, 4, 5, 6
'Gipsy Queen'	purple	4, 5, 6
'Hagley Hybrid'	pink	3, 4, 5, 6
'Mme. Edouard André'	red	4, 5, 6
'Rouge Cardinal'	red	4, 5, 6

CLEMATIS GROUPS
Clematis are typically classified in three groups:

Group I includes species that flower in early spring (*C. alpina, C. macropetala, C. montana*); they should be pruned immediately after they bloom. Prune only to keep the plant in bounds or to remove dead or weak stems.

Group II consists of the late-spring and mid-season large-blossom clematis (*C.* 'Nelly Moser', *C.* 'Henryi', *C.* 'Elsa Spath'); they should be pruned severely (cut back to about a foot from the soil line) in late winter or early spring.

Group III is made up of large-flowered, late-season cultivars and late-season species (*C. jackmanii, C.* 'Ernest Markham', *C. terniflora, C. viticellas*). Although their flowers are produced on new wood, they should be pruned severely in late winter or early spring.

SMALL-FLOWERED CLEMATIS

Too many gardeners are blinded by the brilliance of large-flowered clematis, the plants commonly stocked by garden centers and nurseries. They forget that there are also hardy species with small flowers, everything from the white sweet autumn clematis to Russian virgin's bower, which has bell-like yellow blooms. A good number of small-flowered clematis, including *C. montana* cultivars and sweet autumn clematis, are fragrant.

Group I: spring flowers

'Pamela Jackman' (*C. alpina*)	blue	4/5, 6
Alpine clematis (*C. alpina*)	blue	4/5, 6
'Markham's Pink' (*C. macropetala*)	pink	3, 4, 5, 6
'Elizabeth' (*C. montana*)	pink	5, 6
'Pink Perfection' (*C. montana*)	pink	5, 6
'Grandiflora' (*C. montana grandiflora*)	white	4/5, 6

Group III: late summer/autumn flowers

'Betty Corning'	lilac	4, 5, 6
'Dutchess of Albany'	pink	4, 5, 6
'Etoile Violette'	purple	4, 5, 6
'Gravetye Beauty'	red	5, 6
'Huldine'	white	4, 5, 6
'Perle d'Azur'	blue	4, 5, 6
'Polish Spirit'	purple-blue	5, 6
'Venosa Violacea'	white	5, 6
'Paul Farges' (*C. fargesioides*)	white	4/5, 6

Russian virgin's bower (*C. tangutica*)	yellow	4, 5, 6
Sweet autumn clematis (*C. terniflora*)	white	4, 5, 6
Scarlet clematis (*C. texensis*)	red	4, 5, 6

"Small-flowered clematis are generally the earliest of the hardy clematis to flower in spring. They're tough and will accept situations which are unsuitable for other varieties, but they will not tolerate boggy areas or wet feet in the winter. Because of their compact growth habit, they're good choices for gardens with limited space. Plant them in an eastern exposure."
Sue Austin, owner, Completely Clematis, Ipswich, Massachusetts

CHOICE CLEMATIS FROM A MASSACHUSETTS NURSERYWOMAN

CLEMATIS

Sue Austin is the owner of Completely Clematis, a speciality retail (May to September) and mail-order nursery located in Ipswich, Massachusetts. Her catalog contains over 100 different clematis, all two-year-old plants, which are small enough to be shipped successfully and mature enough to thrive once they've been hardened-off and planted in your garden. With so many gorgeous choices, it's hard to pick favorites, but these are Austin's recommendations for New England gardens. Austin says all these vines are hardy to Zone 4, "probably lower in areas with reliable snowcover."

'Betty Corning'	small-flowered lilac	4, 5, 6
'Etoile Violette'	small-flowered dark purple	4, 5, 6
'Gipsy Queen'	large-flowered purple	4, 5, 6
'Huldine'	large-flowered white	4, 5, 6
'Madame Julia Correvon'	small-flowered red	4, 5, 6
'Perle d' Azur'	large-flowered blue	4, 5, 6
'Ville de Lyon'	large-flowered red	4, 5, 6
'Constance' (*C. alpina*)	small-flowered pink	4, 5, 6
'Jan Lindmark' (*C. macropetala*)	small-flowered red-purple	4, 5, 6
'Burford Variety' (*C. orientalis*)	small-flowered yellow	4, 5, 6
Sweet autumn clematis (*C. terniflora*)	small-flowered white	4, 5, 6
Viticella clematis (*C. viticella*)	small-flowered purple	4, 5, 6

"Wilt, the clematis's only serious foe, is devastating. Healthy vines suddenly wither, but it usually isn't terminal. The best treatment is to remove any affected stems, cutting them to the plant crown. Regrowth may be slow but be patient—most plants recover."
Don Avery, owner, Cady's Falls Nursery, Morrisville, Vermont

OLD-TIME CLIMBERS

No self-respecting Victorian house, according to Marilyn Barlow, would have been without a flowering vine. Barlow, who runs the Select Seed/Antique Flowers seed company in Union, Connecticut, specializes in heirloom plants, open-pollinated flowers and vines that have been grown for at least fifty years. The vines on Barlow's list—a mix of annuals (A) and tender perennials (TP)—have been around for decades and will please you as much as they pleased earlier generations. To get an early start, sow seeds indoors well before your frost-free date. (For more annual vines, see the chapter on annuals, biennials, and tender perennials.)

Creeping gloxinia (*Asarina erubescens*)	TP
Balloon vine/love-in-a-puff (*Cardiospermum halicacabum*)	TP
'Alba' cup-and-saucer vine (*Cobaea scandens*)	TP
Cardinal climber (*Ipomoea multifida*)	A
'Grandpa Otts' morning glory (*Ipomoea purpurea*)	TP
Star glory (*Ipomoea quamoclit*)	TP
'Blue Star' morning glory (*Ipomoea tricolor*)	TP
'Ruby Moon' hyacinth bean (*Lablab purpureus*)	TP
Bottle gourd (*Lagenaria siceraria*)	A
Spanish flag (*Mina lobata*)	A
'Painted Lady' runner bean (*Phaseolus coccineus*)	TP
Black-eyed Susan vine (*Thunbergia alata*)	TP
Canary creeper (*Tropaeolum peregrinum*)	TP

CANARY
CREEPER

> "Love-in-a-puff is one of my favorite old-fashioned vines. It's a perfect name, because the plant's small white flowers are followed by light green inflated seed capsules. Inside each capsule are three seeds, each marked with a perfect white heart."
> **Marilyn Barlow, owner, Select Seeds/Antique Flowers, Union, Connecticut**

BOTANICAL COVERUPS: VINES FOR FENCES, WALLS, AND ARBORS

Vines are first-rate plants for blocking the view—either yours or someone else's. They can hide your neighbor's trash cans or the side of your house that refuses to retain its paint; they can disguise ugly fences, blocking the view into your garden at the same time. Or you can use a vine to create a living ceiling by sending it up and over an arch, arbor, or pergola. Northern New England gardeners have few evergreen vine choices—*Hedera* spp. and winter creeper are two possibilities—so remember that coverage will be scant in winter, privacy only partial. But during the growing season, you can camouflage, screen, or cover with complete success.

Don't forget that most vines need some help in scaling. Tie them loosely to the support as they make their way upward. For a flat surface, be sure to grow a climber that clings, such as Boston ivy or Virginia creeper.

Vines in this list without hardiness zone information are annuals or treated as annuals in New England.

Vines for fences

Porcelain berry (*Ampelopsis brevipedunculata*)	3/4, 5, 6
Dutchman's pipe (*Aristolochia macrophylla*)	3/4, 5, 6
Balloon vine/love-in-a-puff (*Cardiospermum halicacabum*)	
Clematis (*Clematis* spp. and cvs.)	3, 4, 5, 6
'Alba' cup-and-saucer vine (*Cobaea scandens*)	
Wintercreeper (*Euonymus fortunei*)	4/5, 6
Moonflower (*Ipomoea alba*)	
Morning glory (*Ipomoea purpurea*)	
Bottle gourd (*Lagenaria siceraria*)	
Sweet pea (*Lathyrus odoratus*)	

Honeysuckle (*Lonicera* spp.)	3, 4, 5, 6
Moonseed (*Menispermum canadense*)	4, 5, 6
Black-eyed Susan vine (*Thunbergia alata*)	
Canary creeper (*Tropaeolum peregrinum*)	
Asparagus bean (*Vigna unguiculata* ssp. *sesquipedalis*)	
Grape (*Vitis* spp.)	3, 4, 5, 6

Vines for flat walls

Trumpet creeper (*Campsis radicans*)	4, 5, 6
Wintercreeper (*Euonymus fortunei*)	4/5, 6
English ivy (*Hedera helix*)	4, 5, 6
Climbing hydrangea (*Hydrangea petiolaris*)	3/4, 5, 6
Virginia creeper (*Parthenocissus quinquefolia*)	3, 4, 5, 6
Boston ivy (*Parthenocissus tricuspidata*)	4, 5, 6

Vines for arbors

Silver vine (*Actinidia polygama*)	3/4, 5, 6
American bittersweet (*Celastrus scandens*)	2, 3, 4, 5, 6
Sweet autumn clematis (*Clematis terniflora*)	4, 5, 6
Wild cucumber (*Echinocystis lobata*)	5, 6
Carolina yellow jessamine (*Gelsemium sempervirens*)	6/7
Japanese hop (*Humulus japonicus*)	4, 5, 6
Common hop (*Humulus lupulus*)	3, 4, 5, 6
'Ruby Moon' hyacinth bean (*Lablab purpureus*)	
Bottle gourd (*Lagenaria siceraria*)	
Honeysuckle (*Lonicera* spp.)	3, 4, 5, 6
'Scarlet Runner' runner bean (*Phaseolus coccineus*)	
Silver lace vine/fleece vine (*Polygonum aubertii*)	4, 5, 6
Climbing rose (*Rosa* cvs.)	5, 6
Grape (*Vitis* spp.)	3, 4, 5, 6
Japanese wisteria (*Wisteria floribunda*)	4, 5, 6
American wisteria (*Wisteria frutescens*)	5, 6

VINES FOR SHADE

There's shade and there's shade. Few vines are willing to put up with a location where the sun never shines, but the climbers on this list will thrive in less than bright light. Partial shade is ideal for these vines, especially protection from afternoon sun. Dutchman's pipe is famous for climbing 50 feet on the north side of Victorian houses, and Boston ivy blankets the north side of the majority of New England colleges and universities. When it comes to growing vines, full sun is not required. One warning: Flowers are fewer when vines are grown in deep shade.

Climbing fumitory (*Adlumia fungosa*)	5
Five-leaf akebia/chocolate vine (*Akebia quinata*)	5, 6
Porcelain berry (*Ampelopsis brevipedunculata*)	3/4, 5, 6
Dutchman's pipe (*Aristolochia macrophylla*)	3/4, 5, 6
Sweet autumn clematis (*Clematis terniflora*)	4, 5, 6
Winter creeper (*Euonymus fortunei*)	4/5, 6
English ivy (*Hedera helix*)	4, 5, 6
Climbing hydrangea (*Hydrangea petiolaris*)	3/4, 5, 6
Honeysuckle (*Lonicera* spp.)	3, 4, 5, 6

Moonseed (*Menispermum canadense*)	4, 5, 6
Virginia creeper (*Parthenocissus quinquefolia*)	3, 4, 5, 6
Boston ivy (*Parthenocissus tricuspidata*)	4, 5, 6
Grape (*Vitis* spp.)	3, 4, 5, 6

FRAGRANT CLIMBERS

You can double your pleasure by not just planting vines that produce flowers but by planting vines that produce flowers that produce fragrance. Some of the most perfumed climbers, alas, are far too tender for New England gardens. We're not entirely out of luck, however. All the vines on this list bear scented blossoms. If you have a heated greenhouse, consider Chilean jasmine (*Mandevilla laxa*), golden trumpet vine (*Allamanda catharatica*), Madagascar jasmine (*Stephanotis floribunda*), Confederate, or star, jasmine (*Trachelospermum jasminoides*), or one of the true *Jasminum* species.

One scented climber to avoid is Japanese honeysuckle (*Lonicera japonica*)—and its popular cultivar 'Halliana', or Hall's honeysuckle. Both are rampant naturalizers that overwhelm everything in their path. Chinese wisteria (*Wisteria sinensis*), another fragrant vine, is invasive in the warmer parts of our region. Plants in this list without hardiness zone information are annuals or treated as annuals in New England.

Silvervine (*Actinidia polygama*)	3/4, 5, 6
Five-leaf akebia/chocolate vine (*Akebia quinata*)	5, 6
Clematis (*Clematis montana*)	4/5, 6
Sweet autumn clematis (*Clematis terniflora*)	4, 5, 6
Cup-and-saucer vine (*Cobaea scandens*)	
Carolina jasmine (*Gelsemium sempervirens*)	6/7
Moonflower (*Ipomoea alba*)	
Morning glory (*Ipomoea purpurea*)	
Sweet pea (*Lathyrus odoratus*)	
Goldflame honeysuckle (*Lonicera heckrottii*)	5, 6
Woodbine/common honeysuckle (*Lonicera periclymenum*)	4, 5, 6
Silver lace vine/fleece vine (*Polygonum aubertii*)	4, 5, 6
Climbing rose (*Rosa* cvs.)	5, 6
Canarybird flower (*Tropaeolum peregrinum*)	
'Lawrence' Japanese wisteria (*Wisteria floribunda*)	4, 5, 6
American wisteria (*Wisteria frutescens*)	5, 6

TREES

In my previous life as a magazine editor, I rejected an article that began "I'm a tree person." While deploring the writer's lack of originality, I couldn't help agreeing with his sentiment. New Englanders, too, have always been "tree people," although our ancestors viewed the hard- and softwoods they found in North America primarily as a source of raw materials and ready cash. By 1850, much of our region had been cleared. The disastrous effects were not lost on Vermonter George Perkins Marsh.

In 1864, Marsh published his pioneering *Man and Nature*, the first book to detail the damage humans had inflicted on the natural environment. In particular, Marsh decried the destruction of New England's forests: "With the disappearance of the forest, all is changed.... The earth, stripped of its vegetable glebe, grows less and less protective ... gradually it becomes altogether barren and ... is rendered no longer fit for the habitation of man."

Marsh's views weren't universally embraced, but many New England citizens realized that reforestation was important. Their enthusiasm spread, and dovetailed with Arbor Day, which was first celebrated in 1872. The invention of J. Sterling Morton, a Nebraska farmer and politician, Arbor Day was to be a national day for tree planting. America's settlement, Morton believed, was "a diary of destruction." He noted "too much activity in cutting down and too little in planting out of trees." New England responded, as did the rest of the country. By 1887, 600 million trees had been planted; today, the figure runs into the billions. Every state and several foreign countries recognize the holiday—and the importance of trees.

Real estate brokers recognize the importance of trees too, estimating that mature trees can increase the value of homes by as much as 25 percent. If that weren't reason enough to get you planting, trees make homes more comfortable, shading them in summer and protecting them from wind in winter. They add structure to yards and outdoor living areas, add color and form and beauty.

In addition to familiar names, the lists in this chapter (and those in the "Vegetables, Herbs and Fruit" chapter) contain many out-of-the-ordinary species and cultivars, trees you're unlikely to find stocked by general garden centers. To find these trees, you'll have to visit a specialist, such as the Twombly Nursery in Connecticut, or shop by mail (see "The Mail-Order Garden" in this book). Mail-order trees, of course, tend to be much smaller than those purchased at a nursery, perhaps not taller than 2 or 3 feet. I'm not recommending you buy 10-inch seedlings, unless you're reforesting a large area, but don't hesitate to purchase small, young trees.

Although they don't reach their mature size in a year or two, as an herbaceous perennial like astilbe does, trees grow more quickly than you might expect. It's not necessary to spend many hundreds of dollars on a 15-foot oak. In fact, purchasing a young tree not only saves money but usually gives just as good results over time. That's because small trees recover far more quickly from being transplanted. They grow more quickly than large specimens, often outdistancing them in only a few years. In four years, the foot-tall balsam firs I dug from the roadside overtook the 5-footer that friends gave us.

Once you find what you've been looking for, be sure to follow the latest guidelines for tree planting. For container and balled-and-burlaped (B&B) trees:

1. Dig a hole that is at least three times the width but only as deep as the root ball. Set aside the soil. Loosen the soil in the bottom of the hole to a depth of 2 or 3 inches.

2. Unless the soil from the hole is hopelessly heavy (clay) or light (sand), do not amend the soil. If the soil is extremely poor, add compost or other composted organic matter to the soil you've removed.

3. Remove the tree from its container; remove any twine *and* the burlap from a B&B tree. If your tree is potbound, try to untangle the roots with your hands; work carefully so that you damage the roots as little as possible.

4. Set the tree in the hole and fill around the root ball with soil until the hole is half full. Water generously. Once the water has drained, fill the hole to the soil level. If the location is a very windy one or the trunk is extremely narrow, loosely stake the tree.

5. Mulch the planting area with about 3 inches of coarse organic matter, such as shredded bark; keep the mulch 2 or 3 inches away from the trunk to avoid disease and pest problems.

6. Keep the tree well watered for at least six months.

Bare-root trees should be handled similarly except that you should create a mound of dirt in the planting hole, set the tree on top of the mound, and spread the roots around it. When you fill the hole—be sure to tamp the soil around the roots—the tree should be sitting at the same level at which it was previously growing.

LEAF-PEEPER SPECIALS: TREES FOR FALL COLOR

Several million tourists travel to New England every fall to see our brilliant foliage—Vermont's population nearly doubles during September and October—so a list of trees with colorful leaves may be the ultimate in preaching to the converted. But if your landscape is blank, or filled with nothing but conifers, it's time to add some new trees to your garden palette. If you like bright shades, you can't go wrong with maples. For more subtle hues, try an American beech or a white oak.

Hardy to Zone 3	Foliage color
Red maple (*Acer rubrum*)	red
Silver maple (*Acer saccharinum*)	yellow
Sugar maple (*Acer saccharum*)	yellow, red, or orange
Amur maple (*Acer tataricum* subsp. *ginnala*)	yellow or reddish brown
Apple serviceberry (*Amelanchier grandiflora*)	orange or red
Paper birch (*Betula papyrifera*)	yellow
American hornbeam (*Carpinus caroliniana*)	yellow or orange-red
Yellowwood (*Cladrastis lutea*)	yellow
American beech (*Fagus grandifolia*)	golden bronze
Quaking aspen (*Populus tremuloides*)	yellow
Korean mountain ash (*Sorbus alnifolia*)	yellow to orange or red
Blackhaw viburnum (*Viburnum prunifolium*)	reddish purple

Hardy to Zone 4

Washington hawthorn (*Crataegus phaenopyrum*)	orange-red
White ash (*Fraxinus americana*)	yellow to maroon
Ginkgo/maidenhair tree (*Ginkgo biloba*)	golden yellow
Japanese larch (*Larix kaempferi*)	yellow
Tulip tree (*Liriodendron tulipifera*)	yellow
Sourwood (*Oxydendrum arboreum*)	yellow, red, and purple
Persian parrotia (*Parrotia persica*)	yellow, rose, orange, red
White oak (*Quercus alba*)	burgundy to purple-brown
Japanese stewartia (*Stewartia pseudocamellia*)	yellow to orange and red

Hardy to Zone 5

Fringe tree (*Chionanthus virginicus*)	yellow
Kousa dogwood (*Cornus kousa*)	crimson-purple
European beech (*Fagus sylvatica*)	bronze or russet
Sweet gum (*Liquidambar styraciflua*)	yellow to purple-red
Black gum (*Nyssa sylvatica*)	scarlet, orange, or purple
Scarlet oak (*Quercus coccinea*)	scarlet
Sassafras (*Sassafras albidum*)	red or orange

Hardy to Zone 6

Franklin tree (*Franklinia alatamaha*)	red
'Mount Fuji' flowering cherry (*Prunus*)	orange and red

> Early spring—about the time when the forsythia flowers—is the best time to plant trees in New England, especially bare-root trees. Be sure to mulch with wood chips or shredded bark (2 to 3 inches) and keep the tree watered during its first growing season.

FLOWERING TREES

Brilliantly colored leaves in autumn are New England's stock-in-trade, but that doesn't mean that we don't enjoy flowering trees. Most bloom in spring—that unpredictable time of year that is known as "mud season" in parts of our region—and are a welcome sight after a long winter. The exceptions to spring or very early summer bloom are catalpa, goldenrain tree, Japanese pagoda tree, mimosa, smoke tree, and sourwood, which flower in summer, and Franklin tree, which blooms in early fall.

This list contains trees that are landscape regulars, such as the Bradford pear, but also many names that may be unfamiliar. Now's the time to plant something new!

Dogwoods, crabapples, and magnolias are such spectacular flowering trees that they have lists of their own elsewhere in this chapter.

HAWTHORN

Hardy to Zone 3

Ohio buckeye (*Aesculus glabra*)	yellow-white
Apple serviceberry (*Amelanchier grandiflora*)	white
Yellowwood (*Cladrastis lutea*)	white
Korean mountain ash (*Sorbus alnifolia*)	white
Lilac tree (*Syringa reticulata*)	cream-white

Hardy to Zone 4

Downy serviceberry (*Amelanchier arborea*)	white
Northern catalpa (*Catalpa speciosa*)	white
Eastern redbud (*Cercis canadensis*)	pink or white
Cockspur hawthorn (*Crataegus crus-galli* var. *inermis*)	white
'Snowbird' hawthorn (*Crataegus mordenensis*)	white
Sourwood (*Oxydendrum arboreum*)	white
Bradford pear (*Pyrus calleryana*)	white
Japanese pagoda tree (*Sophora japonica*)	cream-white
European mountain ash (*Sorbus aucuparia*)	white

Hardy to Zone 5

Fringe tree (*Chionanthus virginicus*)	white
Smoke tree (*Cotinus coggygria*)	pink to purple
'Paul's Scarlet' English hawthorn (*Crataegus laevigata*)	pink
Goldenrain tree (*Koelreuteria paniculata*)	yellow
Golden-chain tree (*Laburnum anagyroides*)	yellow
Korean stewartia (*Stewartia koreana*)	white
Japanese stewartia (*Stewartia pseudocamellia*)	white
Japanese snowbell (*Styrax japonicus*)	white

Hardy to Zone 6

Mimosa/silk tree (*Albizia julibrissin*)	pink
Franklin tree (*Franklinia alatamaha*)	white
Flowering cherry (*Prunus* hybs.)	pink or white
Fragrant snowbell (*Styrax obassia*)	white

RUSH ORDER: TREES THAT GROW QUICKLY

If you're in a rush for a decent-sized tree or two but can't afford to buy a 25-footer at the local nursery (and who can?), consider the trees in this list. The good news is that they all grow quickly. The bad news is that they all can have problems as mature trees. Most, for example, are susceptible to wind and storm damage. One note of caution: Tree of heaven (*Ailanthus altissima*), made famous by the novel *A Tree Grows in Brooklyn*, is considered an arboreal pest in that city and in warmer parts of New England.

Box elder (*Acer negundo*)	2, 3, 4, 5, 6
Silver maple (*Acer saccharinum*)	3, 4, 5, 6
Tree of heaven (*Ailanthus altissima*)	4, 5, 6
European black alder (*Alnus glutinosa*)	2, 3, 4, 5, 6
Leyland cypress (*Cupressocyparis leylandii*)	6
Silver poplar (*Populus alba*)	3, 4, 5, 6
Eastern cottonwood (*Populus deltoides*)	3, 4, 5, 6
'Italica' lombardy poplar (*Populus nigra*)	3, 4, 5, 6
Bradford pear (*Pyrus calleryana*)	4, 5, 6
White willow (*Salix alba*)	3, 4, 5, 6

MAKING SHADE: TREES THAT CAST SHADOWS

This list of shade trees comes from New Englander Rita Buchanan, a botanist, enthusiastic horticulturist, and author—her most recent book is *Taylor's Master Guide to Landscaping* (2000). She's been gardening since 1992 on a two-acre clearing in Winsted, Connecticut, that is "surrounded by woods and straddles a brook and pond." She says her true passions are "doing stone work and collecting evergreens of all kinds," but she also has broad perennial borders, a tidy vegetable garden, and a greenhouse full of tropicals. All these trees are widely available, trouble-free, and reach heights of 40 feet or more. They provide good shade, Buchanan says, "but don't drop burdensome amounts of leaves in fall."

'October Glory' red maple (*Acer rubrum*)	3, 4, 5, 6
River birch (*Betula nigra*)	3, 4, 5, 6
European hornbeam (*Carpinus betulus*)	4, 5, 6
Yellowwood (*Cladrastis lutea*)	3, 4, 5, 6
Green ash (*Fraxinus pennsylvanica*)	3, 4, 5, 6
Thornless honey locust (*Gleditsia triacanthos* var. *inermis*)	3, 4, 5, 6
Kentucky coffee tree (*Gymnocladus dioica*)	4, 5, 6
Carolina silverbell (*Halesia carolina*)	4, 5, 6
Sargent cherry (*Prunus sargentii*)	5, 6
Oak (*Quercus* spp.)	3, 4, 5, 6
Japanese pagoda tree (*Sophora japonica*)	4, 5, 6
Littleleaf linden (*Tilia cordata*)	3, 4, 5, 6
Chinese elm/lacebark elm (*Ulmus parvifolia*)	5, 6

 "If you're doing any building, remember that tree roots extend far beyond the perimeter of the crown. Disturbing the soil with heavy equipment can damage enough roots to kill a tree even at a distance of 12 feet from the trunk. And don't raise the soil level within the perimeter of the crown. If more than a few inches is added, its weight will compact air spaces and drive out the oxygen required by the roots."
Sydney Eddison, garden author and lecturer, Newtown, Connecticut

SMALL WONDERS

If your garden is small or if you're looking for a diminutive tree to ornament but not overwhelm an outdoor living space, here are some possibilities that will fit under the powerlines. None has aggressive roots that will crack your patio or invade your sewer lines, and with the possible exception of the crabapples, none will blanket your deck with large, messy fruits or prickly seed pods. They're perfect for a small space—or for any space.

Paperbark maple (*Acer griseum*)	4, 5, 6
Japanese maple (*Acer palmatum*)	4/5, 6
Amur maple (*Acer tataricum* subsp. *ginnala*)	3, 4, 5, 6
Downy serviceberry (*Amelanchier arborea*)	4, 5, 6
Apple serviceberry (*Amelanchier grandiflora*)	3, 4, 5, 6
American hornbeam (*Carpinus caroliniana*)	3, 4, 5, 6
Eastern redbud (*Cercis canadensis*)	4, 5, 6
Fringe tree (*Chionanthus virginicus*)	5, 6
Pagoda dogwood (*Cornus alternifolia*)	3, 4, 5, 6

Flowering dogwood (*Cornus florida*)	5, 6
Kousa dogwood (*Cornus kousa*)	5, 6
Cornelian cherry (*Cornus mas*)	4, 5, 6
'Winter King' hawthorn (*Crataegus viridis*)	4/5, 6
Carolina silverbell (*Halesia carolina*)	5, 6
Goldenrain tree (*Koelreuteria paniculata*)	5, 6
'Ballerina', 'Leonard Messel' Loebner magnolia (*Magnolia loebneri*)	5, 6
Star magnolia (*Magnolia stellata*)	4, 5, 6
'Adams', 'Harvest Gold', 'Prairiefire', 'Sugar Tyme' crabapple (*Malus*)	4, 5, 6
Ironwood (*Ostrya virginiana*)	3, 4, 5, 6
Sourwood (*Oxydendrum arboreum*)	4, 5, 6
Persian parrotia (*Parrotia persica*)	4, 5, 6
'Okame', 'Hally Jolivette', 'Snow Goose' flowering cherry (*Prunus*)	5, 6
Japanese stewartia (*Stewartia pseudocamellia*)	4, 5, 6
Japanese snowbell (*Styrax japonicus*)	5, 6
Tree lilac (*Syringa reticulata*)	3, 4, 5, 6
Blackhaw viburnum (*Viburnum prunifolium*)	3, 4, 5, 6

 "We focus on slow-growing and dwarf conifers, which are valuable for the sense of scale they lend to the rock garden, and some of the larger, exotic forms, including those with weeping habits. With some adventurous pruning and staking, many of the faster growing varieties can be coaxed into striking, sculptural specimens. Conifers are susceptible to foliage and/or bud burn from winter sun. We recommend you plant them where they can receive shade from buildings or other plants during the winter months. Minimizing stress through proper siting is the single most important factor in succeeding with conifers."
Don Avery, owner, Cady's Falls Nursery, Morrisville, Vermont

TREES FOR FRAGRANCE

Fragrant shrubs are commonplace in New England gardens, but fragrant trees are less frequently cultivated. This list contains the names of some possibilities for your landscape, and offers a wide range of scents. Sweetbay, or swamp magnolia, has a fragrance that combines roses and lemons; in contrast, the lilac tree, *Syringa reticulata*, has a slightly astringent smell, off-putting to some but appreciated by others. (A list of lilacs appears in the "Shrubs and Vines" chapter.)

For fragrance in summer, plant a linden. Bigleaf linden, *Tilia platyphyllos*, is described by one odor expert as "having the simple sweetness of watermelon."

Fringe tree (*Chionanthus virginicus*)	5, 6
Yellowwood (*Cladrastis lutea*)	3, 4, 5, 6
Pagoda dogwood (*Cornus alternifolia*)	3, 4, 5, 6
Russian olive (*Elaeagnus angustifolia*)	3, 4, 5, 6
Loebner magnolia (*Magnolia loebneri* cvs.)	5, 6
Willow-leaf magnolia (*Magnolia salicifolia*)	5, 6
Saucer magnolia (*Magnolia soulangiana* cvs.)	4, 5, 6
Star magnolia (*Magnolia stellata* cvs.)	4, 5, 6
Sweetbay (*Magnolia virginiana*)	5, 6
Crabapple (*Malus* cvs.)	3, 4, 5, 6
Hardy orange (*Poncirus trifoliata*)	6
Amur chokecherry (*Prunus maackii*)	2, 3, 4, 5, 6

European bird cherry (*Prunus padus*)	4, 5, 6
Black locust (*Robinia pseudoacacia*)	4, 5, 6
Fragrant snowbell (*Styrax obassia*)	6
Tree lilac (*Syringa reticulata*)	3, 4, 5, 6
Littleleaf linden (*Tilia cordata*)	3, 4, 5, 6
Bigleaf linden (*Tilia platyphyllos*)	4/5, 6

TREES WITH INTERESTING CONTOURS

Some places in the landscape not only call out for a tree, they call out for a particularly shaped tree—tall and thin, perhaps, or vase shaped. Your choice may be controlled by space or simply by aesthetic reasons: That spot in the corner needs an eye-catching, unusual tree such as 'Rustic' shore pine (*Pinus contorta*) or a corkscrew willow. Weeping, columnar, and multi-trunked trees have lists of their own elsewhere in this chapter. Here are a few other tree shapes for your consideration.

Vase-Shaped Trees

Yellowwood (*Cladrastis lutea*)	3, 4, 5, 6
Honey locust (*Gleditsia triacanthos*)	3, 4, 5, 6
Crabapple (*Malus* spp.)	3, 4, 5, 6
'Umbraculifera' Japanese tabletop pine (*Pinus densiflora*)	4, 5, 6
Red oak (*Quercus rubra*)	3, 4, 5, 6
'Washington' American elm (*Ulmus americana*)	3, 4, 5, 6
Japanese zelkova (*Zelkova serrata*)	4, 5, 6

Pyramid-Shaped Trees

'Tenuiorifolia' European silver fir (*Abies alba*)	4, 5, 6
'Coerulescens' balsam fir (*Abies balsamea*)	3, 4, 5, 6
'Nanaimo' Korean fir (*Abies koreana*)	5, 6
'Glauca' Himalayan cedar (*Cedrus deodara*)	6
Common hackberry (*Celtis occidentalis*)	2, 3, 4, 5, 6
Katsura tree (*Cercidiphyllum japonicum*)	4, 5, 6
Ginkgo/maidenhair tree (*Ginkgo biloba*)	4, 5, 6
'Aurea' tamarack (*Larix laricina*)	2, 3, 4, 5, 6
'Argenteospica' Norway spruce (*Picea abies*)	4, 5, 6
'Vanderwolf's Blue Pyramid' Engelmann spruce (*Picea engelmannii*)	2, 3, 4, 5, 6
'Atrovirens' oriental spruce (*Picea orientalis*)	4, 5, 6
'Baby Blue Eyes' Colorado spruce (*Picea pungens*)	4, 5, 6
'Variegata' Austrian pine (*Pinus nigra*)	4, 5, 6
Golden larch (*Pseudolarix kaempferi*)	4, 5, 6
Scarlet oak (*Quercus coccinea*)	5, 6
Pin oak (*Quercus palustris*)	3/4, 5, 6
Tree lilac (*Syringa reticulata*)	3, 4, 5, 6
Littleleaf linden (*Tilia cordata*)	3, 4, 5, 6
European white linden (*Tilia tomentosa*)	6
'Feasterville' Canadian hemlock (*Tsuga canadensis*)	4, 5, 6

Unusual/Contorted Trees

'Contorta' European silver fir (*Abies alba*)	4, 5, 6
'Pendula' white mulberry (*Morus alba*)	4, 5, 6
'Kingsville Fluke' Norway spruce (*Picea abies*)	4, 5, 6
'Rustic' shore pine (*Pinus contorta*)	5, 6

'Virgata' Scotch pine (*Pinus sylvestris*)   3, 4, 5, 6
'Contorta', 'Crazy Form' eastern white pine (*Pinus strobus*)   3, 4, 5, 6
'Tortuosa' corkscrew willow (*Salix matsudana*)   4, 5, 6
'Scarlet Curls' red corkscrew willow (*Salix matsudana*)   5, 6

Horizontal Trees

Japanese maple (*Acer palmatum*)   5/6
Pagoda dogwood (*Cornus alternifolia*)   3, 4, 5, 6
Cockspur hawthorn (*Crataegus crus-galli*)   3, 4, 5, 6
European beech (*Fagus sylvatica*)   5, 6
'Viminalis' Norway spruce (*Picea abies*)   4, 5, 6
Dragon spruce (*Picea asperata* var. *notabilis*)   5, 6
'Green Shadow' eastern white pine (*Pinus strobus*)   3, 4, 5, 6
Pin oak (*Quercus palustris*)   3/4, 5, 6
Japanese snowbell (*Styrax japonicus*)   5, 6

Rounded Trees

'Compacta' European silver fir (*Abies alba*)   4, 5, 6
Ohio buckeye (*Aesculus glabra*)   3, 4, 5, 6
European hornbeam (*Carpinus betulus*)   4, 5, 6
'Casuarinifolia' Lawson false cypress (*Chamaecyparis lawsoniana*)   5, 6
American beech (*Fagus grandifolia*)   3, 4, 5, 6
European beech (*Fagus sylvatica*)   5, 6
Franklin tree (*Franklinia alatamaha*)   5/6
'Corley' European larch (*Larix decidua*)   3, 4, 5, 6
'Nigra Nana' dwarf black spruce (*Picea mariana*)   4, 5, 6
'Bloomers Dark Globe' eastern white pine (*Pinus strobus*)   3, 4, 5, 6
Japanese pagoda tree (*Sophora japonica*)   4, 5, 6
Korean mountain ash (*Sorbus alnifolia*)   3, 4, 5, 6
'Little Giant' American arborvitae (*Thuja occidentalis*)   3, 4, 5, 6
'Ammerland' Canadian hemlock (*Tsuga canadensis*)   4, 5, 6

The late Josephine Nuese's immense horticultural knowledge and her sense of humor are displayed in *The Country Garden* (1970), her book about gardening in northwest Connecticut. Trees, she explains, can be used to frame a focal point, which is "any unexpected and pleasurable sight ... which surprises and delights the eye. Like ... an old-fashioned bathtub with claw feet filled with Sophia Loren.... The point is that you can create a focal point out of almost anything if you frame it."

DISEASE-RESISTANT FLOWERING CRABAPPLES

There's no shortage of flowering crabapples (*Malus*) with glorious spring flowers, but all too many are easy targets for leaf diseases—and all too often these are the cultivars you'll find at the local garden center. 'Radiant', one of the most common crabapples, is also one the least disease-resistant. Breeders have been busy improving the disease-resistance of crabs and improving the persistence of their fruits, and growers all over the country have been busy testing them. Here are names that consistently score well.

The fruits of these cultivars are for ornament; although edible, most are too small to use. For jellies, choose 'Adams' or 'Robinson', disease-resistant crabs bred for larger apples. 'Louisa' and 'Red Jade' are weeping crabapples, which have drooping branches like a weeping willow's.

These crabapples do fine in Zones 3 to 6. The Siberian crabapple (M. *baccata*) is hardy to Zone 2.

	Flowers	Fruits
'Adams'	red-pink	dark red
'Bob White'	white	yellow
'Donald Wyman'	white	red
'Indian Magic'	pink	red-orange
'Louisa'	pink	yellow-gold
'Molazam', 'Molten Lava'	white	red
'Ormiston Roy'	white	yellow-orange
'Prairiefire'	purple-red	dark red
'Professor Sprenger'	white	red-orange
'Profusion'	rose-pink	dark red
'Red Jade'	white	red
'Red Splendor'	pink	red
'Robinson'	pink	dark red
'Jackii' Siberian crabapple (M. *baccata*)	white	red

WELL-KEPT SECRETS

Nothing but littleleaf lindens and blue spruce in your neighborhood? Then take a good look at this list of underplanted trees that comes from Renée Beaulieu, a staff member of the Litchfield, Connecticut, nursery White Flower Farm. All of Beaulieu's favorites are planted too rarely and will enhance your landscape twelve months a year. *Persian parrotia*, for example, offers fine form and fabulous exfoliating bark in winter, small burgundy flowers in early spring, glossy green leaves in summer, and brilliantly colored foliage in fall.

'Heritage' river birch (*Betula nigra*)	3, 4, 5, 6
Eastern redbud (*Cercis canadensis*)	4, 5, 6
Yellowwood (*Cladrastis lutea*)	3, 4, 5, 6
Sourwood (*Oxydendrum arboreum*)	4, 5, 6
Persian parrotia (*Parrotia persica*)	4, 5, 6
Lacebark pine (*Pinus bungeana*)	4, 5, 6
'Ivory Silk' tree lilac (*Syringa reticulata*)	3, 4, 5, 6

TREES WITH MULTIPLE TRUNKS

There is a good-sized group of trees that naturally produce more than one trunk, or can be encouraged to produce more than one. They are stunning additions to the home landscape, eye-catching silhouettes in winter and equally lovely in summer. Several—Japanese maple, river birch, and lacebark pine are three—also have ornamental bark, adding even more interest to New England gardens. Don't resist turning some of these beauties into the centerpiece of a beautiful island by underplanting them with ground covers or flowers.

Hedge maple (*Acer campestre*)	4, 5, 6
Paperbark maple (*Acer griseum*)	4, 5, 6
Japanese maple (*Acer palmatum*)	5/6
Amur maple (*Acer tataricum* subsp. *ginnala*)	2/3, 4, 5, 6
Apple serviceberry (*Amelanchier grandiflora*)	3, 4, 5, 6
River birch (*Betula nigra*)	3, 4, 5, 6

American hornbeam (*Carpinus caroliniana*)	3, 4, 5, 6
Eastern redbud (*Cercis canadensis*)	4, 5, 6
Fringe tree (*Chionanthus virginicus*)	5, 6
Pagoda dogwood (*Cornus alternifolia*)	3, 4, 5, 6
Flowering dogwood (*Cornus florida*)	5, 6
Kousa dogweed (*Cornus kousa*)	5, 6
Franklin tree (*Franklinia alatamaha*)	5/6
Saucer magnolia (*Magnolia soulangiana*)	4, 5, 6
Star magnolia (*Magnolia stellata*)	4, 5, 6
Persian parrotia (*Parrotia persica*)	4, 5, 6
Lacebark pine (*Pinus bungeana*)	4, 5, 6
Japanese pagoda tree (*Sophora japonica*)	4, 5, 6
Japanese stewartia (*Stewartia pseudocamellia*)	5, 6
Japanese snowbell (*Styrax japonicus*)	5, 6
Tree lilac (*Syringa reticulata*)	3, 4, 5, 6

MORE MAPLES FOR NEW ENGLAND

Recommending planting a maple to a New England gardener is like carrying coals to Newcastle: If our region had an official tree, it would have to be a maple (*Acer* spp.). Picking which maple, however, would be a tricky business. There are more than 120 species and many, many more subspecies, hybrids, and cultivars. There's absolutely nothing wrong with transplanting a sugar or red maple from the woods (assuming you have the owner's permission), but before you race off with a shovel and a full head of steam, consider some of the less familiar names on this list. Each has its own special merits.

Large Maples

'Atropurpureum' sycamore maple (*Acer pseudoplantanus*)	4, 5, 6
Sycamore maple (*Acer pseudoplantanus* f. *erythrocarpum*)	4, 5, 6
'Schlesingeri', 'Morgan' red maple (*Acer rubrum*)	3, 4, 5, 6
'Legacy', 'Flax Mill Majesty' sugar maple (*Acer saccharum*)	3, 4, 5, 6
Sugar maple (*Acer saccharum*)	3, 4, 5, 6

Compact/Small Maples

'Atropurpureum', 'Attraction', 'Bloodgood', 'Fireglow', 'Katsura', 'Whitney Red' Japanese maple (*Acer palmatum*)	5/6
'Crimson Sentry', 'Golden Globe' Norway maple (*Acer platanoides*)	3, 4, 5, 6
'Brilliantissimum', 'Spring Gold' sycamore maple (*Acer pseudoplantanus*)	4, 5, 6

Multistemmed Maples

Paperbark maple (*Acer griseum*)	4, 5, 6
'Aconitifolium' full-moon maple (*Acer japonicum*)	5, 6
Striped maple (*Acer pensylvanicum*)	3, 4, 5, 6
'Flame' amur maple (*Acer tataricum* subsp. *ginnala*)	3, 4, 5, 6

Fastigiate/Columnar Maples

'Erectum' sycamore maple (*Acer pseudoplantanus*)	4, 5, 6
'Bowhall', 'Columnare' red maple (*Acer rubrum*)	3, 4, 5, 6
'Pyramidale' silver maple (*Acer saccharinum*)	3, 4, 5, 6
'Goldspire', 'Newton Sentry' sugar maple (*Acer saccharum*)	3, 4, 5, 6

Weeping/Pendulous Maples

'Crimson Queen', Green Lace' Japanese maple (*Acer palmatum*)	5/6
'Charles Joly' Norway maple (*Acer platanoides*)	4, 5, 6
'Beebe's Cutleaf Weeping' silver maple (*Acer saccharinum*)	3, 4, 5, 6

Maples With Ornamental Bark

Père David's maple (*Acer davidii*)	5, 6
Paperbark maple (*Acer griseum*)	4, 5, 6
'Arakawa' Japanese maple (*Acer palmatum*)	5/6
'Erythrocladum' striped maple (*Acer pensylvanicum*)	3, 4, 5, 6
Three-flower maple (*Acer triflorum*)	5, 6
Purpleblow maple (*Acer truncatum*)	4, 5, 6

Maples With Outstanding Fall Color

'Aconitifolium' full-moon maple (*Acer japonicum*)	5, 6
Striped maple (*Acer pensylvanicum*)	3, 4, 5, 6
'Morgan', 'October Glory', 'Red Sunset' red maple (*Acer rubrum*)	3, 4, 5, 6
'Louise Lad' sugar maple (*Acer saccharum*)	3, 4, 5, 6
'Flame', 'Fire' amur maple (*Acer tataricum* subsp. *ginnala*)	3, 4, 5, 6

Maples With Variegated Leaves

'Carnival' hedge maple (*Acer campestre*)	6
'Flamingo', 'Variegatum' box elder (*Acer negundo*)	2, 3, 4, 5, 6
'Drummondii' harlequin maple (*Acer platanoides*)	3/4, 5, 6
'Simon Louis Frères' sycamore maple (*Acer pseudoplantanus*)	4, 5, 6

 The average sugar maple tree yields about 12 gallons of sap each season, and it takes between 30 and 50 gallons of maple sap to make 1 gallon of syrup.

BERRY NICE: TREES WITH ORNAMENTAL FRUITS

Shrubs get more credit for colorful berries and fruits than trees do, but there is a good-sized group of arboreal species that produce not only flowers and foliage but ornamental fruits. At a time when most trees offer nothing but green leaves, or bare limbs, these bits of upper-story brightness are especially welcome. Some of these fruits, while not recommended for human consumption, will be appreciated by high-flying and climbing wildlife visitors to your garden. (Crabapples, which are colorful fruit-producers *par excellence*, have a list of their own elsewhere in this chapter.)

Amur maple (*Acer tataricum* subsp. *ginnala*)	2/3, 4, 5, 6
Flowering dogwood (*Cornus florida*)	5, 6
Kousa dogwood (*Cornus kousa*)	5, 6
Cockspur hawthorn (*Crataegus crus-galli*)	3, 4, 5, 6
Washington hawthorn (*Crataegus phaenopyrum*)	4, 5, 6
'Winter King' hawthorne (*Crataegus viridis*)	4/5, 6
American holly (*Ilex opaca*)	5, 6
Goldenrain tree (*Koelreuteria paniculata*)	5, 6
Magnolia (*Magnolia* spp.)	4, 5, 6
Black gum (*Nyssa sylvatica*)	5, 6

Sourwood (*Oxydendrum arboreum*)	4, 5, 6
Sargent cherry (*Prunus sargentii*)	5, 6
European mountain ash (*Sorbus aucuparia*)	4, 5, 6
Blackhaw viburnum (*Viburnum prunifolium*)	3, 4, 5, 6
Chinese date/Chinese jujuba (*Ziziphus jujuba*)	6

WHEN THE WIND BLOWS: TREES WHOSE BOUGHS WON'T BREAK

Strong winds, especially during New England winters, can wreak havoc on trees by drying them out, snapping off their limbs, even uprooting them. The stress can be so severe that the trees that aren't killed are permanently stunted. The species on this list are better than most at standing up to icy blasts, good candidates for creating a windbreak if your garden needs one. Not only will these trees dance in the wind, they won't die from it.

White fir (*Abies concolor*)	3, 4, 5, 6
Norway maple (*Acer platanoides*)	3, 4, 5, 6
Siberian pea tree (*Caragana arborescens*)	2, 3, 4, 5, 6
Common hackberry (*Celtis occidentalis*)	2, 3, 4, 5, 6
Leyland cypress (*Cupressocyparis leylandii*)	6
Russian olive (*Elaeagnus angustifolia*)	3, 4, 5, 6
Eastern red cedar (*Juniperus virginiana*)	3, 4, 5, 6
Osage orange (*Maclura pomifera*)	4, 5, 6
Norway spruce (*Picea abies*)	3, 4, 5, 6
Colorado spruce (*Picea pungens*)	3, 4, 5, 6
Austrian pine (*Pinus nigra*)	4, 5, 6
Eastern white pine (*Pinus strobus*)	3, 4, 5, 6
Scotch pine (*Pinus sylvestris*)	3, 4, 5, 6
'Pyramidalis' silver poplar (*Populus alba*)	3, 4, 5, 6
'Italica' Lombardy poplar (*Populus nigra*)	3, 4, 5, 6
Douglas fir (*Pseudotsuga menziesii*)	6
Willow oak (*Quercus phellos*)	6
American arborvitae (*Thuja occidentalis*)	3, 4, 5, 6
Siberian elm (*Ulmus pumila*)	5, 6

"You may want to build snowframes to keep small conifers and evergreen hedges from being damaged by heavy snow in winter. (A snowframe, which can be made from scrap wood, is like a sawhorse with its two sides covered.) And be careful if you try to remove snow or ice from trees: Limbs are brittle and snap easily when temperatures are below freezing."
Meg Smith, garden publicist for Gardener's Supply, Charlotte, Vermont

AN OFFERING OF OAKS

It's been many decades since British admirals reputedly tramped through the English countryside tossing out acorns and muttering, "There's another ship for the royal navy." Here are some good oaks for New England gardens, even if you're not into shipbuilding. Don't forget that these are tall trees, 50 feet and more, and often as wide as they are high.

If you want to begin with an acorn, F.W. Schumacher Co. in Sandwich, Massachusetts, can help: They sell seeds of more than 1,000 tree species, including eighteen oaks.

Sawtooth oak (*Quercus acutissima*)	5, 6
White oak (*Quercus alba*)	3/4, 5, 6
Swamp white oak (*Quercus bicolor*)	3/4, 5, 6
Scarlet oak (*Quercus coccinea*)	5, 6
Northern pin oak (*Quercus ellipsoidalis*)	3, 4, 5, 6
Southern red oak (*Quercus falcata*)	5/6
Shingle oak (*Quercus imbricaria*)	4, 5, 6
Overcup oak (*Quercus lyrata*)	6
Bur oak (*Quercus macrocarpa*)	2/3, 4, 5, 6
Chinkapin oak (*Quercus muehlenbergii*)	4/5, 6
Pin oak (*Quercus palustris*)	3/4, 5, 6
Willow oak (*Quercus phellos*)	6
Chestnut oak (*Quercus prinus*)	5, 6
English oak (*Quercus robur*)	5, 6
Red oak (*Quercus rubra*)	3, 4, 5, 6
Black oak (*Quercus velutina*)	4, 5, 6

OAK

No one should miss reading Rebecca Rupp's *Red Oaks & Black Birches: The Science and Lore of Trees* (1990). Rupp, who gardens in both Shaftsbury and Swanton, Vermont, points out that oaks are hit by lightning more than any other trees. "One reason the hapless oak is singled out for all this heavenly fury is its bark, a rough, ridged production three to four inches thick." When lightning hits a smooth-barked tree, it follows the surface water to the ground. When it hits the unevenly wet bark of an oak, it seeks out the liquid sap channels inside the trunk. "The resultant explosion blasts the luckless oak to oblivion.... The best place to spend a thunderstorm, safety-conscious citizens agree is indoors—preferable in bed, with a glass of brandy."

EVERGREENS OF A DIFFERENT HUE

In winter, there are no blossoms or green tree leaves in most New England gardens, but you can add color to your landscape by planting a mix of non-deciduous trees. Most of the familiar conifers—pines, spruce, yews, hemlocks, and more—will provide green accents. For shades of blue plus silver and gold, try some of these not-so-green evergreens. (These cultivars are unlikely to be carried by general garden centers, but are available from specialist and mail-order nurseries.) All grow 15 feet or more and are upright in habit, so choose your site accordingly.

Yellow/Gold/Cream

'Aureovariegata' Nordmann fir (*Abies nordmanniana*)	5, 6
'Crisppsii' (*Chamaecyparis obtusa*)	4, 5, 6
'Aurea Jacobsen' Norway spruce (*Picea abies*)	3/4, 5, 6
'Aurea Magnifica' Norway spruce (*Picea abies*)	4, 5, 6

'Dent' white spruce (*Picea glauca*)	3, 4, 5, 6
'Aurea' black spruce (*Picea mariana*)	3, 4, 5, 6
'Stanley Gold' Colorado spruce (*Picea pungens*)	3, 4, 5, 6
'Aureopicta' Scotch pine (*Pinus sylvestris*)	3, 4, 5, 6
'Greg's Variegated' Scotch pine (*Pinus sylvestris*)	3, 4, 5, 6
'Aureovariegata' Douglas fir (*Pseudotsuga menziesii*)	4, 5, 6
'Sudsworthii' American arborvitae (*Thuja occidentalis*)	3, 4, 5, 6
'Canadian Gold' western red cedar (*Thuja plicata*)	5, 6
'Aurea' Canadian hemlock (*Tsuga canadensis*)	3/4, 5, 6
'Femii' Canadian hemlock (*Tsuga canadensis*)	3/4, 5, 6
'Lutea' Canadian hemlock (*Tsuga canadensis*)	3/4, 5, 6

White/Silver/Gray

'Variegata' balsam fir (*Abies balsamea*)	3, 4, 5, 6
'Argentea' white fir (*Abies concolor*)	3, 4, 5, 6
'Chandler's Silver' Rocky Mountain juniper (*Juniperus scopulorum*)	4, 5, 6
'Argentea' Engelmann spruce (*Picea engelmannii*)	3, 4, 5, 6

Blue

'Select Blue', 'Sherwood Blue' white fir (*Abies concolor*)	3, 4, 5, 6
'Glauca' atlas cedar (*Cedrus libani* ssp. *atlantica*)	6
'Blue Broom', 'Blue Sport' Atlantic white cedar (*Chamaecyparis thyoides*)	4, 5, 6
'Pyramidalis' Chinese juniper (*Juniperus chinensis*)	3/4, 5, 6
'Blue Heaven' Rocky Mountain juniper (*Juniperus scopulorum*)	4, 5, 6
'Coerulea' Norway spruce (*Picea abies*)	4, 5, 6
'Vanderwolf's Blue Pyramid' Engelmann spruce (*Picea engelmannii*)	3, 4, 5, 6
'Hoopsii' Colorado spruce (*Picea pungens*)	3, 4, 5, 6
'Blue Giant' Japanese white pine (*Pinus parviflora*)	5, 6
Japanese white pine (*Pinus parviflora* f. *glauca*)	5, 6
'Glauca' eastern white pine (*Pinus strobus*)	3, 4, 5, 6
'Hess's Select Blue' Douglas fir (*Pseudotsuga menziesii*)	4, 5, 6

TREES THAT CAN TAKE CARE OF THEMSELVES

On weekends, Sally Williams travels from her Boston garden to her garden in foothills of the White Mountains in western Maine. "There I've planted trees that are cold hardy, have year-round beauty, and vary in shape and texture. They must be wildlife-friendly, low-maintenance and have good resistance to diseases, especially to cedar-apple rust." The publisher/editor of *Garden Literature*, an annual index to articles and book reviews about plants and gardens (Garden Literature Press, 398 Columbus Ave, No. 181, Boston, MA 02116), Williams recommends these trees—evergreen and deciduous, large and small, common and unusual. All are perfect for gardens that must fend for themselves, and for gardens that are fended for.

'Commemoration' sugar maple (*Acer saccharum*)	3, 4, 5, 6
'Legacy' sugar maple (*Acer saccharum*)	3, 4, 5, 6
Downy serviceberry (*Amelanchier arborea*)	4, 5, 6
'Pendula' Alaska cedar (*Chamaecyparis nootkatensis*)	4, 5, 6
White cedar (*Chamaecyparis thyoides*)	3, 4, 5, 6
'Argentea' variegated pagoda dogwood (*Cornus alternifolia*)	3, 4, 5, 6
Pagoda dogwood (*Cornus alternifolia*)	3, 4, 5, 6
American smoke tree (*Cotinus obovatus*)	4, 5, 6

'Arnold Pink' Carolina silverbell (*Halesia carolina*)	4, 5, 6
Tulip tree (*Liriodendron tulipifera*)	4, 5, 6
'Miss Scarlet' sour gum (*Nyssa sylvatica*)	4, 5, 6
Black Hills spruce (*Picea glauca* var. *densata*)	2, 3, 4, 5, 6
Lijiang spruce (*Picea likangensis*)	4, 5, 6
'Minnesota Red' purpleleaf sand cherry (*Prunus cistena*)	4, 5, 6
Purpleleaf sand cherry (*Prunus cistena*)	4, 5, 6
'Green Vase' Japanese zelkova (*Zelkova serrata*)	4, 5, 6

"I always mulch young trees to keep lawn mowers and other equipment from compacting the soil or damaging the trunk, to conserve moisture, and to protect roots from heaving in late winter and early spring when temperatures alternate between freezing and thawing. Around conifers I use bark mulch, making sure the mulch is not in contact with the trunk. Around deciduous trees, I use leaves that I chop in an inexpensive electric leaf-shredder or run over with the lawn mower. Shredded leaves are less likely to smother perennials and bulbs that may be planted underneath than whole leaves, which mat when they become wet. I add an extra layer of chopped leaves in winter, waiting until the ground is fully frozen—and when I can be more certain that small critters have already found homes and won't nest in the mulch, where they could easily reach the trunk under the snow and gnaw its bark."
Sally Williams, garden writer, editor, and publisher (*Garden Literature*, an index of horticultural articles and reviews), Boston, Massachusetts

DOWN BY THE SEASHORE

Although their growth may be slightly slowed or stunted by the challenging conditions of a seaside setting, these trees are able to withstand strong winds and moderate saltspray. If you're lucky enough to be living oceanside, try some of these species in your garden.

Norway maple (*Acer platanoides*)	3, 4, 5, 6
Sycamore maple (*Acer pseudoplantanus*)	4, 5, 6
Red maple (*Acer rubrum*)	3, 4, 5, 6
Black alder (*Alnus glutinosa*)	4, 5, 6
European white birch (*Betula pendula*)	2, 3, 4, 5, 6
Siberian pea tree (*Caragana arborescens*)	2, 3, 4, 5, 6
Atlantic white cedar (*Chamaecyparis thyoides*)	4, 5, 6
Russian olive (*Elaeagnus angustifolia*)	3, 4, 5, 6
Eastern red cedar (*Juniperus virginiana*)	3, 4, 5, 6
Black gum (*Nyssa sylvatica*)	5, 6
Norway spruce (*Picea abies*)	3, 4, 5, 6
Jack pine (*Pinus banksiana*)	3, 4, 5, 6
Japanese black pine (*Pinus thunbergii*)	5, 6
Silver poplar (*Populus alba*)	4, 5, 6
Black cherry (*Prunus serotina*)	3/4, 5, 6
Blackthorn (*Prunus spinosa*)	4, 5, 6
Holly oak (*Quercus ilex*)	6
White willow (*Salix alba*)	3, 4, 5, 6
Littleleaf linden (*Tilia cordata*)	3, 4, 5, 6

JACK PINE

Henry David Thoreau, Massachusetts' most famous nineteenth-century naturalist-gardener, was clear about where the value of trees lay: "I am occasionally asked if I know what shrub oaks were made for. But worthless as the woodman regards it, it is to me one of the most interesting of trees and, like the white birch, is associated in my mind with New England. For whatever we have perceived to be in the slightest degree beautiful is of infinitely more value to us than what we have only as yet discovered to be useful and to serve our purpose."

WEEPING CONIFERS

The editors wouldn't let me title this list "Hang Down Your Head, *Picea glauca*," but hanging down their head is what weeping conifers do. It makes them one of the most eye-catching tree forms that you can add to a landscape. They call attention to themselves. The first time a Maine friend of mine saw a weeping white pine, he asked the nurseryman if the tree needed water. Discovering it was perfectly healthy, he bought it on the spot! Weeping conifers range from giant to dwarf, so there is a cultivar for every garden, large or small, formal or informal. They're also expensive to propagate and expensive to purchase, but worth every penny, oops, dollar.

CANADIAN
HEMLOCK

'Fagerhult', 'Gable's Weeping' white fir (*Abies concolor*)	3, 4, 5, 6
'Glauca Pendula' atlas cedar (*Cedrus libani* ssp. *atlantica*)	6
'Gracilis Pendula', 'Pendula' Lawson false cypress (*Chamaecyparis lawsoniana*)	5, 6
'Pendula' Nootka false cypress (*Chamaecyparis nootkatenis*)	4, 5, 6
'Mint Julep' Chinese juniper (*Juniperus chinensis*)	4, 5, 6
'Jensen', 'Pendula' common juniper (*Juniperus communis*)	3, 4, 5, 6
'Cincinnati', 'Depressa', 'Inversa', 'Pendula Major', 'Reflexa', 'Weeping Blue' Norway spruce (*Picea abies*)	3, 4, 5, 6
'Fendleri' Engelmann spruce (*Picea engelmannii*)	3, 4, 5, 6
'Pendula' white spruce (*Picea glauca*)	2/3, 4, 5, 6
'Weeping Dwarf' oriental spruce (*Picea orientalis*)	4, 5, 6
'Glauca Pendula', 'Kosteri Pendula', 'Shilo Weeping' Colorado spruce (*Picea pungens*)	3, 4, 5, 6
'Pendula' weeping Japanese red pine (*Pinus densiflora*)	5, 6
'Bennett's Contorted', 'Inversa', 'Old Softie', 'Pendula' eastern white pine (*Pinus strobus*)	3, 4, 5, 6
'Carnefix Weeping', 'Graceful Grace', 'Pendula' weeping Douglas fir (*Pseudotsuga menziesii*)	6
'Gracilis Pendula' English yew (*Taxus baccata*)	6
'Pendula' American arborvitae (*Thuja occidentalis*)	3, 4, 5, 6
'Dawsoniana', 'Pendula' Canadian hemlock (*Tsuga canadensis*)	3/4, 5, 6
'Sargentii', 'Valentine', 'Youngcone' Canadian hemlock (*Tsuga canadensis*)	4, 5, 6

URBAN GUERRILLAS: TREES FOR CITIES

Looking for something to grow in an urban setting in addition to *Ailanthus altissima*, an overly agressive species whose seeds can sprout in a sidewalk crack? Here are some alternatives, trees that not only will thrive in Brooklyn but in your city or town. Some grow 50 feet and taller, so choose your location carefully. Among the giants are red maple, green ash, London plane, pin oak, red oak, littleleaf linden, and European white linden, all large enough to shade your city yard and your neighbors'.

However, all the trees on this list are reasonably tolerant of city life, willing to put up with compacted soil, air pollution, and being watered with Coca-Cola and Starbucks coffee. They even endure car alarms without complaining, which is more than most of us can say.

Red maple (*Acer rubrum*)	3, 4, 5, 6
Common hackberry (*Celtis occidentalis*)	2, 3, 4, 5, 6
Cornelian cherry (*Cornus mas*)	4, 5, 6
'Stricta' singleseed hawthorn (*Crataegus monogyna*)	5, 6
Russian olive (*Elaeagnus angustifolia*)	3, 4, 5, 6
White ash (*Fraxinus americana*)	4, 5, 6
'Summit' green ash (*Fraxinus pennsylvanica*)	4, 5, 6
Ginkgo/maidenhair tree (*Ginkgo biloba*)	4, 5, 6
Thornless honey locust (*Gleditsia triacanthos* var. *inermis*)	3, 4, 5, 6
London plane tree (*Platanus hispanica*)	5, 6
Bradford pear (*Pyrus calleryana*)	4, 5, 6
Pin oak (*Quercus palustris*)	3/4, 5, 6
Red oak (*Quercus rubra*)	3, 4, 5, 6
'Greenspire' littleleaf linden (*Tilia cordata*)	4, 5, 6
European white linden (*Tilia tomentosa*)	6

"Proper siting is key to low maintenance and a tree's success. Get accurate information about the tree's height and branch spread when mature before you plant, and its rate of growth. Set trees far enough from the house that snow and ice won't fall from sloping roofs onto young plants and, when the trees are mature, branches won't rub against the house or fall on it, or root spread interfere with foundations, septic systems, or garden beds. Consider prevailing wind patterns, especially in winter. If you want a tall tree in an exposed site, select species with strong branch habit and plant an understory layer of smaller trees and shrubs or tall grasses between the tree and the direction of the wind."

Sally Williams, garden writer, editor, and publisher (*Garden Literature*, an index of horticultural articles and reviews), Boston, Massachusetts

THE THIN MEN: TREES THAT GROW TALL AND SLIM

Many landscapes require tall trees that don't spread as they ascend—and there are plenty of trees to fit the bill. If you're thumbing a nursery catalog, look for words like *fastigiate* (which means tall and narrow) or some form of the word column, such as *columnare* and *columnaris*. Even on this short list there is great variation—some cultivars are far more tall or narrow than others. Not all of them, as Vermont nurseryman Don Avery described *Acer saccharum* 'Monumentale', will look like "a telephone pole with sugar maple leaves."

Deciduous

'Columnare' Norway maple (*Acer platanoides*)	4, 5, 6
'Monumentale' sugar maple (*Acer saccharum*)	3, 4, 5, 6
'Fastigiata' European white birch (*Betula pendula*)	3, 4, 5, 6
'Columnaris' hornbeam (*Carpinus betulus*)	4, 5, 6
'Stricta' singleseed hawthorn (*Crataegus monogyna*)	5, 6
'Fastigiata' European beech (*Fagus sylvatica*)	5, 6
'Princeton Sentry' ginkgo/maidenhair tree (*Ginkgo biloba*)	4, 5, 6
'Fastigiatum' tulip tree (*Liriodendron tulipifera*)	4, 5, 6

'Harvest Gold' flowering crabapple (*Malus*)	4, 5, 6
'Columnaris' Siberian crabapple (*Malus baccata*)	3, 4, 5, 6
'Italica' Lombardy poplar (*Populus nigra*)	3, 4, 5, 6
'Erecta' upright European aspen (*Populus tremula*)	2, 3, 4, 5, 6
'Amanogawa' Japanese flowering cherry (*Prunus serrulata*)	3, 4, 5, 6
'Fastigiata' English oak (*Quercus robur*)	5, 6
'Fastigiata' European mountain ash (*Sorbus aucuparia*)	4, 5, 6
'Prairie Sentinel' pond cypress (*Taxodium distichum* var. *nutans*)	6

Evergreen

'Columnaris' European silver fir (*Abies alba*)	4, 5, 6
'Columnaris' balsam fir (*Abies balsamea*)	3, 4, 5, 6
'Fastigiata' Himalayan cedar (*Cedrus deodara*)	6
'Fastigiata' atlas cedar (*Cedrus libani* ssp. *atlantica*)	6
'Strict Weeping' Alaskan cedar (*Chamaecyparis nootkatensis*)	4, 5, 6
'Breviramea' Hinoki false cypress (*Chamaecyparis obtusa*)	4, 5, 6
'Columnaris Glauca' Chinese juniper (*Juniperus chinensis*)	4, 5, 6
'Erecta' common juniper (*Juniperus communis*)	3, 4, 5, 6
'Glauca', 'Sparkling Skyrocket' eastern red cedar (*Juniperus virginiana*)	3/4, 5, 6
'Cupressina' Norway spruce (*Picea abies*)	4, 5, 6
'Pendula' white spruce (*Picea glauca*)	2/3, 4, 5, 6
'Pendula' Siberian spruce (*Picea omorika*)	4, 5, 6
'Fastigiata', 'Iseli Fastigate' Colorado spruce (*Picea pungens*)	2, 3, 4, 5, 6
'Arnold Sentinel', 'Obelisk' Austrian pine (*Pinus nigra*)	4, 5, 6
'Brevifolia' eastern white pine (*Pinus strobus*)	3, 4, 5, 6
'Fastigiata', 'Obelisk' American arborvitae (*Thuja occidentalis*)	3, 4, 5, 6
'Kingsville', 'Schramm' Canadian hemlock (*Tsuga canadensis*)	3, 4, 5, 6

IN A NUTSHELL

The spreading chestnut is no longer with us (nor is the village smithy), although the fungus that killed the chestnut is still around. But that doesn't mean there are no nut trees for New England gardeners to plant. This list is short and most of these nuts won't end up in a candy box covered with chocolate. But a few, such as black walnuts, have superb flavor, and the beech nut is responsible for a confectionery company. All the trees on this list produce edible nuts, although some may be more popular with wildlife than they will be with you.

One warning: The roots of black walnut trees produce juglone, a substance that is toxic to many other plants, especially food crops. Plant it at least 50 feet away from your vegetable garden.

AMERICAN
BEECH

Shagbark hickory (*Carya ovata*)	4, 5, 6
Chinese chestnut (*Castanea mollissima*)	5/6
American hazelnut (*Corylus americana*)	3, 4, 5, 6
Turkish filbert (*Corylus colurna*)	4, 5, 6
American beech (*Fagus grandifolia*)	3, 4, 5, 6
'Broadview', 'Idaho' Carpathian walnut (*Juglans*)	4, 5, 6
Japanese walnut (*Juglans ailantifolia*)	5, 6
Butternut (*Juglans cinerea*)	3/4, 5, 6
Black walnut (*Juglans nigra*)	4, 5, 6
English walnut/Persian walnut (*Juglans regia*)	4, 5, 6
Korean pine (*Pinus koraiensis*)	4, 5, 6

> "When I spot a tree house on someone's property, I know civilized people live there, people whose idea of happiness goes beyond the provision of color TV. At the very least, they have made the gift of privacy and independence to a child, and if the child rejects those, he is past saving."
> Eleanor Perényi, Connecticut gardener and author of *Green Thoughts: A Writer in the Garden* (1981)

LILLIPUTIAN CONIFERS

Les Wyman, who lives in Hanson, Massachusetts, grows more than 250 conifers. A former garden columnist for the Brockton *Enterprise*, he now keeps busy working for the American Conifer Society as a member of the board of directors and chair of the membership committee (if you're interested in conifers, contact him about becoming a member: 86 Tavern Waye, Hanson, MA 02341). Coming up with a dozen favorite dwarf conifers was difficult, he says, "because there are so many great ones." Here are Wyman's choices and their approximate height at maturity.

Miniature

'Silberzwerg' Korean fir (*Abies koreana*)	6

One foot

'Golden Sprite' Hinoki false cypress (*Chamaecyparis obtusa*)	4/5, 6

Two feet

'Archer's Dwarf' concolor/white fir (*Abies concolor*)	3/4, 5, 6
'Little Gem' Norway spruce (*Picea abies*)	3, 4, 5, 6
'Pocono' red spruce (*Picea rubens*)	3, 4, 5, 6
'Chief Joseph' shore pine (*Pinus contorta*)	5, 6
'Jervis' Canada hemlock (*Tsuga canadensis*)	3/4, 5, 6

Three feet

'Kosteri' false cypress (*Chamaecyparis obtusa*)	4/5, 6
'Verdoni' false cypress (*Chamaecyparis obtusa*)	4/5, 6
'Alberta Globe' white spruce (*Picea glauca*)	3, 4, 5, 6
'St. Mary's Broom' Colorado spruce (*Picea pungens*)	3, 4, 5, 6
'Blue Shag' eastern white pine (*Pinus strobus*)	3, 4, 5, 6

MAGNOLIA CUM LAUDE

When anyone says the word "magnolia," most of us think of *Magnolia grandiflora*, the magnificent southern species that bears huge waxy white flowers. Hardy only to Zone 7, it's forbidden fruit in 99.9 percent of New England. That doesn't mean we can't grow magnolias, however, although their blooms are sometimes damaged by late frosts. More often than not, you will have glorious flowers in spring, and handsome foliage the rest of the year.

These hardiness zone recommendations, consistently lower than those given in plant encyclopedias, come from magnolia growers in New England, Michigan, Minnesota, and Ottawa, Canada. If you want to take a chance with *Magnolia grandiflora*, try the cultivar 'Edith Bogue'.

'Ann', 'Betty', 'Jane', Little Girl hybrid magnolia (*Magnolia*)	4, 5, 6
'Galaxy', hybrid magnolia (*Magnolia*)	5, 6

Cucumber tree (*Magnolia acuminata*)	4, 5, 6
Fraser magnolia (*Magnolia fraseri*)	4, 5, 6
'Borealis' Asian magnolia (*Magnolia kobus*)	4, 5, 6
'Merrill' Loebner's magnolia (*Magnolia loebneri*)	4, 5, 6
'Snow Spring' Loebner's magnolia (*Magnolia loebneri*)	5, 6
Willow-leaf magnolia (*Magnolia salicifolia*)	5, 6
'Lennei', 'Lennei Alba', 'Verbanica' saucer magnolia (*Magnolia soulangiana*)	4, 5, 6
'Royal Star' magnolia (*Magnolia stellata*)	4, 5, 6
Umbrella magnolia (*Magnolia tripetala*)	4, 5, 6

TREES WITH SHOWY BARK

All these attractive trees have exfoliating, or peeling, bark, which adds interest to the home landscape. Bark colors range from the white of the familiar paper birch, *Betula papyrifera*, to the flaking orange and brown bark of the Chinese, or lacebark, elm, *Ulmus parvifolia*. Exfoliating bark is interesting and ornamental throughout the year, but it really comes into its own in winter when it is no longer hidden by foliage.

Trident maple (*Acer buergeranum*)	5, 6
Paperbark maple (*Acer griseum*)	4, 5, 6
Three-flower maple (*Acer triflorum*)	5, 6
Chinese paper birch (*Betula albosinensis*)	5, 6
Yellow birch (*Betula alleghaniensis*)	4, 5, 6
River birch (*Betula nigra*)	3, 4, 5, 6
Paper birch (*Betula papyrifera*)	2, 3, 4, 5, 6
European white birch (*Betula pendula*)	2, 3, 4, 5, 6
Chinese fringe tree (*Chionanthus retusus*)	6
Kousa dogwood (*Cornus kousa*)	5, 6
Cornelian cherry (*Cornus mas*)	4, 5, 6
Turkish filbert (*Corylus colurna*)	4, 5, 6
Lacebark pine (*Pinus bungeana*)	4, 5, 6
Amur chokecherry (*Prunus maackii*)	2, 3, 4, 5, 6
Japanese stewartia (*Stewartia pseudocamellia*)	5, 6
Chinese elm/lacebark elm (*Ulmus parvifolia*)	5, 6

MOTH MAGNETS: TREES LOVED BY THE GYPSY MOTH

Gypsy moths, who lay eggs by the hundreds, are a periodic plague in New England. During years of heavy infestations, the ravenous caterpillars can denude entire forests. There are no really effective methods of controlling gypsy moths, although sticky bands around tree trunks will stop the caterpillars, which are about 2 to 3 inches long and have pairs of red and blue spots on their backs. (For more information about gypsy moths, contact your local extension service.)

Since there are no effective natural predators of the gypsy moth, your best defense from these pests is to avoiding planting the trees they prefer. These are the easy targets.

Box elder (*Acer negundo*)	2, 3, 4, 5, 6
Paper birch (*Betula papyrifera*)	2, 3, 4, 5, 6
Gray birch (*Betula populifolia*)	2, 3, 4, 5, 6
Hawthorn (*Crataegus* spp.)	4, 5, 6
Sweet gum (*Liquidambar styraciflua*)	5, 6
Crabapple (*Malus* spp.)	3, 4, 5, 6

Quaking aspen (*Populus tremuloides*)	2, 3, 4, 5, 6
Oak (*Quercus* spp.)	3, 4, 5, 6
Willow (*Salix* spp.)	3, 4, 5, 6
Basswood (*Tilia americana*)	3, 4, 5, 6

Garden writer Rita Buchanan, who gardens in Winsted, Connecticut, suggests that gardeners with wildlife problems "plant defensively. If deer are a problem in your area, the trees that will interest them least are Japanese maples, birches, hawthorns, ashes, ginkgo, magnolias, spruces, and pines."

BEYOND *CORNUS FLORIDA*: HARDY DOGWOODS

Form, flower, foliage, fruits—dogwoods have it all. Some dogwoods also have leaf and stem anthracnose and borers, plagues that are ravishing flowering dogwood, *Cornus florida*, trees in Connecticut and other parts of New England. These botanical banes don't mean your garden must be a dogwood-free zone. There are plenty of *Cornus* candidates for Yankees, including disease-resistant *C. florida* cultivars, as well as hardy dogwoods for Zone 3 dwellers. *Cornus* species range from 30-foot trees to bunchberry, which grows about 8 inches tall. It and most shrub species are easily propagated by cuttings made in spring—good news, because one dogwood is never enough.

Trees

'Argentea' variegated pagoda dogwood (*Cornus alternifolia*)	3, 4, 5, 6
Pagoda dogwood (*Cornus alternifolia*)	3, 4, 5, 6
'Variegata' variegated giant dogwood (*Cornus controversa*)	5, 6
'Cherokee Princess' flowering dogwood (*Cornus florida*)	5, 6
'Cherokee Sunset' red flowering dogwood (*Cornus florida*)	5, 6
'Rosabella', 'Santomi' pink kousa dogwood (*Cornus kousa*)	5, 6
Kousa dogwood (*Cornus kousa* var. *chinensis*)	5, 6
Japanese cornel (*Cornus officinalis*)	5, 6
'Constellation' (*Cornus rutgersiensis*)	5, 6

Shrubs

'Elegantissima' variegated redtwig dogwood (*Cornus alba*)	2, 3, 4, 5, 6
'Spaethii' variegated redtwig dogwood (*Cornus alba*)	2, 3, 4, 5, 6
'Flava' Cornelian cherry (*Cornus mas*)	4, 5, 6
'Cardinal' red osier dogwood (*Cornus stolonifera*)	2, 3, 4, 5, 6
'Flaviramea' red osier dogwood (*Cornus stolonifera*)	2, 3, 4, 5, 6

Ground Cover

Bunchberry/creeping dogwood (*Cornus canadensis*)	2, 3, 4, 5, 6

DEALING WITH DAMP: TREES FOR WET SITES

Here's a list of deciduous trees that do well in damp sites—not swamplike conditions, mind you, but moist places. They have all sorts of other merits in addition to putting up with wet feet. Box elder, for example is fast-growing; look for 'Variegatum', which has green-and-white leaves. River birch has beautiful exfoliating bark. Tulip trees have yellow-orange flowers, while the small flowers of the silver linden are fragrant. The corkscrew willow has an eye-catching form. All are worth planting even if your landscape doesn't have a damp spot!

Box elder (*Acer negundo*)   2, 3, 4, 5, 6
Striped maple (*Acer pensylvanicum*)   3, 4, 5, 6
Red maple (*Acer rubrum*)   3, 4, 5, 6
River birch (*Betula nigra*)   3, 4, 5, 6
American hornbeam (*Carpinus caroliniana*)   3, 4, 5, 6
Shellbark hickory (*Carya laciniosa*)   5, 6
European/common larch (*Larix decidua*)   3, 4, 5, 6
Sweet gum (*Liquidambar styraciflua*)   5, 6
Tulip tree (*Liriodendron tulipifera*)   4, 5, 6
Kobus magnolia (*Magnolia kobus*)   5, 6
Sycamore (*Platanus occidentalis*)   4, 5, 6
Silver poplar (*Populus alba*)   3, 4, 5, 6
Swamp white oak (*Quercus bicolor*)   3/4, 5, 6
Pin oak (*Quercus palustris*)   4, 5, 6
Weeping willow (*Salix babylonica*)   3, 4, 5, 6
'Tortuosa' corkscrew willow (*Salix matsudana*)   4, 5, 6
Bald cypress (*Taxodium distichum*)   5, 6
Littleleaf linden (*Tilia cordata*)   3, 4, 5, 6
Pendent silver linden (*Tilia petiolaris*)   5, 6

TREES FOR DRY LOCATIONS

Many New England gardeners are cursed with rocky soil that retains water about as well as a slotted spoon. At the same time, we're blessed with a substantial list of deciduous trees, both natives and arboreal immigrants, that can tolerate dry conditions. If your landscape contains a micro-desert or two and you don't want to spend the rest of your life watering, consider some of these.

Current recommendations say *not* to amend the soil in the planting hole unless the soil is extremely poor, but mulching with organic matter is always a good idea.

HACKBERRY

Box elder (*Acer negundo*)   2, 3, 4, 5, 6
Tatarian maple (*Acer tataricum*)   2/3, 4, 5, 6
Amur maple (*Acer tataricum* subsp. *ginnala*)   2/3, 4, 5, 6
Ohio buckeye (*Aesculus glabra*)   3, 4, 5, 6
Devil's walking stick (*Aralia spinosa*)   5, 6
European hornbeam (*Carpinus betulus*)   4, 5, 6
Northern catalpa (*Catalpa speciosa*)   4, 5, 6
Common hackberry (*Celtis occidentalis*)   2, 3, 4, 5, 6
Russian olive (*Elaeagnus angustifolia*)   3, 4, 5, 6
Green ash (*Fraxinus pennsylvanica*)   3, 4, 5, 6
Ginkgo/maidenhair tree (*Ginkgo biloba*)   4, 5, 6
Thornless common honey locust (*Gleditsia triacanthos* var. *inermis*)   3, 4, 5, 6
Eastern red cedar (*Juniperus virginiana*)   3, 4, 5, 6
Goldenrain tree (*Koelreuteria paniculata*)   5, 6
White mulberry (*Morus alba*)   4, 5, 6
Ironwood (*Ostrya virginiana*)   3, 4, 5, 6
Jack pine (*Pinus banksiana*)   3, 4, 5, 6
Austrian pine (*Pinus nigra*)   4, 5, 6
Eastern white pine (*Pinus strobus*)   3, 4, 5, 6
'Chanticleer' callery pear (*Pyrus calleryana*)   4, 5, 6
Scarlet oak (*Quercus coccinea*)   5, 6

Bur oak (*Quercus macrocarpa*)	2/3, 4, 5, 6
Chestnut oak (*Quercus prinus*)	5, 6
Black oak (*Quercus velutina*)	4, 5, 6
Japanese pagoda tree (*Sophora japonica*)	4, 5, 6
Japanese yew (*Taxus cuspidata*)	3, 4, 5, 6
Littleleaf linden (*Tilia cordata*)	3, 4, 5, 6
Chinese elm/lacebark elm (*Ulmus parvifolia*)	5, 6
Siberian elm (*Ulmus pumila*)	5, 6

It's routine for nurseries to sell trees that are marginally hardy in your USDA hardiness zone. Trees are expensive, so talk to other gardeners if you have any doubts about the ability of a species to survive in your garden. Unless it's something that you feel you absolutely can't live without, planting a tree that will always need extra care or protection is a mistake.

CRY-BEAUTIES: WEEPING DECIDUOUS TREES

Weeping trees are graceful show-stoppers—at least one belongs in every garden. Fortunately for New Englanders, there are plenty to choose from, starting with a Young's weeping birch, which has irregular, almost contorted pendulous branches. Or choose 'Red Jade', a small weeping crabapple that looks as if it's raining fire when its fruits appear in fall. A list of weeping conifers appears elsewhere in this chapter.

'Crimson Queen', 'Waterfall' weeping Japanese maple (*Acer palmatum*)	5/6
Young's weeping birch (*Betula pendula*)	3, 4, 5, 6
Walker cutleaf weeping caragana (*Caragana arborescens*)	2, 3, 4, 5, 6
'Pendula' weeping European hornbeam (*Carpinus betulus*)	4/5, 6
'Pendulum' weeping katsura tree (*Cercidiphyllum magnificum*)	5, 6
'Pendula', 'Purple Fountain' weeping European beech (*Fagus sylvatica*)	5, 6
'Pendulum' weeping golden-chain tree (*Laburnum anagyroides*)	5, 6
'Pendula' weeping European larch (*Larix decidua*)	4, 5, 6
'Red Jade', 'Oekonomierat Echtermeyer', White Cascade', 'Louisa', 'Sinai Fire' weeping crabapple (*Malus*)	4, 5, 6
'Chaparral' white mulberry (*Morus alba*)	4, 5, 6
'Pendula Rosea Plena' Higan cherry (*Prunus subhirtella*)	6
'Prairie Cascade' weeping willow (*Salix babylonica*)	3, 4, 5, 6
'Tristis' golden weeping willow (*Salix babylonica*)	3, 4, 5, 6
'Pendula' weeping pagoda tree (*Sophora japonica*)	5, 6
'Carilon' weeping Japanese snowbell (*Styrax japonicus*)	5, 6
Pendent silver linden (*Tilia petiolaris*)	5, 6

SALT-RESISTANT TREES

While more and more local towns and cities are finding new ways to keep their roads clear of ice, spreading salt in winter is still common practice in our region. Some of New England's most cherished trees—sugar maple, American beech, balsam fir, Canadian hemlock, and white birch—are also among the species most susceptible to salt damage to their roots. If you're planting roadside trees and the salt truck is a regular feature of winter, choose one of species listed below. While their roots aren't impervious to salt, they are more resistant than most.

Yellow birch (*Betula alleghaniensis*)	4, 5, 6
Sweet birch (*Betula lenta*)	3, 4, 5, 6
Russian olive (*Elaeagnus angustifolia*)	3, 4, 5, 6
Honey locust (*Gleditsia triacanthos*)	3, 4, 5, 6
European/common larch (*Larix decidua*)	3, 4, 5, 6
Colorado spruce (*Picea pungens*)	3, 4, 5, 6
Austrian pine (*Pinus nigra*)	4, 5, 6
Silver poplar (*Populus alba*)	3, 4, 5, 6
White oak (*Quercus alba*)	3/4, 5, 6
Red oak (*Quercus rubra*)	3, 4, 5, 6
Black locust (*Robinia pseudoacacia*)	4, 5, 6
White willow (*Salix alba*)	3, 4, 5, 6

LARCH

NATIVE PLANTS

None of the New England states can match California, which has more than 5,500 native species, plants that were growing here before Europeans began to settle the continent. But New England doesn't do too badly. At last count, Connecticut has 1,914 native species, Massachusetts 2,116, New Hampshire 1,686, Rhode Island 1,490, and Vermont 1,723.

These were the flora that the European colonists ohhhhed and ahhhhed over when they first arrived in the seventeenth century. According to their letters home, trees and berries especially impressed them, but "arematicall herbs and plants" also caught their eye. John Josselyn, an early observer, wrote that, "The plants in New England for the variety, number, beauty, style and vertues, may stand in Competition with the plants of any Countrey in Europe." His *New-England Rarities Discovered*, subtitled *Birds, Beasts, Fishes, Serpents, and Plants of that Country*, was published in 1672 and became a minor best-seller.

Of course these same colonists immediately set to work cutting down the native trees and clearing the land of its indigenous shrubs, wildflowers, and grasses. Only in the last few decades has there been wide-spread interest in native plants, in protecting them and bringing them into our gardens. Many of the plants in this chapter are difficult to find. In case you're tempted to cut corners and collect plants that you see growing in the wild, here's a word of caution.

Wildcrafting is the term for gathering plants from the countryside, and it's becoming so popular that many species are being threatened by over-collection. Irresponsible collectors who take plants for profit are only part of the problem. The other part is that familiar feeling that we all have when we see a stand of goldenseal or bloodroot: "Oh, it won't matter if I take just a few." Of course everyone else has the same feeling, so multiply "take a few" by 100 or 1,000 and you see the problem.

The U.S. Fish and Wildlife Service coordinates the list of federally protected plants, but your state may have placed many more plants on a threatened-and-endangered list of its own. Those species should not be collected at all. Check with state authorities—it may be the Department of Agriculture, the Fish and Wildlife Department, or some other agency—for the rules in your area. The New England Wild Flower Society is also a first-rate source of information about plants in the wild.

Here are some other rules of the plant-collecting road:

- Get permission to harvest; most public lands have regulations that you must follow when collecting plant material. Collect away from trails and roads. Be careful, too, that you don't damage the environment.
- Be sure you're collecting what you think you're collecting.
- Collect only from large, healthy stands of plants.
- Never dig more than 5 percent (5 in 100) of any stand of plants.
- Collect seeds or take cuttings rather than dig plants. Collect from several plants and be sure you leave at least three-fourths of the seeds behind.

- Don't harvest more than you can replant or sow.
- If the area is about to be bulldozed for a new road or condominium, feel free to dig everything you can.

Nearly all native plants, including those on "endangered" and "threatened" lists, are available for sale from nurseries. Make sure the company you patronize *propagates* its plants—actually grows them from seeds or cuttings—rather than takes them in the wild, puts them in pots, and calls them "nursery grown." Ask sellers where they get their plants, and don't buy from the unscrupulous. Better still, start from seed, as seeds are now sold for most native plants.

Remember that native species need the same conditions in the garden that they came from in the wild. Plant a clump of Thomas Jefferson's namesake twinleaf, *Jeffersonia diphylla*, which grows naturally in shady woodlands, in a sunny flower bed and you'll have a bare spot to fill in no time at all.

The lists in this chapter are made up primarily of plants that were born and bred in New England. I've also added some native North Americans from outside our region who have made themselves at home here, such as queen-of-the-prairie. Queen-of-the-prairie, pussy toes, Jack-in-the-pulpit, winecups, pink turtlehead, Dutchman's breeches, Virginia bluebells, hairy beardtongue, lady's tresses. The names alone are enough to make you want to plant native species!

NEW ENGLAND WILDFLOWERS: THE PROPAGATOR'S PICKS

Bill Cullina is the plant propagator and nursery manager for Garden in the Woods, the native-plant showcase of the New England Wild Flower Society. He's also the author of *The New England Wild Flower Society Guide to Growing and Propagating Wildflowers* (2000), which details how to start and cultivate New England wildflowers. Cullina began this list with the idea of choosing his favorite dozen natives, but as you see, his list grew. Understandably so—who could resist the striking red-orange flowers of butterfly weed, or golden yellow blooms of the forest dwelling of blue-stemmed goldenrod? Or resist curly-heads, which produces seed heads with golden tails, or umbrella leaf, whose small white flowers are followed by blue fruits that contain purple-crimson seeds?

Don't disregard Cullina's site recommendations in your enthusiasm to add these natives to your garden: Either too much or too little light can be fatal.

Southern monkshood (*Aconitum uncinatum*)	part shade/shade	5, 6
Rue anemone (*Anemonella thalictroides*)	part sun/shade	4, 5, 6
Butterfly weed (*Asclepias tuberosa*)	sun/part sun	3, 4, 5, 6
Prairie aster (*Aster turbinellus*)	sun/part sun	3, 4, 5, 6
White wild indigo (*Baptisia alba*)	sun/light shade	5, 6
Great red paintbrush (*Castilleja miniata*)	sun/part sun	3, 4, 5, 6
Curly heads (*Clematis ochroleuca*)	sun/light shade	5, 6
Bead lily (*Clintonia umbellulata*)	shade	4, 5, 6
Cumberland rosemary (*Conradina verticillata*)	sun/part sun	5, 6
Kentucky lady's slipper (*Cypripedium kentuckiense*)	light shade	4, 5, 6
Showy lady's slipper (*Cypripedium reginae*)	sun/part sun	3, 4, 5, 6
Umbrella plant (*Darmera peltatum*)	part sun/shade	5, 6
Cut-leaf toothwort (*Dentaria laciniata*)	shade	3, 4, 5, 6
Western bleeding heart (*Dicentra formosa*)	sun/shade	4, 5, 6
Umbrella leaf (*Diphylleia cymosa*)	shade	4, 5, 6
Fairy bells (*Disporum maculatum*)	shade	4, 5, 6
Tennessee coneflower (*Echinacea tennesseensis*)	sun	4, 5, 6

White dog-tooth violet (*Erythronium albidum*)	summer shade	3, 4, 5, 6
Spotted Joe-Pye weed (*Eupatorium maculatum*)	sun	3, 4, 5, 6
Flowering spurge (*Euphorbia corollata*)	sun/part sun	3, 4, 5, 6
Fringed gentian (*Gentianopsis crinita*)	sun/part sun	3, 4, 5, 6
Swamp sunflower (*Helianthus angustifolius*)	sun/part sun	5, 6
Round-lobed hepatica (*Hepatica americana*)	part shade/shade	3, 4, 5, 6
Cyclamen-leaved ginger (*Hexastylis minor*)	shade	5, 6
Crested iris (*Iris cristata*)	part sun/shade	4, 5, 6
Wood lily (*Lilium philadelphicum*)	sun/part sun	3, 4, 5, 6
Canada mayflower (*Maianthemum canadense*)	part sun/shade	2/3, 4, 5, 6
Virginia bluebells (*Mertensia virginica*)	part sun/shade	3, 4, 5, 6
Rock beardtongue (*Penstemon rupicola*)	sun	5, 6
Wild blue phlox (*Phlox divaricata*)	part sun/shade	3, 4, 5, 6
Salmon polemonium (*Polemonium carneum*)	part sun	5, 6
Furry Jacob's ladder (*Polemonium reptans* var. *villosum*)	part sun/part shade	3, 4, 5, 6
Broad-leaved mountain mint (*Pycnanthemum muticum*)	sun/part shade	3, 4, 5, 6
Plymouth gentian (*Sabatia kennedyana*)	sun/part sun	4, 5, 6
White trumpet (*Sarracenia leucophylla*)	sun	5, 6
Allegheny skullcap (*Scutellaria serrata*)	sun/shade	4, 5, 6
Oconee bells (*Shortia galacifolia*)	shade	4, 5, 6
Idaho blue-eyed grass (*Sisyrinchium idahoense*)	sun/part shade	4, 5, 6
Blue-stemmed goldenrod (*Solidago caesia*)	sun/shade	3, 4, 5, 6
Indian pink (*Spigelia marilandica*)	part sun/part shade	4, 5, 6
Clumping foamflower (*Tiarella cordifolia* var. *collina*)	sun/shade	4, 5, 6
White trillium (*Trillium grandiflorum*)	part sun/part shade	3, 4, 5, 6
Large-flowered bellwort (*Uvularia grandiflora*)	part sun/shade	3, 4, 5, 6
Appalachian violet (*Viola appalachiensis*)	part sun/shade	4, 5, 6
Bird's-foot violet (*Viola pedata*)	sun/part sun	3, 4, 5, 6
Turkey beard (*Xerophyllum asphodeloides*)	sun/part sun	5, 6

 "The secret to starting wildflowers from seeds is that the seeds should never dry out. When sowing wildflower seeds, scarecrows and cats are a good thing. Another warning: Seeds that are given a deep bed or lots and lots of cover may stay dormant rather than germinate."
Ruth Vroman Gorius, co-owner, Windham Wildflowers, Westminster Station, Vermont

BIGGEST AND BEST TREES OF NEW ENGLAND

New England is famous for its deciduous trees, especially for the autumn colors of many of its native species. Here's a short list of a few of our biggest and best deciduous and evergreen trees. Planting natives is always a good idea. They're well adapted to our region, able to withstand our rugged climate, and resistant to naturally occurring diseases and pests. In addition, they're the food of choice of some of New England's favorite wildlife.

Balsam fir (*Abies balsamea*)	3, 4, 5, 6
Red maple (*Acer rubrum*)	3, 4, 5, 6
Sugar maple (*Acer saccharum*)	3, 4, 5, 6
River birch (*Betula nigra*)	3, 4, 5, 6
Paper birch (*Betula papyrifera*)	2, 3, 4, 5, 6
American hornbeam (*Carpinus caroliniana*)	3, 4, 5, 6

Pagoda dogwood (*Cornus alterniflolia*)	3, 4, 5, 6
Hawthorn (*Crataegus submollis*)	3/4, 5, 6
White ash (*Fraxinus americana*)	4, 5, 6
American hop hornbeam (*Ostrya virginiana*)	3, 4, 5, 6
White spruce (*Picea glauca*)	3, 4, 5, 6
Red pine (*Pinus resinosa*)	3, 4, 5, 6
White pine (*Pinus strobus*)	3, 4, 5, 6
Red oak (*Quercus rubra*)	3, 4, 5, 6
American mountain ash (*Sorbus americana*)	3, 4, 5, 6
American arborvitae (*Thuja occidentalis*)	3, 4, 5, 6
Eastern hemlock (*Tsuga canadensis*)	3, 4, 5, 6

SUGAR MAPLE

FAVORITE NEW ENGLAND SHRUBS

Every one of these flowering shrubs is a native New Englander, a woody plant that is well adapted to our climate. Many are widely available at garden centers and nurseries; others, such as wild lilac and silky dogwood, may be more difficult to find. The nonprofit New England Wild Flower Society, which was begun exactly a century ago, is a good source of information about native plants and sources for obtaining them. The society also owns and operates the Garden in the Woods in Framingham, Massachusetts, where you can see many of the native plants listed in this chapter.

Bottlebrush buckeye (*Aesculus parviflora*)	4, 5, 6
Serviceberry/shadbush (*Amelanchier canadensis*)	3, 4, 5, 6
Bog rosemary (*Andromeda polifolia*)	2, 3, 4, 5, 6
Carolina allspice/sweetshrub (*Calycanthus floridus*)	4, 5, 6
Wild lilac (*Ceanothus ovatus*)	4, 5, 6
Summersweet (*Clethra alnifolia*)	3, 4, 5, 6
Silky dogwood (*Cornus amomum*)	4, 5, 6
Dwarf fothergilla (*Fothergilla gardenii*)	5, 6
Large fothergilla (*Fothergilla major*)	4, 5, 6
Common witch hazel (*Hamamelis virginiana*)	3, 4, 5, 6
Hills of snow (*Hydrangea arborescens*)	3, 4, 5, 6
Oakleaf hydrangea (*Hydrangea quercifolia*)	5, 6
Sheep laurel (*Kalmia angustifolia*)	2, 3, 4, 5, 6
Mountain laurel (*Kalmia latifolia*)	4/5, 6
Beach plum (*Prunus maritima*)	4, 5, 6
Rhododendron (*Rhodondendron canadense*)	3, 4, 5, 6
Great laurel (*Rhododendron maximum*)	4, 5, 6
Pinxterbloom azalea (*Rhododendron periclymenoides*)	5, 6
Pinkshell azalea (*Rhododendron vaseyi*)	4, 5, 6
Swamp azalea (*Rhododendron viscosum*)	4, 5, 6
American cranberry bush (*Viburnum trilobum*)	2/3, 4, 5, 6

"I often see New England gardeners overdoing things when they try to grow native New England plants. The soil is crucial, but if you have reasonably fertile, slightly acid soil to begin with, don't add anything to it. Sometimes amendments, even things like peat moss, do more harm than good."
Mark Stavish, owner, Eastern Plant Specialties, Georgetown, Maine

UNTAMED BEAUTIES: NEW ENGLAND AZALEAS

These native azaleas, a few of the more than 800 species in the *Rhododendron* genus, are guaranteed to enhance your landscape. For the record, all azaleas, which have medium or small leaves, are rhododendrons, but not all rhododendrons are azaleas. Azaleas demand acid soil (5.0 to 5.8 pH) that has good drainage and has been supplemented with plenty of organic matter. To lower your soil's pH, add peat moss or superphosphate to the planting hole, and be sure to mulch your plants with compost or some other water-permeable organic material, such as pine needles.

Sweet azalea (*Rhododendron arborescens*)	white	4/5, 6
Coast azalea (*Rhododendron atlanticum*)	white	5, 6
Flame azalea (*Rhododendron calendulaceum*)	orange, yellow	6
Piedmont azalea (*Rhododendron canescens*)	pale pink	4, 5, 6
Cumberland azalea (*Rhododendron cumberlandense*)	orange-red	5, 6
Oconee azalea (*Rhododendron flammeum*)	red, orange	6
Pinxterbloom azalea (*Rhododendron periclymenoides*)	pink, white	5, 6
Roseshell azalea (*Rhododendron prinophyllum*)	rose-pink	4, 5, 6
Plumleaf azalea (*Rhododendron prunifolium*)	red	6
Pinkshell azalea (*Rhododendron vaseyi*)	pink, white	4, 5, 6
Swamp azalea (*Rhododendron viscosum*)	white	4, 5, 6

NEW ENGLAND'S FLOWERING TREES

If you're weary of seeing nothing but flowering crabs and Bradford pears, consider planting one or two of these native trees. All bear flowers, are wonderfully ornamental, and are appropriate for either large or small yards. A few offer a bonus in addition to their blossoms: Pawpaws produce edible fruits, and sourwood foliage turns brilliant red and purple in autumn.

Downy serviceberry (*Amelanchier arborea*)	4, 5, 6
Pawpaw (*Asimina triloba*)	5, 6
Eastern redbud (*Cercis canadensis*)	4, 5, 6
Fringe tree (*Chionanthus virginicus*)	5, 6
Pagoda dogwood (*Cornus alternifolia*)	3, 4, 5, 6
Franklin tree (*Franklinia alatamaha*)	6
Carolina silverbell (*Halesia carolina*)	5, 6
Sweet bay (*Magnolia virginiana*)	5, 6
Sourwood (*Oxydendrum arboreum*)	4, 5, 6
American mountain ash (*Sorbus americana*)	3, 4, 5, 6

WATER BABIES: WILDFLOWERS FOR WET SITES

The vast number of native New England wildflowers prefer moist conditions—humus-rich soil that retains moisture but drains well. Some natives, however, like their feet damp and are happy growing where drainage is slow and the ground stays wet. Here are some of the best of that group, perennials that thrive in bogs and boglike places. (A list of wildflowers willing to put up with dry conditions appears elsewhere in this chapter.)

Bog arum (*Calla palustris*)	4, 5, 6
Marsh marigold (*Caltha palustris*)	3, 4, 5, 6
Camas lily (*Camassia esculenta*)	5, 6
Pink turtlehead (*Chelone lyonii*)	3, 4, 5, 6

BOG
ARUM

Swamp pink (*Helonias bullata*)	5, 6
Marsh mallow (*Hibiscus moscheutos*)	4/5, 6
Blue flag (*Iris versicolor*)	3, 4, 5, 6
Cardinal flower (*Lobelia cardinalis*)	3, 4, 5, 6
Great lobelia (*Lobelia siphilitica*)	3, 4, 5, 6
Allegheny monkey flower (*Mimulus ringens*)	4, 5, 6
Wild bergamot (*Monarda fistulosa*)	3, 4, 5, 6
False dragonhead (*Physostegia virginiana*)	3, 4, 5, 6
Meadow beauty (*Rhexia virginica*)	5, 6
Pitcher plant (*Sarracenia purpurea*)	2, 3, 4, 5, 6
Skunk cabbage (*Symplocarpus foetidus*)	3, 4, 5, 6
Purple meadow rue (*Thalictrum dasycarpum*)	3, 4, 5, 6
Spreading globeflower (*Trollius laxus*)	4, 5, 6
False hellebore (*Veratrum viride*)	3, 4, 5, 6
Narrow-leaved ironweed (*Vernonia angustifolia*)	4, 5, 6

EPHEMERALS: SPRING WILDFLOWERS

When most New Englanders think of wildflowers, we think of our woodland species, those lovely flowers that bloom for only a short time in spring before the deciduous trees put out their leaves. They tend to be small plants, not more than a foot tall—Canada anemone, Solomon's seal, false Solomon's seal, and large-flowered bellwort are taller—and do best in the moist, humus-rich soil beneath the canopy of a mature woods. They also can be grown in perennial beds and borders, but remember that they need soil that has been amended with plenty of organic matter, such as compost; and once summer comes, these flowers must be shaded from the sun.

Canada anemone (*Anemone canadensis*)	2, 3, 4, 5, 6
Jack-in-the-pulpit (*Arisaema triphyllum*)	3, 4, 5, 6
Wild ginger (*Asarum canadense*)	3, 4, 5, 6
Spring beauty (*Claytonia virginica*)	3, 4, 5, 6
Cut-leaf toothwort (*Dentaria laciniata*)	3, 4, 5, 6
Squirrel corn (*Dicentra canadensis*)	3, 4, 5, 6
Dutchman's breeches (*Dicentra cucullaria*)	3, 4, 5, 6
Trout lily (*Erythronium americanum*)	3, 4, 5, 6
Wild geranium (*Geranium maculatum*)	3, 4, 5, 6
Round-lobed hepatica (*Hepatica americana*)	3, 4, 5, 6
Crested iris (*Iris cristata*)	4, 5, 6
Twinleaf (*Jeffersonia diphylla*)	4, 5, 6
Twinflower (*Linnaea borealis*)	2, 3, 4, 5, 6
Canada mayflower/deerberry (*Maianthemum dilatatum*)	4, 5, 6
Virginia bluebells (*Mertensia virginica*)	4, 5, 6
Partridgeberry (*Mitchella repens*)	3, 4, 5, 6
Creeping phlox (*Phlox stolonifera*)	3, 4, 5, 6
May apple (*Podophyllum peltatum*)	3, 4, 5, 6
Solomon's seal (*Polygonatum biflorum*)	3, 4, 5, 6
Bloodroot (*Sanguinaria canadensis*)	3, 4, 5, 6
False Solomon's seal (*Smilacina racemosa*)	3, 4, 5, 6
Celandine/wood poppy (*Stylophorum diphyllum*)	4, 5, 6
Foamflower (*Tiarella cordifolia*)	3, 4, 5, 6
Trillium (*Trillium* spp.)	3, 4, 5, 6
Large-flowered bellwort/great merrybells (*Uvularia grandiflora*)	3, 4, 5, 6

NATIVE WILDFLOWERS TO START FROM SEED

Most native wildflowers can be started from seeds, although some, such as trillium, take years to bloom for the first time. The wildflowers on this list are among the easiest perennials to start from seed; most will bloom in their first or second year. To see New England wildflowers in their native habitats, visit the Garden in the Woods. Located in Framingham, Massachusetts, the garden is maintained by the nonprofit New England Wild Flower Society, which also sells seeds and plants of native species.

Nodding onion (*Allium cernuum*)	3, 4, 5, 6
Eastern wild columbine (*Aquilegia canadensis*)	3, 4, 5, 6
Jack-in-the-pulpit (*Arisaema triphyllum*)	3, 4, 5, 6
Swamp milkweed (*Asclepias incarnata*)	3, 4, 5, 6
Smooth aster (*Aster laevis*)	3, 4, 5, 6
New England aster (*Aster novae-angliae*)	3, 4, 5, 6
Blue false indigo (*Baptisia australis*)	3/4, 5, 6
Pink turtlehead (*Chelone lyonii*)	3, 4, 5, 6
Purple coneflower (*Echinacea purpurea*)	3, 4, 5, 6
Joe-Pye weed (*Eupatorium fistulosum*)	3, 4, 5, 6
American alumroot/rock geranium (*Heuchera americana*)	4, 5, 6
Marsh mallow (*Hibiscus moscheutos*)	4/5, 6
Twinleaf (*Jeffersonia diphylla*)	4, 5, 6
Cardinal flower (*Lobelia cardinalis*)	3, 4, 5, 6
Great lobelia (*Lobelia siphilitica*)	3, 4, 5, 6
Wild bergamot (*Monarda fistulosa*)	3, 4, 5, 6
Beardtongue (*Penstemon serrulatus*)	5, 6
Foamflower (*Tiarella cordifolia*)	3, 4, 5, 6
Downy yellow violet (*Viola pubescens* var. *eriocarpa*)	4, 5, 6

William Cullina, plant propagator for Garden in the Woods in Farmington, Massachusetts, and author of *The New England Wild Flower Society Guide to Growing and Propagating Wildflowers of the United States and Canada* (2000), recommends that gardeners grow native plants from seed when they can. "Starting from seeds means that the new plants will have the genetic diversity that is lost when plants are propagated vegetatively, and they are often much easier for the home gardener to grow as well. If you harvest your own seeds, be sure to collect from plants that are healthy and vigorous, two good signs that they are well adapted to your region's conditions. Avoid collecting seeds from wild plants without permission and never collect the seed of rare/endangered species. We sow most of our seeds in November and put the seed flats in outdoor coldframes for the winter. I find that the seed germinates more uniformly and the plants need less care than if I raised them in the greenhouse."

AMERICAN GOLD: DAISIES

Daisies and daisylike flowers are composites, which means that each "flower" is actually many flowers. A single bloom is made up of scores of tiny tubular florets, or disk flowers, which are surrounded by strap-shaped florets, the so-called petals. Give your love a daisy, and you're giving a bouquet. All the daisies and daisylike perennial flowers listed below are American natives, pure American gold, both yellow and platinum white, with dark centers. (For daisies of different colors, see the list in "Daisies Pied: Colorful Choices for New England Gardens.")

SNEEZEWEED	Big-flower coreopsis (*Coreopsis grandiflora*)	3/4, 5, 6
	Lanceleaf coreopsis (*Coreopsis lanceolata*)	3, 4, 5, 6
	Maryland golden aster (*Coreopsis mariana*)	4, 5, 6
	Tall tickseed (*Coreopsis tripteris*)	3, 4, 5, 6
	Threadleaf coreopsis (*Coreopsis verticillata*)	3, 4, 5, 6
	Yellow coneflower (*Echinacea paradoxa*)	4, 5, 6
	Blanket flower (*Gaillardia aristata*)	3, 4, 5, 6
	Sneezeweed (*Helenium autumnale*)	3, 4, 5, 6
	Woodland sunflower (*Helianthus divaricatus*)	3, 4, 5, 6
	Swamp sunflower (*Helianthus giganteus*)	3, 4, 5, 6
	Jerusalem artichoke (*Helianthus tuberosus*)	3, 4, 5, 6
	Ox-eye (*Heliopsis helianthoides*)	3, 4, 5, 6
	Hairy golden aster (*Heterotheca villosa*)	3, 4, 5, 6
	'Goldsturm' (*Rudbeckia fulgida* var. *sullivantii*)	3, 4, 5, 6
	Large black-eyed Susan (*Rudbeckia grandiflora*)	5, 6
	Common black-eyed Susan (*Rudbeckia hirta* var. *pulcherrima*)	3, 4, 5, 6
	Cutleaf coneflower (*Rudbeckia laciniata*)	3, 4, 5, 6
	Brown-eyed Susan (*Rudbeckia triloba*)	3, 4, 5, 6
	Compass plant (*Silphium laciniatum*)	3, 4, 5, 6
	Mule's ears (*Wyethia amplexicaulis*)	3, 4, 5, 6

DAISIES PIED: COLORFUL CHOICES FOR NEW ENGLAND GARDENS

William Wordsworth mentioned daisies again and again in his poetry, "bright flowers, whose home is everywhere." But Wordsworth's daisy, his "poet's darling," was the English daisy, *Bellis perennis*, which grows far better in England than in New England. While our most familiar native daisies are yellow or white (see the list called "American Gold: Daisies"), there are plenty of daisies or daisylike flowers of different hues. Some have so many ray florets, or "petals," that plucking them one by one may take several hours. Nevertheless, these American beauties can still reveal if he or she loves you.

The flowers in this list are perennial, except for rosering blanket flower (*Gaillardia pulchella*), which is an annual but self-sows easily in sandy soils.

Prairie heart-leaved aster (*Aster azureus*)	blue	3, 4, 5, 6
Blue wood aster (*Aster cordifolius*)	violet	3, 4, 5, 6
Smooth aster (*Aster laevis*)	violet	3, 4, 5, 6
Big-leaf aster (*Aster macrophyllus*)	pale violet	3, 4, 5, 6
New England aster (*Aster novae-angliae*)	violet, purple, or rose	3, 4, 5, 6
New York aster (*Aster novae-belgii*)	violet, purple, rose, or white	3, 4, 5, 6
Lobed tickseed (*Coreopsis auriculata*)	orange	4, 5, 6
Pink coreopsis (*Coreopsis rosea*)	pink	4, 5, 6
Appalachian coneflower (*Echinacea laevigata*)	rose	5, 6
Purple coneflower (*Echinacea purpurea*)	dark rose	3, 4, 5, 6
Tennessee coneflower (*Echinacea tennesseensis*)	rose	4, 5, 6
Common fleabane (*Erigeron philadelphicus*)	pale red-purple	2/3, 4, 5, 6

Robin's plantain (*Erigeron pulchellus*)	magenta	3/4, 5, 6
Blanket flower (*Gaillardia aristata*)	red and yellow	3, 4, 5, 6
Rosering blanket flower (*Gaillardia pulchella*)	purple/burgundy and yellow	

WILDFLOWERS FOR DRY, SUNNY SITES

Not all wildflowers grow in the deep, damp woods, as this list of perennials for sunny, dry sites shows. The plant recommendations, many of which would be ideal for planting in a meadow or field, come from experts at the Garden in the Woods in Framingham, Massachusetts, as well as from members of the New England Wild Flower Society, which has chapters throughout our region and is our very best source of information about native plants.

Nodding onion (*Allium cernuum*)	3, 4, 5, 6
Common mildweed (*Asclepias syriaca*)	3, 4, 5, 6
Butterfly weed (*Asclepias tuberosa*)	3, 4, 5, 6
Eastern silvery aster (*Aster concolor*)	5, 6
Ground plum (*Astragalus crassicarpus*)	4, 5, 6
Poppy mallow/winecups (*Callirhoe involucrata*)	4, 5, 6
Bluebell/harebell (*Campanula rotundifolia*)	3, 4, 5, 6
Lanceleaf coreopsis (*Coreopsis lanceolata*)	3, 4, 5, 6
Threadleaf coreopsis (*Coreposis verticillata*)	3, 4, 5, 6
Small coneflower (*Echinacea angustifolia*)	3, 4, 5, 6
Purple coneflower (*Echinacea purpurea*)	3, 4, 5, 6
Flowering spurge (*Euphorbia corollata*)	3, 4, 5, 6
Blanket flower (*Gaillardia pulchella*)	4, 5, 6
Ox-eye (*Heliopsis helianthoides*)	3, 4, 5, 6
Hairy golden aster (*Heterotheca villosa*)	3, 4, 5, 6
New England blazing star (*Liatris scariosa* var. *novae-angliae*)	4, 5, 6
Perennial flax (*Linum perenne* var. *lewisii*)	4, 5, 6
Sundial lupine (*Lupinus perennis*)	4, 5, 6
Spotted horsemint (*Monarda punctata*)	4, 5, 6
Ozark sundrops (*Oenothera macrocarpa*)	4, 5, 6
Hairy beardtongue (*Penstemon hirsutus*)	4, 5, 6
Moss phlox (*Phlox subulata*)	3, 4, 5, 6
Black-eyed Susan (*Rudbeckia fulgida* var. *sullivantii*)	3, 4, 5, 6
Thin-leaf coneflower (*Rudbeckia triloba*)	4, 5, 6
Wild petunia (*Ruellia humilis*)	4, 5, 6
Blue sage (*Salvia azurea*)	4, 5, 6
Compass plant (*Silphium laciniatum*)	3, 4, 5, 6
Gray goldenrod (*Solidago nemoralis*)	3, 4, 5, 6
Stiff goldenrod (*Solidago rigida*)	3, 4, 5, 6
Showy goldenrod (*Solidago speciosa*)	3, 4, 5, 6
Rose verbena (*Verbena canadensis*)	5, 6
Ironweed (*Vernonia lettermannii*)	6
Adam's needle (*Yucca filamentosa*)	4, 5, 6

"Native plants are ideal for country gardens like mine. The deer ate two dozen hostas to the ground a month after I planted them, but milkweeds, asters, may apples, columbines, coneflowers, wild geraniums, false Solomon's seal, goldenrods, and lupines all seem to be deer-proof."
Carol Haddock, owner, Wool Hollow Farm, Jericho, Vermont

FLOODED WITH FERNS

New England is home to an enormous number of fern species, more than almost any other temperate region. Ferns, remember, are flowerless plants that produce spores rather than fruits and seeds, and fronds rather than leaves. All the native ferns on this list should thrive in your garden with little care as long as you provide humus-rich soil and the proper amount of light and moisture. Species requiring moist soil are marked with an asterisk (*).

Maidenhair fern (*Adiantum pedatum*)*	shade	2, 3, 4, 5, 6
Lady fern (*Athyrium filix-femina*)	shade	2, 3, 4, 5, 6
Wooly lip fern (*Cheilanthes lanosa*)	sun/partial shade	5, 6
Fragile bladder fern (*Cystopteris fragilis*)	shade	2, 3, 4, 5, 6
Hay-scented fern (*Dennstaedtia punctilobula*)	sun/partial shade	3, 4, 5, 6
Glade fern (*Diplazium pycnocarpon*)	shade	4, 5, 6
Goldie's wood fern (*Dryopteris goldiana*)*	partial/full shade	3, 4, 5, 6
Marginal shield fern (*Dryopteris marginalis*)*	shade	2, 3, 4, 5, 6
Oak fern (*Gymnocarpium dryopteris*)*	shade	2, 3, 4, 5, 6
Ostrich fern (*Matteuccia struthiopteris*)	sun/partial shade	2, 3, 4, 5, 6
Sensitive fern (*Onoclea sensibilis*)*	sun/shade	2, 3, 4, 5, 6
Cinnamon fern (*Osmunda cinnamomea*)*	shade/partial sun	2, 3, 4, 5, 6
Interrupted fern (*Osmunda claytoniana*)*	shade/partial sun	2, 3, 4, 5, 6
Royal fern (*Osmunda regalis*)*	shade/partial sun	2, 3, 4, 5, 6
Christmas fern (*Polystichum acrostichoeids*)*	shade	3, 4, 5, 6
New York fern (*Thelypteris noveboracensis*)*	sun/partial shade	4, 5, 6
Blunt-lobed woodsia (*Woodsia obtusa*)	shade	3, 4, 5, 6

LOVERS OF THE GARISH SUN: WILDFLOWERS FOR BRIGHT LIGHT

Not all New England wildflowers are timid woodland species, shade seekers that depend on the forest canopy to protect them from the garish sun. This list of light-lovers are happiest when nothing is blocking their view of Apollo. While many will put up with dappled shade at midday, give these natives full sun and moist, humus-rich soil, and they will flower best.

Butterfly weed (*Asclepias tuberosa*)	3, 4, 5, 6
New England aster (*Aster novae-angliae*)	3, 4, 5, 6
White wild indigo (*Baptisia alba*)	5, 6
Blue false indigo (*Baptisia australis*)	3/4, 5, 6
Yellow wild indigo (*Baptisia shaerocarpa*)	4, 5, 6
Boltonia (*Boltonia asteroides*)	3, 4, 5, 6
Poppy mallow/winecups (*Callirhoe involucrata*)	4, 5, 6
Pink tickseed (*Coreopsis rosea*)	4, 5, 6
Small coneflower (*Echinacea angustifolia*)	3, 4, 5, 6
Pale purple coneflower (*Echinacea pallida*)	4, 5, 6
Purple coneflower (*Echinacea purpurea*)	3, 4, 5, 6
Joe-Pye weed (*Eupatorium fistulosum*)	3, 4, 5, 6
Flowering spurge (*Euphorbia corollata*)	3, 4, 5, 6
White gaura (*Gaura lindheimeri*)	5, 6
Prairie smoke (*Geum triflorum*)	2/3, 4, 5, 6
Swamp sunflower (*Helianthus angustifolius*)	5, 6
Willow-leaf sunflower (*Helianthus salicifolius*)	4, 5, 6

Blazing star/rough gayfeather (*Liatris aspera*)	3, 4, 5, 6
Spike gayfeather (*Liatris spicata*)	3, 4, 5, 6
Sundial lupine (*Lupinus perennis*)	4, 5, 6
Spotted horsemint (*Monarda punctata*)	4, 5, 6
False dragonhead (*Physostegia virginiana*)	3, 4, 5, 6
Black-eyed Susan (*Rudbeckia fulgida* var. *sullivantii*)	3, 4, 5, 6
Thin-leaf coneflower (*Rudbeckia triloba*)	4, 5, 6
Wild petunia (*Ruellia humilis*)	4, 5, 6
Stiff goldenrod (*Solidago rigida*)	3, 4, 5, 6
Rough-stem goldenrod (*Solidago rugosa*)	4, 5, 6
Seaside goldenrod (*Solidago sempervirens*)	4, 5, 6
Showy goldenrod (*Solidago speciosa*)	3, 4, 5, 6
Stokes' aster (*Stokesia laevis*)	5, 6
Carolina bush pea (*Thermopsis villosa*)	3, 4, 5, 6
Tall ironweed (*Vernonia altissima*)	4, 5, 6
Culver's root (*Veronicastrum virginicum*)	3, 4, 5, 6
Adam's needle (*Yucca filamentosa*)	4, 5, 6

LEAVES OF ORNAMENTAL GRASS

Many of the cultivated ornamental grasses that are so popular today are not native New Englanders, but there are native North American grasses that do well in our gardens. Stem and plume colors vary, so you may want to do a little research before you plant. Spring is the best time to plant grasses. Early spring is also the best time to cut back the old shoots, which are wonderfully decorative in the winter landscape.

Grasses that spread by way of above-ground stems called stolons or underground stems called rhizomes can be invasive, so think twice before you introduce them into your perennial border. Potentially invasive species in this list are ribbon grass (*Phalaris arundinacea* var. *picta*) and prairie cord grass (*Spartina pectinata*).

Elliott's broom sedge (*Andropogon elliottii*)	5, 6
Big bluestem (*Andropogon gerardii*)	4, 5, 6
Split-beard broomsedge (*Andropogon ternarius*)	5/6
Broomsedge (*Andropogon virginicus*)	3, 4, 5, 6
Northern sea oats (*Chasmanthium latifolium*)	5, 6
Purple love grass (*Eragrostis spectabilis*)	5, 6
Coastal switch grass (*Panicum amarum*)	5, 6
Deer tongue grass (*Panicum clandestinum*)	4, 5, 6
Switch grass (*Panicum virgatum*)	5, 6
Ribbon grass (*Phalaris arundinacea* var. *picta*)	4, 5, 6
Little bluestem (*Schizachyrium scoparium*)	3, 4, 5, 6
Indian grass (*Sorghastrum nutans*)	4, 5, 6
Prairie cord grass (*Spartina pectinata*)	4, 5, 6
Purpletop (*Tridens flavus*)	5, 6

NATIVE FERNS HARDY TO ZONE 2

Gardeners in Zone 2 can get discouraged—there are so many choice plants that simply can't survive winters where the mercury dips as low as 50 degrees below zero. One bright note is that this group of native ferns can take the rugged weather that Zone 2 gardens and gardeners endure: long, cold winters and, fortunately for the ferns, a reliable snowcover. Interestingly, the fragile-looking maidenhair fern is one of the species that can take these near-arctic conditions. New England gardeners in warmer zones also can succeed with these cold-hardy plants.

Maidenhair fern (*Adiantum pedatum*)
Alpine lady fern (*Athyrium alpestre*)
Fragile bladder fern (*Cystopteris fragilis*)
Mountain wood fern (*Dryopteris campyloptera*)
Marginal shield fern (*Dryopteris marginalis*)
Oak fern (*Gymnocarpium dryopteris*)
Ostrich fern (*Matteuccia struthiopteris*)
Sensitive fern (*Onoclea sensibilis*)
Cinnamon fern (*Osmunda cinnamomea*)
Interrupted fern (*Osmunda claytoniana*)
Royal fern (*Osmunda regalis*)

Susan Romanoff, an enthusiastic gardener who lives in Huntington, Vermont, is an art director for Gardener's Supply, the Burlington, Vermont, horticultural tool and equipment company. Her country garden is rich with native ferns, which "help soften the transition between the borders and the woods. I like to mix them with pulmonaria, which deer don't eat. Ferns transplant well and require absolutely no care. They're ideal garden plants!"

TOUCH NOT, TAKE NOT—AND PROBABLY BUY NOT!

The increased demand for native plants—by home gardeners and commercial traders—has placed many North American species in peril. If you see native wildflowers for sale at a nursery or in a mail-order catalog, make sure to ask if they were nursery propagated. "Nursery propagated" means that they were started from seed or from cuttings, divisions, or some other vegetative technique by the seller or another grower. The term "nursery grown" is not the same as nursery propagated, and is often used by unethical firms. The native species listed below, many of which are very slow-growing, may be wild-collected by commercial growers who are unwilling to spend the several years required to produce sellable plants. These native plants should not be purchased unless the seller can show that they didn't come from the wild. Remember, too, if you are walking in the New England woods and come across one of the species in this list, don't dig it up.

Jack-in-the-pulpit (*Arisaema triphyllum*)	3, 4, 5, 6
Blue cohosh (*Caulophyllum thalictroides*)	3, 4, 5, 6
Lady's slipper (*Cypripedium* spp.)	3, 4, 5, 6
Dutchman's breeches (*Dicentra cucullaria*)	3, 4, 5, 6
Trout lily (*Erythronium americanum*)	3, 4, 5, 6
Wandflower (*Galax urceolata*)	4/5, 6
Fringed orchid (*Habenaria* spp.)	5, 6
May apple (*Podophyllum peltatum*)	3, 4, 5, 6
Solomon's seal (*Polygonatum* spp.)	3, 4, 5, 6
Bloodroot (*Sanquinaria canadensis*)	3, 4, 5, 6
Pitcher plant (*Sarracenia purpurea*)	2, 3, 4, 5, 6
Lady's tresses (*Spiranthes* spp.)	3, 4, 5, 6
Trillium (*Trillium* spp.)	3, 4, 5, 6

COVERING SUNNY GROUND

Not all these ground covers grow as densely as vinca or spread as quickly as ajuga—or stay green twelve months a year—but they're all trouble-free natives, well-adapted for the conditions offered by New England gardens. Native plants are famous for not needing much help from the gardener, but every plant on this list will benefit from soil that has been amended with generous amounts of humus or other decayed organic material. A few ferns, such as sweet fern, *Comptonia peregrina*, also make good ground covers for sunny locations (a list of native ferns appears elsewhere in this chapter).

Nodding onion (*Allium cernuum*)	3, 4, 5, 6
Pussy toes (*Antennaria rosea*)	3, 4, 5, 6
Bearberry (*Arctostaphylos uva-ursi*)	2, 3, 4, 5, 6
Showy aster (*Aster spectabilis*)	3, 4, 5, 6
Green and gold (*Chrysogonum virginianum*)	5/6
Sweet fern (*Comptonia peregrina*)	4, 5, 6
Threadleaf coreopsis (*Coreopsis verticillata*)	3, 4, 5, 6
Wild bleeding heart (*Dicentra eximia*)	3/4, 5, 6
Wintergreen (*Gaultheria procumbens*)	3, 4, 5, 6
American alumroot/rock geranium (*Heuchera americana*)	4, 5, 6
Foxglove penstemon (*Penstemon digitalis*)	3, 4, 5, 6
Sand phlox (*Phlox bifida*)	4, 5, 6
Creeping phlox (*Phlox stolonifera*)	3, 4, 5, 6
Moss phlox (*Phlox subulata*)	3, 4, 5, 6
Three-toothed cinquefoil (*Potentilla tridentata*)	3, 4, 5, 6
Wild stonecrop (*Sedum ternatum*)	4, 5, 6

> The late Senator George Aiken, who lived in Putney, Vermont, was one of the early champions of both protecting and growing wildflowers. In his groundbreaking *Pioneering with Wildflowers* (1933), he wrote that he wanted people to enjoy and love native New England wildflowers, but that "the sad part of the story is that the loveliest wildflowers are being almost exterminated in the most accessible places."

COVERING SHADY GROUND

As with native ground covers for sun, not all these ground covers grow as densely as English ivy, or spread as quickly as ajuga, or stay green throughout the year. They are all trouble-free natives, however, and will thrive in New England gardens. Like their sun-loving friends, these species don't need much help from the gardener but will benefit from soil that has been amended with generous amounts of humus or other decayed organic material. Ferns also make fine ground covers in shaded locations (a separate list of native ferns appears elsewhere in this chapter).

WILD GINGER

Wood anemone (*Anemone quinquefolia*)	3, 4, 5, 6
Heartleaf wild ginger (*Asarum arifolium*)	4, 5, 6
Wild ginger (*Asarum canadense*)	3, 4, 5, 6
White wood aster (*Aster divaricatus*)	3, 4, 5, 6
Plantain sedge (*Carex plantaginea*)	4, 5, 6
Goldenstar (*Chyrysogonum virginianum*)	5, 6
Bunchberry (*Cornus canadensis*)	2, 3, 4, 5, 6

Wild bleeding heart (*Dicentra eximia*)	3/4, 5, 6
Wintergreen (*Gaultheria procumbens*)	3, 4, 5, 6
Dwarf crested iris (*Iris cristata*)	4, 5, 6
Canada mayflower (*Maianthemum canadense*)	2/3, 4, 5, 6
Partridgeberry (*Mitchella repens*)	3, 4, 5, 6
Allegheny spurge (*Pachysandra procumbens*)	4, 5, 6
Creeping phlox (*Phlox stolonifera*)	3, 4, 5, 6
May apple (*Podophyllum peltatum*)	3, 4, 5, 6
Bloodroot (*Sanguinaria canadensis*)	3, 4, 5, 6
False Solomon's seal (*Smilacina racemosa*)	3, 4, 5, 6
Foamflower (*Tiarella cordifolia*)	3, 4, 5, 6

NATIVE PLANTS FOR A MEADOW

Meadow gardens aren't as easy as the garden articles and seed vendors would have you believe—you can't just dump a can of seeds on the ground and walk away. To keep weeds from overtaking your flowers, you'll need to clear and cultivate the soil. But if you have a sunny field or even a sunny bed that needs flowers, try some of these light-loving natives. You'll want to add some native grasses, too (see the "Leaves of Ornamental Grass" list).

Nodding onion (*Allium cernuum*)	3, 4, 5, 6
Showy milkweed (*Asclepias speciosa*)	2, 3, 4, 5, 6
Butterfly weed (*Asclepias tuberosa*)	3, 4, 5, 6
Calico aster (*Aster lateriflorus*)	4, 5, 6
New England aster (*Aster novae-angliae*)	3, 4, 5, 6
Blue false indigo (*Baptisia australis*)	3/4, 5, 6
Boltonia (*Boltonia asteroides*)	3, 4, 5, 6
Maryland golden aster (*Chrysopsis mariana*)	4, 5, 6
Big-flower coreopsis (*Coreopsis grandiflora*)	3/4, 5, 6
Threadleaf coreopsis (*Coreopsis verticillata*)	3, 4, 5, 6
Coneflower (*Echinacea* spp.)	3, 4, 5, 6
Rattlesnake master (*Eryngium yuccifolium*)	4, 5, 6
Joe-Pye weed (*Eupatorium fistulosum*)	3, 4, 5, 6
Flowering spurge (*Euphorbia corollata*)	3, 4, 5, 6
Ox-eye (*Heliopsis helianthoides*)	3, 4, 5, 6
Blazing star/rough gayfeather (*Liatris aspera*)	3, 4, 5, 6
Scaly blazing star (*Liatris squarrosa*)	4, 5, 6
Foxglove penstemon (*Penstemon digitalis*)	3, 4, 5, 6
Hairy beardtongue (*Penstemon hirsutus*)	4, 5, 6
Black-eyed Susan (*Rudbeckia hirta*)	2, 3, 4, 5, 6
Early goldenrod (*Solidago juncea*)	3, 4, 5, 6
Rough-stem goldenrod (*Solidago rugosa*)	4, 5, 6
Showy goldenrod (*Solidago speciosa*)	3, 4, 5, 6
New York ironweed (*Vernonia noveboracensis*)	4, 5, 6
Culver's root (*Veronicastrum virginicum*)	3, 4, 5, 6

NATIVE PLANTS THAT THRIVE IN PERENNIAL BEDS AND BORDERS

If their soil, sun, and moisture requirements are met, most wildflowers are good neighbors in an ornamental border or bed. Still, some species are more equal than others in the cultivated garden. A few natives, such as lady's slipper species, are so particular that they rarely do well when grown in perennial beds and borders. Here are recommendations from members of the New England Wild Flower Society and other wildflower devotees for native plants that can hold their own and thrive among the hybrids and cultivars that we commonly use to fill our gardens.

Eastern wild columbine (*Aquilegia canadensis*)	sun/partial shade	3, 4, 5, 6
Goatsbeard (*Aruncus dioicus*)	sun/partial shade	3/4, 5, 6
Smooth aster (*Aster laevis*)	sun	3, 4, 5, 6
New England aster (*Aster novae-angliae*)	sun	3, 4, 5, 6
False goatsbeard (*Astilbe biternata*)	shade	4, 5, 6
Boltonia (*Boltonia asteroides*)	sun	3, 4, 5, 6
Black snakeroot (*Cimicifuga racemosa*)	sun/partial shade	3, 4, 5, 6
Purple coneflower (*Echinacea purpurea*)	sun	3, 4, 5, 6
Joe-Pye weed (*Eupatorium fistulosum*)	sun	3, 4, 5, 6
Marsh mallow (*Hibiscus moscheutos*)	sun	4/5, 6
Turk's-cap lily (*Lilium superbum*)	sun/partial shade	4, 5, 6
Cardinal flower (*Lobelia cardinalis*)	sun/partial shade	3, 4, 5, 6
Bee balm (*Monarda didyma*)	sun/partial shade	3, 4, 5, 6
Sundrops (*Oenothera fruticosa*)	sun	4, 5, 6
Ozark sundrops (*Oenothera macrocarpa*)	sun	4, 5, 6
Wild sweet William (*Phlox maculata*)	sun/partial shade	3, 4, 5, 6
Foamflower (*Tiarella cordifolia*)	shade	3, 4, 5, 6
Spiderwort (*Tradescantia subaspera*)	sun	4, 5, 6
Tall ironweed (*Vernonia altissima*)	sun	4, 5, 6
Culver's root (*Veronicastrum virginicum*)	sun	3, 4, 5, 6

"If you want to begin a wildflower garden, use plants that come from similar natural settings. Trying to mix prairie plants that need sun and woodland species that need partial or full shade in the same bed is a sure prescription for failure."
Jake Chapline, freelance writer and former editor, *Country Journal*, Durham, New Hampshire

VEGETABLES, HERBS, AND FRUITS

Seeds were among the most precious goods that the first colonists brought to New England. Those practical souls carried a few of their favorite flowers, but most of their seeds were "for meate or medicine," to borrow the subtitle of the first of Ann Leighton's three volumes on the history of American gardens. There were herbs for healing (elecampane for lung problems, fever-few for fevers, sage to ease childbirth, and garlic to cure everything from worms to consumption) and vegetables for the table.

Before John Winthrop Jr. sailed to join his father in the Massachusetts Bay Colony in July, 1631, he placed a large order with the English seed merchant Robert Hill, "dwelling at the three Angellis in lumber streete." Winthrop's list was overwhelmingly practical, mostly vegetables. He ordered pumpkins, onions, radishes, parsnips, lettuce, and cabbage seeds in the greatest amounts; cauliflower seeds were the most expensive item on his £160 tab. Herbs, both medicinal and culinary, were well represented too, everything from angelica and basil to savory and thyme.

While the colonists were awed by the fruits they found in the new world, especially the many berries, they carried seeds of their favorite apples, cherries, peaches, pears, and plums. The technique of grafting was known, but most fruits were commonly grown from seed until well into the nineteenth century. By 1642, George Fenwick of Saybrook, Connecticut, reported that he was "prettie well storred with chirrie & peach trees."

Although ornamental plants now dominate New England gardens, we Yankees have never stopped growing vegetables, herbs, and fruits. Our ancestors were responsible for many of the culti-vars that we tend today. 'Molasses Face' beans came from Maine, 'Low's Champion' from the Boston seed company Aaron Low, and 'Vermont Cranberry' from Vermont. 'King of the Garden' lima bean was developed in a New Haven, Connecticut, garden. 'Cannonball' cabbage originated in Marblehead, Massachusetts, in 1868. Livermore, Maine, is the home of 'Boothby's Blond' cucumber, and Massachusetts the starting place of 'Boston Marrow' and a tribe of 'Hubbard' squashes, as well as a yellow tomato named 'Yellow Peach.' Moreover, 'Baldwin', 'Black Gilliflower', 'Blue Permain', 'Hubbard Nonesuch', 'Rhode Island Greening', 'Twenty Ounce', and 'Westfield Seek-No-Further' are just a sample of apples that got their start in New England. The list could go on and on.

In addition to regional seed companies and nurseries that have an interest in old cultivars, the best sources of locally adapted fruits and vegetables are the nonprofit Seed Savers Exchange and the Flower and Herb Exchange. Another source of information, seeds, and plants is the North American Fruit Explorers (NAFEX). For the small membership fees that these organizations request, you receive their publications and access to tens of thousands of vegetables, herbs, and fruits that are nearly impossible to obtain elsewhere. For more information, see "The Mail-Order Garden" in this book.

Only the most long-season, heat-demanding edibles are problematic in New England gardens, and plant breeders are busy trying to solve even those problems. More short-season cultivars are introduced each year—tomatoes that ripen in sixty-five days instead of eighty-five, and corn, chiles, and eggplants that can ripen in cool weather.

In the meantime, consider some of our home-grown cultivars, which are adapted to New England's conditions. You'll find plenty of favorite sons and daughters to choose from, such as the new, early yellow tomato 'Taxi', bred by Johnny's Selected Seeds in Albion, Maine, or the old-timer 'Connecticut Field' pumpkin. Probably cultivated by Native Americans before the colonists "discovered" it, 'Connecticut Field' is still responsible for more New England Jack-o'-lanterns than any other cultivar.

BARS FARM'S BEST TOMATOES, SQUASH, AND PEPPERS

The Bars Farm, located outside historic Deerfield, Massachusetts, has been in Mary Marsh's family since 1820. A well-known market gardener in the area, Marsh and her family grow a wide range of vegetables as well as several dozen different species of flowers for cutting. She buys most of her seeds from Johnny's Selected Seeds, a New England neighbor located in Albion, Maine. These are just a handful of her favorite vegetables cultivars, each chosen from the hundreds she's tried over the years in her Zone 5 garden. For a quick salad, Marsh recommends a mix of 'Sierra' summer crisp lettuce, a red cultivar, and slices of 'Little-Leaf Pickler' cucumber. Marsh plants by the acre, but she says that these cultivars "do fine in home gardens, too."

Tomatoes (*Lycopersicon esculentum*)
'French Carmelo'	red standard
'Majesty'	red standard
'Matt's Wild Cherry'	red cherry
'Sun Gold'	tangerine-orange cherry
'Sunbeam'	red standard

Winter Squash (*Cucurbita*)
'Buttercup'	buttercup type
'Delicata'	sweet potato type
'Sugar Loaf'	sweet potato type
'Sweet Dumpling'	vegetable gourd type

Sweet Peppers (*Capsicum annuum*)
'Islander' (purple)	purple
'King Arthur' (red)	red
'Orobell' (yellow)	yellow
'Valencia' (red)	orange

Hot Peppers (*Capsicum annuum*)
'Giant Jalepeño'	very hot
'Serrano'	very hot
'Super Chile'	very hot
'Surefire'	moderately hot

"Floating row covers are a wonderful invention. They're inexpensive and easy to put on and take off. In addition to giving young plants protection from the cold, they protect vegetables from insect damage."
Susan Romanoff, Huntington, Vermont

YOU SAY TUH-MAY-TOE, I SAY TUH-MAH-TOE

Or you could say love apple, wolf peach, or Moor's apple. It's all the same vegetable (oops, fruit), *Lycopersicon esculentum*—North America's most popular edible garden crop. Tomato breeders have worked overtime to produce more than 25,000 different cultivars, an astonishing collection that includes the good, the bad, and the ugly. Of that 25,000, about 1,500 are available to home gardeners, although not all are easy to find. New England tomato growers, especially those in northern locations, should look for cultivars that mature quickly. This list is a place to begin.

'Bellstar'	plum/paste
'Big Beef'	beefsteak
'Celebrity'	salad
'Daybreak'	large salad
'Early Cascade'	cherry
'Early Girl'	salad
'Evergreen'	green heirloom salad
'First Lady'	salad
'German'	heirloom beefsteak
'Gold Nugget'	yellow cherry
'Johnny's 361'	beefsteak
'Juliet'	plum/paste
'Lemon Boy'	yellow salad
'Principe Borghese'	heirloom plum/paste
'Red Sun'	large salad
'Roma VF'	plum/paste
'Ruby Cluster'	cherry
'Sub-Arctic Maxi'	salad for extremely cold regions
'Sun Gold'	orange cherry
'Sweet Million'	cherry
'Taxi'	yellow
'Tuscany'	plum/paste
'Wonder Light'	yellow heirloom plum/salad

SUGARY ENHANCED CORNS

Sugary enhanced (SE) corns, hybrids of *Zea mays*, are among the glories of vegetable breeding. Like supersweet cultivars, SE corns are sweeter than traditional sweet corns and remain sweet hours, even days, after being harvested. But better than supersweet types, SE corns germinate more reliably in cold soil and don't require isolation from other corns to avoid cross pollination.

SE corns were first developed in 1980, and there are now well over 100 cultivars. Among the best and most reliable are the

CORN

names on this list. The estimated number of days from germination to harvest is indicated. Gardeners in northern New England will want to grow cultivars that mature in the fewest days.

	Kernel color	Days to harvest
'Advantage'	yellow	65 days
'Bodacious'	yellow	85 days
'First Choice'	bicolor	65 days
'Frosty'	white	70 days
'King Arthur'	yellow	72 days
'Lancelot'	bicolor	80 days
'Miracle'	yellow	78 days
'Platinum Lady'	white	80 days
'Quickie'	bicolor	65 days
'Summer Delicious'	bicolor	90 days
'Trinity'	bicolor	70 days

OUT OF THE PAST: HEIRLOOM VEGETABLES

The Seed Savers Exchange in Decorah, Iowa, is now world famous for preserving cultivars of vegetables and other plants our great-grandparents grew. Tom Stearns is on a similar mission. Most of the seeds he sells have a long history in our region, and all are grown organically on Stearns's Wolcott, Vermont, farm. Every seed, he says, "has been planted, tended, and harvested by hand." Here are recommendations from his High Mowing Organic Seed Farm catalog for vegetables that will thrive in New England gardens—and also would have been at home in a New England garden 100 years ago.

'Evergreen Hardy' bunching onion (*Allium fistulosum*)
'Boston Marrow' winter squash (*Cucurbita maxima*)
'Long Pie' pumpkin (*Cucurbita pepo*)
'Red Deer Tongue' lettuce (*Lactuca sativa*)
'Aunt Mary's Paste' tomato (*Lycopersicon esculentum*)
'Yellow Perfection' tomato (*Lycopersicon esculentum*)
'Low's Champion' dry bean (*Phaseolus vulgaris*)
'True Red Cranberry' pole bean (*Phaseolus vulgaris*)
'Boston Beauty' dry bean (*Phaseolus vulgaris*)
'Dark Green Perfection' pea (*Pisum sativum* ssp. *sativum*)
'French Breakfast' radish (*Raphanus sativus*)
'Roy's Calais' flint corn (*Zea mays*)
'Tom Thumb' popcorn (*Zea mays*)

"To improve your chances of success in the garden, grow heirloom vegetable and flower varieties from New England. They have been growing successfully here for many years and are acclimated to our climate."
Tom Stearns, High Mowing Organic Seed Farm, Wolcott, Vermont

REPEAT PERFORMANCE:
CUT-AND-COME-AGAIN LETTUCES

Cutting lettuces, all *Lactuca sativa* species, are an informal group of nonheading cultivars that will sprout new leaves after they are sliced off an inch or two from the soil surface. They are also called *cut-and-come-again* lettuces. Lettuce guru Shepherd Ogden, founder of The Cook's Garden in Londonderry, Vermont, recommends cutting these cultivars when they are no more than 6 inches tall. Keep sowing—every two weeks—to extend the salad season even further. For more lettuce choices, take a look at The Cook's Garden seed catalog, which lists more than thirty cultivars (see "The Mail-Order Garden" in this book).

LOOSELEAF LETTUCE

'Bionda Liscia'	green
'Brunia'	green with red edges
'Curly Oakleaf'	curled green
'Lollo Bionda'	curled pale green
'Lollo Rossa'	curled green with red
'Merlot'	burgundy
'Red Salad Bowl'	red
'Riccia Rossa d'America'	pale green with red
'Rossa di Trento'	green with red
'Royal Oak Leaf'	green
'Salad Bowl'	lime green
'Valeria'	frizzy-edged red

CULINARY CLIMBERS

While any vine—or any plant, for that matter—has a practical side, climbing plants that produce edible crops are the last word in utility. They're also wonderfully useful if your growing space is small, for they let you garden vertically rather than horizontally. All edible climbers need a strong support to scale. Species with heavy fruits, such as melons, will require your help to stay attached to their trellis, and also may require cloth "slings" to support the fruits. Peas and beans are the best-known culinary climbers, but there are plenty more possibilities—as this list makes clear.

Hardy kiwi (*Actinidia arguta*)
Malabar spinach (*Basella alba*)
'Sugar Baby', 'New Hampshire Midget', 'Festival', 'Garden Baby' watermelon (*Citrullus lanatus*)
'Prior', 'Flyer', 'Minnesota Midget', 'Early Dawn', 'Early Sweet' melon (*Cucumis melo*)
'Suyo Long', 'Sweet Slice', 'English Telegraph', 'Orient Express', 'Lemon', 'Burpless 26' cucumber (*Cucumis sativus*)
'Baby Bear', 'Munchkin', 'Jack Be Little', 'New England Pie', 'Sweetie Pie', 'Baby Pam' pumpkin (*Cucurbita*)
'Early Butternut', 'Butternut Supreme', 'Ambercup', 'Golden Delicious', 'Vegetable Spaghetti' winter squash (*Cucurbita*)
'Zucchetta Rampicante' summer squash (*Cucurbita*)
Chinese yam (*Dioscorea batatas*)
Common hop (*Humulus lupulus*)
'Beaugard', 'Georgia Jet', 'Jewel' sweet potato (*Ipomoea batatas*)
Hyacinth bean (*Lablab purpureus*)
'Cucuzzi' gourd (*Lagenaria siceraria*)
Bitter melon/balsam pear (*Momordica charantia*)

Maypop (*Passiflora incarnata*)

'Scarlet Runner', 'Dutch White', 'Red Knight', 'Butler', 'Painted Lady' runner bean (*Phaseolus coccineus*)

'Christmas Pole', 'Sieva', 'King of the Garden' pole lima bean (*Phaseolus lunatus*)

'Goldmarie', 'Blue Lake', 'Northeaster', 'Trionfo', 'Kentucky Wonder', 'Romano', 'Purple Peacock', 'Kentucky Blue', 'Kentucky Wonder Wax' pole bean (*Phaseolus vulgaris*)

'Sugar Snap', 'Super Sugar Snap', 'Super Sugar Mel' sugarsnap pea (*Pisum*)

'Maxigolt', 'Maestro', 'Tall Telephone', 'Alderman' garden pea (*Pisum sativum* ssp. *sativum*)

'Mammoth Melting Sugar', 'Carouby de Maussane' snow pea (*Pisum sativum* ssp. *sativum* f. *macrocarpon*)

Asparagus pea/winged bean (*Psophacarpus tetragonolobus*)

Asparagus bean (*Vigna unguiculata* ssp. *sesquipedalis*)

Grape (*Vitis* spp. and cvs.)

PLANTS WITH EDIBLE FLOWERS

You can munch on the flowers of any culinary herb, although some of the blossoms are so tiny that it would be hard to find them on your plate. Most have a flavor that is slightly milder than the plant's leaves. Many ornamental plants also have edible blossoms. These are some of the best posies for prettifying salads and other dishes. If the blossom is large, like pot marigold's, use individual petals rather than the entire flower. Plants without hardiness zone information are annuals or treated as annuals in New England.

Anise hyssop (*Agastache foeniculum*)	4, 5, 6
Chives (*Allium schoenoprasum*)	3, 4, 5, 6
Garlic chives (*Allium tuberosum*)	3, 4, 5, 6
Dill (*Anethum graveolens*)	
English daisy (*Bellis perennis*)	4, 5, 6
Borage (*Borago officinalis*)	3, 4, 5, 6
Pot marigold (*Calendula officinalis*)	
Chamomile (*Chamaemelum nobile*)	3, 4, 5, 6
Coriander/cilantro (*Coriandrum sativum*)	
Fennel (*Foeniculum vulgare*)	4, 5, 6
Mint (*Mentha* spp.)	3, 4, 5, 6
Bee balm (*Monarda* spp.)	3, 4, 5, 6
Basil (*Ocimum basilicum*)	
Scarlet runner bean (*Phaseolus coccineus*)	
Rose (*Rosa* spp.)	3, 4, 5, 6
Common sage (*Salvia officinalis*)	4, 5, 6
Marigold (*Tagetes* spp.)	
Red clover (*Trifolium pratense*)	3, 4, 5, 6
Nasturtium (*Tropaeolum majus*)	
Johnny-jump-up (*Viola tricolor*)	3/4, 5, 6
Pansy (*Viola wittrockiana*)	

"You can save space in your garden by trellising vegetable crops like cucumbers, squash, and melons in addition to the usual suspects, such as pole beans and peas. Trellising also tends to increase yields and discourages diseases by keeping the produce off the ground."
Shep Ogden, founder, The Cook's Garden, Londonderry, Vermont

UPSCALE SALADS: MESCLUN

The word "mesclun" is short for *salade de mesclun*, the French phrase for a salad made exclusively of greens. The traditional Provence recipe is one part arugula, one part curly endive, two parts chervil, and four parts lettuce. Today, mesclun is standard fare in upscale restaurants, and salad makers are more adventurous—anything goes, including edible flowers (see "Plants with Edible Flowers" in this chapter).

Be sure to plant a mesclun garden successively—sow in rows or broadcast a mix of plants in small beds—and don't forget to begin harvesting when your greens are still small, only a few inches tall. Most crops will resprout for a second or third harvest.

The traditional mesclun dressing is a vinaigrette made with white wine vinegar, olive oil, and Dijon mustard.

Chives (*Allium schoenoprasum*)
Chervil (*Anthriscus cerefolium*)
Orach (*Atriplex hortensis*)
Mizuna (*Brassica juncea*)
Mustard (*Brassica juncea*)
Good King Henry (*Chenopodium bonushenricus*)
Endive (*Cichorium endivia*)
Chicory (*Cichorium intybus*)

Radicchio (*Cichorium intybus*)
Arugula (*Eruca sativa*)
Garden cress (*Lepidium sativum*)
Miner's lettuce/claytonia (*Montia perfoliata*)
Parsley (*Petroselinum crispum*)
Purslane (*Portulaca oleracea*)
Nasturtium (*Tropaeolum majus*)
Corn salad/mâche (*Valerianella locusta*)
Johnny-jump-up (*Viola tricolor*)

TIMING IS EVERYTHING: STARTING SEEDS INDOORS

Starting from seed in the vegetable garden gives you access to hundreds of cultivars not found on the shelves of garden centers. It also requires good timing so that you'll have young, vigorous plants—not spindly potbound ones—ready to go into the garden at exactly the right moment. Shep Ogden, the founder of The Cook's Garden seed company in Londonderry, Vermont, and a prolific garden writer (his latest is *Straight Ahead Organic*, 1999), recommends this indoor sowing schedule for New England gardeners.

Sow 10-12 Weeks Before Your Frost-Free Date	Sow 6-8 Weeks Before Your Frost-Free Date	Sow 2-4 Weeks Before Your Frost-Free Date
Celeriac	Basil	Annual herbs
Eggplant	Broccoli	Brussels sprouts
Leeks	Cabbage	Cucumbers
Onions	Cauliflower	Dill
Parsley	Celery	Lettuce
Perennial herbs	Endive	Melons
Sweet and hot peppers	Lettuce	Squash
	Okra	
	Tomatoes	

HERBS FOREVER

Many of our favorite culinary herbs, such as basil and rosemary, are either annuals or tender perennials that are unable to survive our winter weather. New England gardeners can have a perennial herb garden, however, filled with plants to harvest for the kitchen.

As for rosemary, *Rosmarinus officinalis*, gardeners in the warmest parts of our region should look for the cultivar 'Arp.' It has grayish foliage and ice-blue to white flowers, and is usually hardy in Zone 6 if it is well protected in winter.

Anise hyssop (*Agastache foeniculum*)	4, 5, 6
Chives (*Allium schoenoprasum*)	3, 4, 5, 6
Garlic chives (*Allium tuberosum*)	3, 4, 5, 6
Horseradish (*Armoracia rusticana*)	3, 4, 5, 6
French tarragon (*Artemisia dracunculus* var. *sativa*)	4/5, 6
Fennel (*Foeniculum vulgare*)	4, 5, 6
Lovage (*Levisticum officinale*)	4, 5, 6
Lemon balm (*Melissa officinalis*)	3, 4, 5, 6
Spearmint (*Mentha spicata*)	3, 4, 5, 6
Greek oregano (*Origanum vulgare* ssp. *hirtum*)	5, 6
Common sage (*Salvia officinalis*)	4/5, 6
Winter savory (*Satureja montana*)	4, 5, 6
Thyme (*Thymus* spp.)	3/4, 5, 6

SAGE

The late Henry Beston, who lived in Nobleboro, Maine, is best known for *The Outermost House* (1928), an account of a year living on Cape Cod. In 1935, he published his classic *Herbs and the Earth,* which he called "part garden book, part musing study of our relation to Nature through the oldest group of plants known to gardeners." When making an herb garden, he wrote, "the emphasis should always rest on the beauty and character of the plants."

THE TEN CONDIMENTS

Biblical plants have been a source of fascination for centuries, although identifying the plants mentioned hasn't been easy. We know what the cedar of Lebanon is, but what species was the forbidden fruit? The apple ended up with honor, although there is no evidence for that conclusion in the Bible itself. Some plants, such as the bulrush (*Cyperus papyrus*), play a starring role in the stories of the Bible, while others are mentioned only in passing. Here are ten herbs to get your biblical garden started. Interested in making it larger? Take a look at *A Fountain of Gardens: Plants and Herbs of the Bible* by Wilma Paterson (1992), a standard work on the subject.

Garlic (*Allium sativum*)
"We remember the fish, which we did eat in Egypt freely; the cucumbers, and the melons, and the leeks, and the onions, and the garlick." Numbers 11:5
Wormwood (*Artemisia absinthium*)
"He hath filled me with bitterness, he hath made me drunken with wormwood.... Remembering mine affliction and my misery, the wormwood and the gall." Lamentations 3:15, 19
Black mustard (*Brassica nigra*)
"The kingdom of heaven is like a grain of mustard seed, which a man took, and sowed in his field." Matthew 13:31, 32
Coriander (*Coriandrum sativum*)
"But now our soul is dried away: there is nothing at all, besides this manna, before our eyes. And the manna was as coriander seed." Numbers 11:6, 7
Saffron (*Crocus sativus*)
"Thy plants are an orchard of pomegranates, with pleasant fruits; camphire with

spikenard and saffron … myrrh and aloes, with all the chief spices." Song of Solomon 4:13, 14

Hyssop (*Hyssopus officinalis*)

"And they filled a sponge with vinegar, and put it upon hyssop, and put it to his mouth." John 19:29

Bay (*Laurus nobilis*)

"I have seen the wicked in great power, and spreading himself like a green bay tree." Psalms 37:35–36

Flax (*Linum usitatissimum*)

"She seeketh wool, and flax, and worketh willing with her hands." Proverbs 31:13

Mint (*Mentha* spp.) Rue (*Ruta graveolens*)

"But woe unto you, pharisees! For ye tithe of mint and rue and all manner of herbs, and pass over judgment and the love of god." Luke 11:42

TEA TIME: POTABLE HERBS

You don't have to be Peter Rabbit to drink chamomile tea: The next time the clock strikes four, brew your cup'a from the garden. The leaves of these herbs can be steeped alone or in combination (a universal favorite is lemon verbena and lemon balm with a sprig of spearmint). The usual recommendation is 2 teaspoons fresh herbs or 1 teaspoon dried herbs per cup of water, but feel free to experiment until you find a flavor, blend, and strength you like. According to tradition, tea should steep as long as it takes you to recite Psalm 51, but some herbs take longer than others, so you may need to recite the Gettysburg Address or read the Constitution aloud.

Plants without hardiness zone information are annuals or treated as annuals in New England.

Anise hyssop (*Agastache foeniculum*)	4, 5, 6
Lemon verbena (*Aloysia triphylla*)	
Borage (*Borago officinalis*)	3, 4, 5, 6
Roman chamomile (*Chamaemelum nobile*)	3, 4, 5, 6
Lemongrass (*Cynbopogon citratus*)	
Lemon balm (*Melissa officinalis*)	3, 4, 5, 6
Mint (*Mentha* spp.)	3, 4, 5, 6
Bee balm (*Monarda didyma*)	3, 4, 5, 6
Sweet Cicely (*Myrrhis odorata*)	3, 4, 5, 6
Catnip (*Nepeta cataria*)	3, 4, 5, 6
Scented geranium (*Pelargonium* spp.)	
Common sage (*Salvia officinalis*)	4, 5, 6
Lemon thyme (*Thymus citriodorus*)	5, 6

HERBS FOR AN ORNAMENTAL BORDER

Aurelia C. Scott has gardened in Massachusetts, California, and New Mexico, but now she grows herbs, perennials, and vegetables within sight of Casco Bay in Portland, Maine. A garden writer and lecturer, she says she feels comfortable in "muddy field boots as a Cooperative Extension Master Gardener and in clean high heels as a Garden Club president." Above all, she's comfortable in the garden, where she likes to combine herbs, vegetables, and flowers in order to create an edible landscape. These are a few of the "useful" perennial herbs that she recommends for an ornamental border. The color of their blooms or foliage is indicated for each plant.

Blue globe onion (*Allium caeruleum*)	cornflower blue	3, 4, 5, 6
Giant allium (*Allium giganteum*)	purple-violet	3/4, 5, 6
Garlic chives (*Allium tuberosum*)	white	3, 4, 5, 6
Southernwood/lad's love (*Artemisia abrotanum*)	white	4, 5, 6
Fringed wormwood (*Artemisia frigida*)	yellow	3, 4, 5, 6
'Silver King' western mugwort (*Artemisia ludoviciana* var. *albula*)	silver foliage	4, 5, 6
'Hopley' oregano (*Origanum laevigatum*)	purple	4/5, 6
Common sage (*Salvia officinalis*)	lilac-purple	4, 5, 6
Lemon thyme (*Thymus citriodorus*)	pale purple	5, 6
Creeping thyme (*Thymus serpyllum*)	pale purple	3, 4, 5, 6
Silver thyme (*Thymus vulgaris* 'Argenteus')	purple	5, 6

"I'm a champion of edible landscaping. Pole beans look as pretty on a trellis as any flowering vine. Choose the reliable 'Kentucky Wonder', a yellow pod variety such as 'Gold Marie', or the purple and green pods of 'Cascade Giant.' I use 'Spicy Bush' basil, 'Brussels Winter' chervil, and a long-season carrot, such as 'Bolero', as edging plants. Harvest the basil and chervil as needed, and the carrots at the end of the season. To attract bees and hummingbirds, I plant mint. But always plant it in gallon pots sunk into the soil so it doesn't take over the entire garden."
Aurelia Scott, Master Gardener, garden writer, and lecturer, Portland, Maine

TUBBY TOYS: HERBS FOR ADDING TO THE BATH

If you want to relax, smell as good as your garden—and give your skin a little TLC—consider growing some of these plants to harvest for your bath. You can use them singly or in combinations. To prepare plants for use in the tub, pour boiling water over the leaves, seeds, and/or flowers, and allow them to steep for six to eight hours; strain and discard the plant matter. Add 1 quart strained herb water to each bath.

Plants without hardiness zone information are annuals or treated as annuals in New England.

LAVENDER

Lady's mantle (*Alchemilla mollis*)	leaves	3, 4, 5, 6
Pot marigold (*Calendula officinalis*)	flowers	
Chamomile (*Chamaemelum nobile*)	flowers, leaves	3, 4, 5, 6
Fennel (*Foeniculum vulgare*)	leaves, seeds	3/4, 5, 6
Marsh mallow (*Hibiscus moscheutos*)	leaves	4/5, 6
Lavender (*Lavandula* spp.)	flowers	4, 5, 6
Lovage (*Levisticum officinale*)	leaves	4, 5, 6
Lemon balm (*Melissa officinalis*)	leaves	3, 4, 5, 6
Mint (*Mentha* spp.)	leaves	3, 4, 5, 6
Rose (*Rosa* spp.)	flowers	3, 4, 5, 6
Common sage (*Salvia officinalis*)	leaves	4, 5, 6
Comfrey (*Symphytum officinale*)	leaves	3, 4, 5, 6
Vervain (*Verbena officinalis*)	leaves	4, 5, 6

RAISING CANES: RASPBERRIES AND BLACKBERRIES

Raspberries and blackberries—botanical cousins—are a terrific crop for Yankee gardeners (and a great lure for Japanese beetles, if that's a problem in your part of our region). You can settle for wild berries, but cultivated bushes are more productive and their fruits larger and their thorns smaller. Raspberries are hollow when picked and tend to be milder flavored than blackberries. Blackberries produce larger crops but are less hardy than raspberries.

If you garden in Zone 3 or 4, stick with summer-bearing raspberry cultivars and avoid fall-bearing bushes, which may not ripen their berries before the first frost. 'Latham', an old favorite in the Northeast, is still carried by garden centers but is no longer recommended because of its susceptibility to disease. Don't forget that summer-bearing raspberries produce fruit on the previous year's canes, so prune (to the ground) only the canes that have already fruited.

RASPBERRY

Raspberries (Rubus idaeus var. strigosus)

'Amity'	fall-bearing red	4/5, 6
'August Red'	fall-bearing red	3, 4, 5, 6
'Autumn Bliss'	fall-bearing red	3/4, 5, 6
'Black Hawk'	summer-bearing black	3/4, 5, 6
'Boyne'	summer-bearing red	3, 4, 5, 6
'Canby'	summer-bearing red	4, 5, 6
'Fall Red'	fall-bearing red	4, 5, 6
'Goldie'	fall-bearing yellow	5, 6
'Heritage'	fall-bearing red	5, 6
'Jewel'	summer-bearing black	3/4, 5, 6
'John Robertson'	summer-bearing black	3/4, 5, 6
'Killarney'	summer-bearing red	3, 4, 5, 6
'Kiwigold'	fall-bearing yellow	5, 6
'Newburg'	summer-bearing red	3, 4, 5, 6
'Nova'	summer-bearing red	4, 5, 6
'Redwing'	fall-bearing red	3/4, 5, 6
'Royality'	summer-bearing purple	3/4, 5, 6
'Ruby'	fall-bearing red	5, 6
'Taylor'	summer-bearing red	3, 4, 5, 6

Blackberries (Rubus occidentalis)

'Cherokee'	thorny	5, 6
'Chester'	thornless	5/6
'Cheyenne'	thorny	6
'Darrow'	thorny	5, 6
'Dirkson'	thornless	5, 6
'Navaho'	thornless	5, 6

ON BLUEBERRY HILL

New England gardeners can grow three of the four types of blueberries; only heat-loving rabbiteyes (Vaccinium ashei) are too tender for our region. Fortunately for us, the other three groups—lowbush, highbush, and half-high—are considered the best of this North American native plant.

Although you'll need to plant more than one cultivar to ensure pollination, blueberries come close to being a perfect crop. The bushes are hardy, attractive (handsome red foliage in autumn), and disease resistant. Only birds and Japanese beetles are pests, and both can be controlled by covering your plants with floating row covers or fine-mesh netting. All of the cultivars listed here have blue fruits except for 'Leucocarpum', which is a white variety.

Lowbush (*Vaccinium angustifolium* var. *laevifolium*)

'Augusta'	2, 3, 4, 5, 6
'Brunswick'	2, 3, 4, 5, 6
'Early Sweet'	2, 3, 4, 5, 6
'Leucocarpum'	2, 3, 4, 5, 6

Half-high (*Vaccinium*)

'Blue Haven'	4, 5, 6
'Chippewa'	3, 4, 5, 6
'Northblue'	3, 4, 5, 6
'Northland'	3, 4, 5, 6
'Northsky'	2/3, 4, 5, 6

Highbush (*Vaccinium corymbosum*)

'Bluecrop'	3/4, 5, 6
'Blueray'	3/4, 5, 6
'Collins'	5, 6
'Coville'	5, 6
'Earliblue'	4, 5, 6
'Ivanhoe'	5, 6
'Jersey'	4/5, 6
'Nelson'	4, 5, 6
'Patriot'	3, 4, 5, 6

"Half-high blueberries, which combine the large fruit of highbush plants and the hardiness and early bloom of lowbush varieties, are a boon for far-north gardeners. Good varieties are 'Northblue', 'Northsky', Northcountry', 'St. Cloud', and 'Friendship.' Mulch your plants with a 5-inch layer of sawdust or pine needles to protect their shallow roots, deter weeds, and retain moisture."
R. E. Gough, fruit specialist, Oakfield, Massachusetts

"Why blueberries? Lovely pinkish bell-shaped flowers in spring, edible fruits in summer, striking red and orange leaves in autumn, and gorgeous bark and stems in winter."
Mark Stavish, owner, Eastern Plant Specialties, Georgetown, Maine

GRAPE EXPECTATIONS

Grapes (*Vitis*) have been grown for as long as there have been gardeners, and there are now thousands and thousands of cultivars. Most of the European wine and table grapes are hardy only in the warmest parts of the country, but 'Concord', the most famous jelly and juice grape, is a native of the Massachusetts town whose name it bears. Most grapes need full sun and at least 150 frost-free days to ripen their fruits. These are some of the grapes that do best in New England, all American or American hybrids.

For Jelly and Juice

'Concord'	blue-black	4, 5, 6
'Beta'	blue-black	3, 4, 5, 6

'Bluebell'	blue	4, 5, 6
'King of the North'	blue	4, 5, 6
'Worden'	purple-black	4, 5, 6

Table Use

'Concord Seedless'	seedless blue-black	4, 5, 6
'Himrod'	seedless yellow	5, 6
'Niagara'	light green	5, 6
'Reliance'	seedless pink-red	4/5, 6
'Steuben'	blue-purple	5, 6
'Valiant'	blue-black	3/4, 5, 6

Wine

| 'Frontenac' | red wine | 4, 5, 6 |
| 'Seyval Blanc' | white wine | 5, 6 |

NO-SPRAY APPLES

Ron and Celia Hackett have been growing and marketing apples, pears, and other fruits for more than thirty years. Located in South Hero, the southern-most of Vermont's Champlain Lake islands, the Hacketts' forty-acre orchard (sixteen acres of apple trees, forty-six different cultivars) lies in Zone 5. They recommend that New England home gardeners choose disease-resistant cultivars (all species of *Malus domestica*), especially those bred to resist apple scab. At the head of the list are their three favorite no-sprays that combine good flavor and superior disease resistance. All of these apples are hardy to at least Zone 5, 'Spartan' to Zone 4, and 'Mantet' to Zone 3.

No-Spray Apples

'Freedom'	red
'Liberty'	red
'Sunrise'	red

Other Disease-Resistant Apples

'Burgundy'	red
'Mantet'	red and amber
'Novamac'	red
'Redfree'	yellow-green
'Spartan'	red

In her *Red Oaks & Black Birches: The Science and Lore of Trees* (1990), Rebecca Rupp, who gardens both in Shaftsbury and Swanton, Vermont, points out that apples "have a nasty reputation dating back to the Book of Genesis. Unlike women and snakes, however—whose hypothetical past activities have been largely forgiven and forgotten—the apple's part in the fiasco in the Garden of Eden has been immortalized in scientific Latin. The generic name of the modern apple is *Malus*, from the Latin for bad.... It seems unfair that the apple should have been saddled with this moral stigma, since biblical scholars now agree that the fatal fruit probably wasn't an apple at all."

PROFESSOR GREENE'S APPLE FAVORITES

Professor Duane W. Greene is a member of the Department of Plant and Soil Sciences at the University of Massachusetts in Amherst, where he's been involved for several years in research evaluating apple cultivars for both commercial and home growers. For the backyard orchard he recommends cultivars that are resistant to apple scab "so that you won't have to spray several times." All of the apples in this list are hardy in Greene's Zone 5 location, "and probably in Zone 4 as well."

Disease-Resistant Cultivars

'Liberty'	red
'Priscilla'	red
'Pristine'	yellow
'Redfree'	yellow-green with red
'Scarlet O'Hara'	red
'Williams Pride'	red with yellow

Good Cultivars Without Disease-Resistance

'Akane'	red
'Gala'	yellow with red
'Ginger Gold'	yellow
'Golden Delicious'	yellow
'Honeycrisp'	yellow
'Jonagold'	red and yellow
'McIntosh'	red
'Mutsu'	yellow with red

"Dwarf apple trees—which are created by grafting standard varieties on dwarfing rootstock—produce fruit when they are young and are easy to care for. While small trees are better choice for the home gardener, most of the dwarfing rootstocks that are used to shrink a standard tree are not very hardy. To get around that problem, nurseries also sell your favorite apple variety grafted on top of a piece of dwarfing interstem (which makes the tree smaller) that is grafted on top of vigorous rootstock. Reading nursery catalogs is a serious matchmaking effort, as you seek compatibility between the varieties of fruit and roots and the unalterable conditions of your site."
Paul Dunphy, organic grower and freelance garden writer, Haydenville, Massachusetts

THE APPLES OF MY EYE

It's too cold in Zones 3 and 4 to grow some of the most popular apples, such as 'Granny Smith', but Yankees in the most frigid parts of our region can grow apples. The hardy cultivars on this list don't all produce high-quality, overly large fruits—some run only about 3 inches in diameter—or the heaviest crops, but these trees do thrive in cold. Many were bred in Canada but have immigrated to New England and made themselves at home. New England gardeners in Zone 5 and 6 can grow nearly any apple cultivar.

'Breakey'	yellow with red blush	4, 5, 6
'Brookland'	red	4, 5, 6
'Burgundy'	red	3, 4, 5, 6
'Carrol'	striped red and green	4, 5, 6

'Chestnut'	bronze-red	3, 4, 5, 6
'Cortland'	red	4, 5, 6
'Dutchess'	red striped	3, 4, 5, 6
'Fall Red'	red	3, 4, 5, 6
'Freedom'	red	2/3, 4, 5, 6
'Garland'	red	3, 4, 5, 6
'Goodland'	red	3, 4, 5, 6
'Haralson'	yellow with red stripes	3, 4, 5, 6
'Honeycrisp'	red	4, 5, 6
'Honeygold'	yellow	3, 4, 5, 6
'Lodi'	green	4, 5, 6
'Mantet'	red and amber	3, 4, 5, 6
'McIntosh'	red	4, 5, 6
'Norda'	red streaked	4, 5, 6
'Norland'	red	2/3, 4, 5, 6
'Northern Spy'	yellow with red stripes	4/5, 6
'Parkland'	green-yellow with red stripes	2/3, 4, 5, 6
'Roxbury Russet'	green with yellow russet	4, 5, 6
'Spartan'	red	2/3, 4, 5, 6
'State Fair'	red	3, 4, 5, 6
'Sweet 16'	red	3, 4, 5, 6
'Wealthy'	yellow with red stripes	2/3, 4, 5, 6

"Three tips for home gardeners growing apples: Keep your trees healthy by pruning them in late spring, after the worst of the cold weather but before buds break; fertilize young trees with a balanced food spread to the drip line, once in late spring and again in mid-June; and rake up and remove all leaves under the trees in fall. One other tip: use a wire guard around the tree trunks to keep mice from damaging them in winter."
Ron and Celia Hackett, owners, Hackett's Orchard, South Hero, Vermont

LOVELIEST OF TREES: THE CHERRY

Loveliest of trees, the cherry now / Is hung with blooms along the bough. / And stands about the woodland ride / Wearing white for Eastertide." Most New England gardeners can't recite Housman's lines with much authority, as nearly all sweet cherries and many sour cherries aren't hardy in our region. Gardeners in Zone 6 should be able to grow all cherries. If those in colder zones want to take a chance, here are the cultivars to try. Not a gambler? Plant bush cherries, which are hardy but have fruits that are extremely sour.

'Kristin' sweet cherry (*Prunus avium*)	5, 6
'Sam' sweet cherry (*Prunus avium*)	4/5, 6
'Stark Gold' sweet cherry (*Prunus avium*)	4/5, 6
'Summit' sweet cherry (*Prunus avium*)	5, 6
'Van' sweet cherry (*Prunus avium*)	5, 6
'Mando' western sand bush cherry (*Prunus besseyi*)	3, 4, 5, 6
'Meteor' sour cherry (*Prunus ceraus*)	3/4, 5, 6
'Montmorency' sour cherry (*Prunus ceraus*)	4/5, 6
'Morellenfeuer' sour cherry (*Prunus ceraus*)	4, 5, 6

'Northstar' sour cherry (*Prunus ceraus*)	3/4, 5, 6
'Surefire' sour cherry (*Prunus ceraus*)	4, 5, 6
Mongolian cherry/European dwarf cherry (*Prunus fruticosa*)	2, 3, 4, 5, 6
Manchu bush cherry (*Prunus tomentosa*)	3, 4, 5, 6

 Pears, blueberries, plums, sweet cherries, elderberries, and even a few apples and grapes are not self-pollinating. That means that you need to plant two varieties for cross-fertilization. Garden books, nursery catalogs, and local nursery people can advise you on what other variety will make the best pollinator for the fruit you want to grow.

PEAR EXCELLENCE

Of the two types of pears, Asian and European, only the latter have been grown in North America for more than 100 years. Asian pears, which derive from different *Pyrus* species, are usually round and large and have sweet, crisp flesh. European pears, all members of *Pyrus communis* and pear shaped, are best suited for the warmest part of New England, Zone 6; gardeners in Zones 4 and 5 may have success growing the hardiest cultivars in a sheltered location. See the recommendations in this list.

Most pears are not reliably self-pollinating, so you must plant more than one cultivar. European pears are best if they are picked before they are fully mature and ripened in a cool room.

PEAR	'Bartlett'	5, 6
	'Flemish Beauty'	4/5, 6
	'Gourmet'	4, 5, 6
	'Harrow Delight'	5, 6
	'Harrow Sweet'	5, 6
	'Harvest Queen'	5, 6
	'Luscious'	4, 5, 6
	'Magness'	5, 6
	'Seckel'	5, 6
	'Stark Honeysweet'	5, 6
	'Tyson'	3/4, 5, 6
	'Vermont Beauty'	3/4, 5, 6

PLUM CRAZY

New England gardeners have an international inventory of plums to choose from: European, Japanese, North American, and assorted other species and hybrids. Japanese plums (*Prunus salicina*) are the ones you find at the grocery store. European plums (*Prunus domestica*) are excellent fresh, but most are destined to become prunes. The small North American plums (*Prunus americana* and beach plums, *Prunus maritima*), usually available only at roadside farm stands, are good for eating fresh or making preserves. Hybrids represent the best of all possible plums. At least that's what the breeders say.

If you live in Zone 6 or the warmer parts of Zone 5, you can grow almost any of the 2,000 plums that are grown worldwide. Yankees with arctic conditions should pick from among the more hardy cultivars on this list. Most plums are not self-pollinating and require a second tree in order to set fruit.

European	
'Fellenberg'	5, 6
'Iroquois'	5, 6
'Mount Royal'	4/5, 6

'President'	5, 6
'Seneca'	5, 6
'Stanley'	4/5, 6
'Valor'	5, 6

North American

Beach plum	3/4, 5, 6
'Bounty'	2, 3, 4, 5, 6
'Norther'	2/3, 4, 5, 6

Japanese

'Brookgold'	2/3, 4, 5, 6
'Brookred'	3, 4, 5, 6
'Burbank'	5, 6

Hybrid

'Elite'	3, 4, 5, 6
'Kahinta'	4, 5, 6
'Ozark Premier'	5, 6
'Pembina'	3, 4, 5, 6
'Superior'	4, 5, 6
'Tecumseh'	3/4, 5, 6
'Underwood'	3/4, 5, 6
'Waneta'	3, 4, 5, 6

Fruit Yields

"How much will I get?" is a common question from gardeners new to growing fruits. There's not an exact answer, of course, as yields are affected by weather, location, the cultivar being grown, pruning, and thinning, to list only five factors. The numbers that follow are approximate for a single *mature* plant, but they give you an idea of the bounty of the backyard fruit garden.

Apple, dwarf	50 pounds	Gooseberry	6 pounds
Apple, standard	250 pounds	Grape	12 pounds
Blueberry, highbush	6 pounds	Pear, dwarf	50 pounds
Cherry, sweet	250 pounds	Pear, standard	250 pounds
Cherry, sour	100 pounds	Raspberry	2 pounds
Currant	6 pounds	Strawberry	2 pounds

DARE TO GROW A PEACH—OR NECTARINE OR APRICOT

J. Alfred Prufrock wondered if he dare eat a peach. New England gardeners wonder if they dare try to grow them—or their cousins, nectarines. Peaches and nectarines are members of the same species, *Prunus persica*. The difference between them—fuzzy skinned or smooth—is a matter of a single gene. Common, or European, apricots are members of *Prunus armeniaca*, while Manchurian apricots belong to the *Prunus armeniaca* var. *mandschurica* species. Make sure, if you buy a grafted peach, nectarine, or apricot tree, that the rootstock is hardy to your location.

Peaches

'Fairhaven'	5, 6
'Garnet Beauty'	5, 6
'Georgia Bell' (white flesh)	5/6
'Hale'	5, 6
'Hale Haven'	6
'Red Haven'	5, 6
'Redskin'	6
'Spring Gold'	5, 6

Nectarines

'Garden Delight'	5, 6
'Hardired'	4/5, 6
'Mericrest'	5, 6
'Red Chief' (white flesh)	6
'Red Gold'	5, 6

Common/European Apricots

'Alfred'	5/6
'Henderson'	5/6
'Goldcot'	5/6
'Moonpark'	5/6

Manchurian Apricots

'Brookcot'	4, 5, 6
'Moongold'	4, 5, 6
'Scout'	4, 5, 6
'Sunrise'	4, 5, 6

BE FRUITFUL: MORE CHOICES FOR YANKEE GARDENERS

Here are a few more berries, drupes, and fruits for the New England garden. Don't forget that some species require two plants for pollination, and that grafted plants are only as hardy as their rootstock. If you have currant wine or gooseberry jelly in mind, be sure that there are no bans in your area on planting currants or other *Ribes* species, which host white pine blister rust. If there are white pines growing in your yard or within 1,000 feet, be sure to purchase *Ribes* that are rust-resistant.

Be warned, too, that strawberries need good protection in winter. On the other hand, cranberries don't have to grow in a bog, and elderberries are so easy that Vermont garden writer Lewis Hill writes, "I'm not including any cultural directions—they take the least work of any of the fruits."

Juneberry/serviceberry (*Amelanchier alnifolia*)	2/3, 4, 5, 6
'Earlyglow', 'Northeaster', 'Veestar' early strawberry (*Fragaria ananassa*)	3, 4, 5, 6
'Kent', 'Allstar' midseason strawberry (*Fragaria ananassa*)	3/4, 5, 6
'Sparkle', 'Glooscap' mid/late strawberry (*Fragaria ananassa*)	3, 4, 5, 6
'Tristar', ever-bearing strawberry (*Fragaria ananassa*)	4, 5, 6
Rhubarb (*Rheum cultorum*)	3, 4, 5, 6
'Welcome' American gooseberry (*Ribes hirtellum*)	4, 5, 6
'Red Lake' red currant (*Ribes rubrum*)	4, 5, 6
'Johns', 'Adams', 'New York 21' elderberry (*Sambucus canadensis*)	3/4, 5, 6
American cranberry (*Vaccinium macrocarpon*)	2/3, 4, 5, 6

SPECIAL LISTS AND GARDENS

This is the *et alia*, the "and others" chapter. It's made up of special lists that don't fit easily into this book's general categories. Some lists, for example, contain both woody and herbaceous plants. Then there are plant lists for special gardens, including a garden intended to be viewed by moonlight and one to bring in hummingbirds. There are even lists of plants you may not want to introduce into your garden: "Alien Invaders: Aggressive Plants to Avoid" and "Botanical Blackguards: Toxic Plants." Another list, "Gardens to Visit," doesn't contain plants at all; instead, it's a state-by-state enumeration of public gardens, display gardens, and specialized collections to inspire you.

Half the fun of gardening, after all, is using your imagination, doing something a little different. An extreme example of an imaginative gardener was the Victorian Sir Frank Crisp, who erected fake mountains, tunnels, caves, and even underground lakes at his Henley estate. His "garden" was lit by electricity and embellished by artificial spiders and other monsters that menaced unexpecting visitors. The resemblance of this nineteenth-century creation to a Disney theme park is so close that one wonders if Crisp's estate should sue the Disney empire for royalties under the laws protecting intellectual property.

You may not want to go as far as Crisp did, but have some fun. The best gardens are personal, even if they begin with someone else's list.

Before You Buy

In this checklist are questions for you to answer before you purchase any plant for your garden—tree, shrub, vine, or flower. It's what you need to know *before* you hand over your credit card. Be realistic about what you can do—if there is no time in your schedule for pruning, stick with plants that don't require that kind of attention.

- Will the plant thrive in the conditions in your garden? Is it hardy enough to survive the extremes of both winter and summer weather?
- Will the plant do well in your garden's soil? Does it need an extreme pH or especially high fertility? Does it like moist soil or dry?
- Can you give the plant as much sun or shade as it requires?
- Will the plant need more water than normal rainfall provides?
- Is the plant resistant to insect pests or diseases or will it require special protection and/or controls?
- How fast does the plant grow and how big will it get? Is it aggressive? How long will it live?
- Will the plant need special care from you, such as pruning, staking, spraying, or watering?

NEW ENGLAND'S FLORA ICONS

Just in case dinner-table conversation lulls—or your first-grader needs something to show-and-tell—here are the plants adopted as our official state flowers and trees in New England. Rumor has it that there have been nasty cracks by Vermonters about New Hampshire not knowing a tree from a flower and Connecticut not knowing a shrub from a flower, but as more than one non-Vermont gardener has pointed out, a state that chooses a European legume grown for fodder as its official flower probably shouldn't criticize.

Flowers

Connecticut	mountain laurel (*Kalmia latifolia*)
Maine	white pine (pinecone and tassel) (*Pinus strobus*)
Massachusetts	trailing arbutus (*Epigaea repens*)
New Hampshire	common lilac (*Syringa vulgaris*)
Rhode Island	violet (*Viola* spp.)
Vermont	red clover (*Trifolium pratense*)

Trees

Connecticut	white oak (*Quercus alba*)
Maine	white pine (*Pinus strobus*)
Massachusetts	American elm (*Ulmus americana*)
New Hampshire	paper birch (*Betula papyrifera*)
Rhode Island	red maple (*Acer rubrum*)
Vermont	sugar maple (*Acer saccharum*)

CARY AWARDS

Sponsored by the Tower Hill Botanic Garden, the Cary Award was established in 1997 as a way to identify "home landscape plants that have proven their performance in New England." Is there an outstanding tree, shrub, ground cover, or vine that thrives in your garden? Anyone can nominate a plant by writing to The Cary Award, Tower Hill Botanic Garden, P.O. Box 598, Boylston, MA 01505-0598. The envelope please.

1997 Winners

'Pendula' Alaskan weeping cedar (*Chamaecyparis nootkatensis*)	4, 5, 6
Redvein enkianthus (*Enkianthus campanulatus*)	4, 5, 6
Large fothergilla (*Fothergilla major*)	4, 5, 6
'Centennial' star magnolia (*Magnolia stellata*)	4, 5, 6
Japanese stewartia (*Stewartia pesudocamellia*)	4, 5, 6

1998 Winners

Climbing hydrangea (*Hydrangea anomala* subsp. *petiolaris*)	3/4, 5, 6
'Red Sprite' dwarf winterberry (*Ilex verticillata*)	3, 4, 5, 6
'Leonard Messel' Loebner magnolia (*Magnolia loebneri*)	4/5, 6
Russian arborvitae/Siberian carpet cypress (*Microbiota decussata*)	3, 4, 5, 6
Pinkshell azalea (*Rhododendron vaseyi*)	4, 5, 6

1999 Winners

'Massachusetts' bearberry (*Arctostaphylos uva-ursi*)	2, 3, 4, 5, 6
Cornelian cherry (*Cornus mas*)	4, 5, 6
'Blue Prince', 'Blue Princess' holly (*Ilex meserveae*)	5, 6

NOT ON THE LEVEL: PLANTS FOR A HILLSIDE

Winsted, Connecticut, garden writer Rita Buchanan provides all sorts of helpful information in *Making a Garden: Reliable Techniques, Outstanding Plants, and Honest Advice* (1999). She follows her own landscaping advice in her two-acre, Zone 5 garden, where she's built stone terraces to solve some of the challenges presented by sloping terrain. If you're among the New England gardeners who aren't on the level, Buchanan recommends any of these plants—and recommends mulching them and the hillside with a coarse material, such as shredded bark, to retain moisture and prevent erosion.

Border pinks (*Dianthus* spp.)	4, 5, 6
'Emerald Gaiety' wintercreeper (*Euonymus fortunei*)	4, 5, 6
Bigroot geranium (*Geranium macrorrhizum*)	3, 4, 5, 6
Perennial candytuft (*Iberis sempervirens*)	3, 4, 5, 6
Creeping junipers (*Juniperus horizontalis* cvs.)	2, 3, 4, 5, 6
Catmints (*Nepeta faassenii* cvs.)	4, 5, 6
'Alba Meidiland', 'Pearl Meidiland', 'Scarlet Meidiland' (*Rosa*)	5, 6
Japanese spirea (*Spiraea japonica* cvs.)	4, 5, 6
'Helene von Stein' big lamb's ears (*Stachys byzantina*)	3, 4, 5, 6

The best way to attract wildlife to your garden is to use native plants and to encourage diversity: Make sure your landscape includes trees, shrubs, vines, and flowering plants.

STOCKING THE HUMMINGBIRD GARDEN

The ruby-throated hummingbird is the only hummingbird species that regularly frequents New England, but it's well worth your hanging feeders and adding plants to your garden that will attract these avian jewels. All the names on this list—flowers, vines, and shrubs—are guaranteed to lure hummingbirds. For immediate results, start with bee balm, *Monarda didyma*. The plants in this list that have no hardiness zone information are annuals or are grown as annuals in New England.

LUPINES

Columbine (*Aquilegia* spp.)	3, 4, 5, 6
Butterfly bush (*Buddleia davidii*)	5, 6
Trumpet creeper (*Campsis radicans*)	4/5, 6
Delphinium (*Delphinium* spp.)	3, 4, 5, 6
Fuchsia (*Fuchsia* hyb.)	
Coralbells (*Heuchera sanguinea*)	3, 4, 5, 6
Jewelweed (*Impatiens capensis*)	2, 3, 4, 5, 6
Morning glory (*Ipomoea purpurea*)	
Red-hot poker (*Kniphofia* hyb.)	4, 5, 6
Beauty bush (*Kolkwitzia amabilis*)	4, 5, 6
Cardinal flower (*Lobelia cardinalis*)	3, 4, 5, 6
Trumpet honeysuckle (*Lonicera sempervirens*)	3, 4, 5, 6
'Arnold Red' tatarian honeysuckle (*Lonicera tatarica*)	4, 5, 6
Lupine (*Lupinus* hyb.)	3, 4, 5, 6
Scarlet monkey flower (*Mimulas cardinalis*)	6
Bee balm (*Mondara didyma*)	3, 4, 5, 6
Scarlet runner bean (*Phaseolus coccineus*)	

Sage (*Salvia officinalis*)	4, 5, 6
Scarlet sage (*Salvia splendens*)	
Nasturtium (*Tropaeolum* cvs.)	
'Red Prince' weigela (*Weigela florida*)	5, 6

THOREAU'S FLOWERS

Few figures have a stronger identification with New England than does Henry David Thoreau, the Massachusetts philosopher-naturalist who not only heard a different drummer but warned others to "beware of all enterprises that require new clothes." Thoreau, who is more famous for growing practical crops than ornamentals, wrote movingly about flowers he encountered as he wandered the countryside. For more about Thoreau's favorite plants, take a look at Peter Loewer's *Thoreau's Garden* (1966).

Jack-in-the-pulpit (*Arisaema triphyllum*)	3, 4, 5, 6
Aster (*Aster* spp.)	3, 4, 5, 6
Joe-Pye weed (*Eupatorium fistulosum*)	3, 4, 5, 6
Cranesbill (*Geranium maculatum*)	3, 4, 5, 6
Common spatterdock/yellow pond lily (*Nuphar advena*)	3, 4, 5, 6
Evening primrose (*Oenothera biennis*)	4, 5, 6
Black-eyed Susan (*Rudbeckia hirta*)	2, 3, 4, 5, 6

ALIEN INVADERS: AGGRESSIVE PLANTS TO AVOID

This list of exotic, or non-native, plants comes from the New England Wild Flower Society. All were imported to North America for use in gardens and roadsides, but over time they have become invasive pests in New England, especially in its warmer areas. Because they have no natural enemies, they bully native species. It's hard to deny the beauty of a roadside stand of purple loosestrife (*Lythrum salicaria*), but it is overwhelming many native wetland plants that are crucial to wildlife. Other names on this list are similarly aggressive. Plant them with care; better still, don't plant them at all.

Norway maple (*Acer platanoides*)	3, 4, 5, 6
Bishop's weed/goutweed (*Aegopodium podagraria*)	3, 4, 5, 6
Tree of heaven (*Ailianthus altissima*)	4, 5, 6
Porcelain berry (*Ampelopsis brevipedunculata*)	3/4, 5, 6
Japanese barberry (*Berberis thunbergii*)	3/4, 5, 6
Common barberry (*Berberis vulgaris*)	3, 4, 5, 6
Oriental bittersweet (*Celastrus orbiculata*)	4, 5, 6
Spotted knapweed (*Centaurea maculosa*)	5, 6
Russian olive (*Elaeagnus angustifolia*)	3, 4, 5, 6
Autumn olive (*Elaeagnus umbellata*)	3, 4, 5, 6
Burning bush (*Euonymus alatus*)	3/4, 5, 6
Cypress spurge (*Euphorbia cyparissias*)	4, 5, 6
Yellow flag (*Iris pseudacorus*)	4, 5, 6
Japanese privet (*Ligustrum obtusifolium*)	3, 4, 5, 6
Common privet (*Ligustrum vulgare*)	4, 5, 6
Japanese honeysuckle (*Lonicera japonica*)	4, 5, 6
Honeysuckle (*Lonicera maackii*)	4/5, 6
Honeysuckle (*Lonicera morrowii*)	4, 5, 6
Tatarian honeysuckle (*Lonicera tatarica*)	3, 4, 5, 6
Purple loosestrife (*Lythrum salicaria*)	3, 4, 5, 6

Common reed (*Phragmites australis*)	5, 6
Mile-a-minute vine (*Polygonum baldschuanicum*)	4, 5, 6
Japanese knotweed (*Polygonum japonicum*)	4/5, 6
Common buckthorn (*Rhamnus cathartica*)	3, 4, 5, 6
Alder buckthorn (*Rhamnus frangula*)	3, 4, 5, 6
Black locust (*Robinia pseudoacacia*)	4, 5, 6
Multiflora rose (*Rosa multiflora*)	4/5, 6
Japanese wisteria (*Wisteria floribunda*)	4/5, 6

"After a divorce, I suddenly had to take care of an overrun country garden. A friend delivered a load of grass clippings from his job mowing cemeteries. I spread the clippings around what I thought were the flowers. I may have smothered a few good guys, but the hot decomposition killed all the weeds between the plants and gave me a garden. Now Johnny-jump-ups and annual asters reseed where I once had weeds."
A. Carman Clark, garden columnist, Union, Maine

LOVELY LAGGARDS: PLANTS TO END THE GARDEN SEASON

A. Carman Clark, whose Zone 5 garden is located in Union, Maine, writes "Down East Garden Ways" for *The Camden Herald*. She keeps up a large garden "in my fashion," she says. "I'm not over-anxious about a few weeds." Most New Englanders get anxious as winter nears, which is one reason that the last flowers of the garden seasons are especially precious. "These plants are still blossoming in early November," Clark says, "when frosts, rains, and winds have wiped color from the trees." To encourage mallow to rebloom in late fall, Clark adds, cut them back in August. The plants in this list that have no hardiness zone information are annuals or are grown as annuals in New England.

BLACK-EYED SUSAN

'Rosea' rose yarrow (*Achillea millefolium*)	3, 4, 5, 6
Snapdragon (*Antirrhinum majus*)	
Strawflower (*Bracteantha bracteata*)	
Pot marigold (*Calendula officinalis*)	
Sweet alyssum (*Lobularia maritima*)	
Black-eyed Susan (*Rudbeckia hirta*)	2, 3, 4, 5, 6
Johnny-jump-up (*Viola tricolor*)	3/4, 5, 6

SHAKESPEARE IN THE GARDEN

Shakespeare knew his plants as well as his fellow human beings. Trees, shrubs, vines, herbs, vegetables, and flowers are sprinkled generously throughout his plays and poetry, usually as metaphors for human qualities. The garden, too, was a frequent image: "Our bodies are gardens; to the which our wills are gardeners." If you love the Bard, why not create a Shakespeare garden in New England, beginning with these perennials?

Monkshood (*Aconitum* spp.)   3, 4, 5, 6
"That the united vessel of their blood, / Mingled with venom of suggestion ... / Shall never leak, though it do work as strong / As aconitum or rash gunpowder."
2 Henry IV

OXEYE DAISY

Columbine (*Aquilegia* spp.)   3, 4, 5, 6
"There's fennel for you, and columbines: / There's rue for you: and here's some for me."
Hamlet

English daisy (*Bellis perennis*)   4, 5, 6
"When daisies pied and violets blue / And lady'smocks all silver white / And cuckoo-buds
of yellow hue / Do paint the meadows with delight." *Love's Labour's Lost*

Lily-of-the-valley (*Convallaria majalis*)   3, 4, 5, 6
"those lily hands / Tremble, like aspen-leaves, upon a lute." *Titus Andronicus*

Bearded iris (*Iris* cvs.)   3, 4, 5, 6
"what sayest thou, my fair flower-de-luce?" *Henry V*

Yellow flag (*Iris pseudacorus*)   4, 5, 6
"Like to a vagabond flag upon the stream, / Goes to and back, lackeying the varying tide."
Anthony and Cleopatra

Lavender (*Lavandula* spp.)   4/5, 6
"Here's flowers for you; / Hot lavender, mints, savory, marjoram." *The Winter's Tale*

Ox-eye daisy (*Leucanthemum vulgare*)   3, 4, 5, 6
"There with fantastic garlands did she come / Of crow-flowers, nettles, daisies, and long
purples." *Hamlet*

Peony, or "pioner" (*Paeonia officinalis*)   3, 4, 5, 6
"Thy banks with pioned and twilled brims, / Which spongy April at thy best betrims."
The Tempest

Cowslip (*Primula veris*)   4, 5, 6
"The even mead, that erst brought sweetly forth / The freckled cowslip, burnet and green
clover." *Henry V*

Sweet violet (*Viola odorata*)   6
"violets dim, / But sweeter than the lids of Juno's eyes / Or Chtherea's breath." *The
Winter's Tale*

BY THE SEA: A CAPE COD GARDEN

Frances Tenenbaum works in Boston—she's been the garden editor at Houghton Mifflin Company
for twenty-five years and is so good at her job that she has her own imprint (A Francis Tenenbaum
Book). Summers she spends at Gay Head on Cape Cod, where she gardens "in a small way. I'm sure
other people could add many more plants," she says of her list, "but I've included only flowers and
shrubs that do especially well for me and can take care of themselves. She also reports that George
Schenk, author of several garden books, sent her the spirea on this list about twenty-five years ago,
"and last year was the first time it even needed pruning."

Plains false indigo (*Baptisia australis*)   3, 4, 5, 6
White gaura (*Gaura lindheimeri*)   5/6
Daylily (*Hemerocallis* cvs.)   3, 4, 5, 6
Coral flower/coralbells (*Heuchera* spp.)   4, 5, 6

St. John's wort (*Hypericum* spp.)	5, 6
Lavender (*Lavandula* spp.)	5, 6
Rugosa rose (*Rosa rugosa* cvs.)	3, 4, 5, 6
'Bumalda', Japanese spirea (*Spiraea japonica*)	4, 5, 6
Common lilac (*Syringa vulgaris*)	3, 4, 5, 6

"Plants for a seasonal home like mine on Cape Cod must be hardy, vigorous, and self-reliant. They shouldn't require regular pruning or other care. And they should bloom when I'm there, not when I'm somewhere else."
Frances Tenenbaum, garden editor, Gay Head, Massachusetts

PODS AND HEADS: PLANTS FOR BOUQUETS

If you're looking for interesting "plant material" to add to your bouquets, both fresh and dried, consider some of the plants on this list. In late summer or fall, they all produce attractive seed heads or seed pods that are as effective in the vase as any flower. Conifers, many of which have wonderful cones, aren't included in this list, but you'll want to include them in your arrangements. The plants in this list that have no hardiness zone information are annuals or are grown as annuals in New England.

Milkweed (*Asclepias speciosa*)	3, 4, 5, 6
Heather (*Calluna vulgaris*)	4, 5, 6
Sedge (*Carex* spp.)	4/5, 6
Indian bean tree (*Catalpa bignonioides*)	5, 6
Clematis (*Clematis* spp.)	3, 4, 5, 6
Fuller's teasel (*Dipsacus fullonum*)	4/5, 6
Hyacinth bean (*Lablab purpureus*)	
Purple coneflower (*Echinacea purpurea*)	3, 4, 5, 6
Globe thistle (*Echinops rito*)	3, 4, 5, 6
Fescue (*Festuca* spp.)	3, 4, 5, 6
Goldenrain tree (*Koelreuteria paniculata*)	5, 6
'Greynog Gold' ligularia (*Ligularia*)	4, 5, 6
Sweet gum (*Liquidambar styraciflua*)	5, 6
Honesty/money plant (*Lunaria annua*)	
Magnolia (*Magnolia* spp.)	4, 5, 6
Love-in-a-mist (*Nigella damascena*)	
Shirley poppy/Flanders Field poppy (*Papaver rhoeas*)	
Opium poppy (*Papaver somniferum*)	
Chinese lanterns (*Physalis alkekengi*)	
Oak (*Quercus* spp.)	3, 4, 5, 6
Castor bean (*Ricinus communis*)	
Black-eyed Susan (*Rudbeckia hirta*)	2, 3, 4, 5, 6
Cattails (*Typha latifolia*)	3, 4, 5, 6

PLANTS FROM PARADISE—WATERLILIES

This list of plants comes from Paradise Water Gardens in Whitman, Massachusetts, not the more famous Paradise, although the waterlilies (*Nymphaeas*) that nursery owner Paul Stetson Sr. recommends for New England gardeners are beautiful enough to have come from the Garden of Eden. Stetson says that it's more difficult to pick only ten—"there are many, many more"—than to grow all ten. He guarantees that all these sun-loving lilies are hardy to Zone 4, maybe Zone 3, as long as your water garden is at least 18 inches deep or does not freeze solid. For partially shaded water gardens, Stetson recommends 'James Brydon', 'Joey Tomocik', 'Chromatella', and 'Helveola.'

'Attraction'	deep red	3/4, 5, 6
'Chromatella'	deep yellow	3/4, 5, 6
'Comanche'	yellow to bronze	3/4, 5, 6
'Escarboucle'	deep red	3/4, 5, 6
'Gloriosa'	strawberry red	3/4, 5, 6
'Indiana'	orange to red	3/4, 5, 6
'Joey Tomocik'	deepest yellow	3/4, 5, 6
'Mayla'	fuchsia pink	3/4, 5, 6
'Pink Sensation'	deep pink	3/4, 5, 6
'Virginalis'	pure white	3/4, 5, 6

"Waterlilies are easy to grow, but they need to be free from competing with other plants. Plant them in 16-inch pots filled with rich garden soil (covered with 1 to 2 inches of sand) set from 6 to 24 inches deep. The corms of the lily should be covered with at least 6 inches of water. The more sun waterlilies get, the better they flower, and if you fertilize them monthly, blooming will be even greater."
Paul W. Stetson Sr., owner, Paradise Water Gardens, Whitman, Massachusetts

MOONLIGHT SERENADE

Previous generations of New England gardeners often planted "moon gardens," beds and borders filled with white flowers and foliage that came into their own at dusk. Many of the plants on this list are also most fragrant in the evening, magnets for night-flying moths and other pollinators. All are either annuals or tender perennials; although a few may self-sow in warmer areas, your moon garden will have to be replanted each year, which will give you an opportunity to add new plants to the mix.

'White Queen' spider flower (*Cleome hassleriana*)
'White Sonata' cosmos (*Cosmos bipinnatus*)
Snow-on-the-mountain/ghost weed (*Euphorbia marginata*)
'Italian White' sunflower (*Helianthus annuus*)
Moonflower (*Ipomoea alba*)
Sweet alyssum (*Lobularia maritima*)
'Grandiflora' jasmine tobacco (*Nicotiana alata*)
'Miss Jekyll Alba' love-in-a-mist (*Nigella damascena*)
'Midnight Candy' night phlox (*Zaluzianskya capensis*)
'White Star' zinnia (*Zinnia haageana*)

THE BEES' KNEES: PLANTS TO ATTRACT POLLINATORS

If you remember any of your elementary school science, you know that bees are crucial to both ornamental and edible plants. As they collect nectar from flowers, bees and insects bump and brush against the flowers' anthers, coating themselves with pollen that they transfer to the stigmas—all of which leads to fertilization and the eventual production of seeds and new plants. The decline of honeybees is well documented—the result of environmental degradation, the varroa mite, and other factors—but you can help their plight by including some of these plants in your landscape. The plants in this list that have no hardiness zone information are annuals or are grown as annuals in New England.

Allium (*Allium* spp.)	3, 4, 5, 6
Columbine (*Aquilegia* spp.)	3, 4, 5, 6
Aster (*Aster* spp.)	3, 4, 5, 6
Borage (*Borago officinalis*)	3, 4, 5, 6
Common foxglove (*Digitalis purpurea*)	
Winter aconite (*Eranthis hyemalis*)	3, 4, 5, 6
Joe-Pye weed (*Eupatorium maculatum*)	3, 4, 5, 6
Sunflower (*Helianthus annuus*)	
Lavender (*Lavandula* spp.)	4, 5, 6
Honeysuckle (*Lonicera* spp.)	4, 5, 6
Lemon balm (*Melissa officinalis*)	3, 4, 5, 6
Bee balm (*Monarda didyma*)	3, 4, 5, 6
Daffodil (*Narcissus* cvs.)	3, 4, 5, 6
Catnip (*Nepeta cataria*)	3, 4, 5, 6
Poppy (*Papaver* spp.)	
Scarlet runner bean (*Phaseolus coccineus*)	
Phlox (*Phlox* spp.)	3, 4, 5, 6
Goldenrod (*Solidago* spp.)	2/3, 4, 5, 6
Lilac (*Syringa vulgaris* cvs.)	3, 4, 5, 6
Thyme (*Thymus* spp.)	3/4, 5, 6
Nasturtium (*Tropaeolum* cvs.)	
Blueberry (*Vaccinium* spp.)	3, 4, 5, 6

FOXGLOVE

BOTANICAL BLACKGUARDS: TOXIC PLANTS

Most New England gardeners don't graze randomly in the garden—or in the wild. A good thing, too, for there are plants growing in our region, both native and exotic, that can irritate, inflame, and even poison. Mushrooms are the most common culprits—especially *Amanita* species. With common names such as death cap and destroying angel they are, excuse the pun, dead giveaways. Fungi aren't the only culprits, however, as you can see from this incomplete list of potentially dangerous plants: Many species are plants that we regularly plant in our gardens. The plants in this list that have no hardiness zone information are annuals or are grown as annuals in New England.

Monkshood (*Aconitum napellus*)	all parts, esp. seeds, roots	3, 4, 5, 6
Common horse chestnut (*Aesculus hippocastanum*)	leaves, flowers, fruits	3, 4, 5, 6
Jack-in-the-pulpit (*Arisaema triphyllum*)	all parts	3, 4, 5, 6
Milkweed (*Asclepias syriaca*)	all parts	3, 4, 5, 6
Deadly nightshade (*Atropa belladonna*)	all parts, esp. berries	5, 6
Water hemlock (*Cicuta maculata*)	all parts, esp. roots	4, 5, 6
Meadow saffron (*Colchicum autumnale*)	all parts, esp. corm, seeds	4, 5, 6

Poison hemlock (*Conium maculatum*)	all parts, esp. roots, seeds	4/5, 6
Lily-of-the-valley (*Convallaria majalis*)	all parts	3, 4, 5, 6
Common foxglove (*Digitalis purpurea*)	leaves, flowers, seeds	
Henbane (*Hyoscyamus niger*)	all parts	
Morning glory (*Ipomoea tricolor*)	seeds	
Mountain laurel (*Kalmia latifolia*)	all parts	4/5, 6
Narcissus/daffodil (*Narcissus* spp.)	bulbs	3, 4, 5, 6
Pokeweed (*Phytolacca americana*)	all parts, esp. roots	4, 5, 6
May apple (*Podophyllum peltatum*)	all parts, esp. roots, fruits	3, 4, 5, 6
Black cherry (*Prunus serotina*)	seeds, leaves	3/4, 5, 6
Rhubarb (*Rheum cultorum*)	leaf blades	3, 4, 5, 6
Elderberry (*Sambucus canadensis*)	all parts except edible berries	3/4, 5, 6
English yew (*Taxus baccata*)	all parts	5/6

A DYER'S GARDEN

Using plants as dyes isn't as straightforward as you might think—a yellow flower won't necessarily turn your T-shirt yellow. If you're just beginning, get a copy of Bobbie McRae's *Colors from Nature: Growing, Collecting and Using Natural Dyes* (1993) or *A Handbook of Dyes from Natural Materials* (1981) by Anne Bliss. Both books provide information about mordents (the substances that bind the dye to the fiber) and their effects on color as well as designating the parts of the plants that are used for dying.

As for the plants themselves, start your dyer's garden with some of these species. The plants in this list that have no hardiness zone information are annuals or are grown as annuals in New England.

Yarrow (*Achillea millefolium*)	3, 4, 5, 6
Dyer's chamomile/golden marguerite (*Anthemis tinctoria*)	3, 4, 5, 6
Absinthe (*Artemisia absinthium*)	3, 4, 5, 6
Mugwort (*Artemisia* spp.)	3, 4, 5, 6
Milkweed (*Asclepias* spp.)	3, 4, 5, 6
Barberry (*Berberis* spp.)	3, 4, 5, 6
Chamomile (*Chamaemelum nobile*)	3, 4, 5, 6
Queen Anne's lace (*Daucus carota*)	3, 4, 5, 6
Foxglove (*Digitalis purpurea*)	
Joe-Pye weed (*Eupatorium purpureum*)	3, 4, 5, 6
Lady's bedstraw (*Galium verum*)	3, 4, 5, 6
Sunflower (*Helianthus annuus*)	
Mint (*Mentha* spp.)	3, 4, 5, 6
Catnip (*Nepeta cataria*)	3, 4, 5, 6
Pokeweed (*Phytolacca americana*)	4, 5, 6
Rhubarb (*Rheum cultorum*)	3, 4, 5, 6
Madder (*Rubia tinctorum*)	5/6
Black-eyed Susan (*Rudbeckia hirta*)	2, 3, 4, 5, 6
Betony (*Stachys officinalis*)	4, 5, 6
Comfrey (*Symphytum officinale*)	3, 4, 5, 6
Marigold (*Tagetes* spp.)	
Tansy (*Tanacetum vulgare*)	3, 4, 5, 6
Great mullein (*Verbascum thapsus*)	4/5, 6

BOTANICAL BONDAGE: PLANTS FOR ESPALIERING

Espalier, a term that comes from the Italian word *spalle*, or shoulder (in the sense of shouldering a load), is a pruning and training system by which non-vining woody plants are made to grow horizontally against a flat, vertical surface like a wall or trellis. Espalier is the last word in control—it requires lots of pruning and tying and training—but the results are both ornamental and practical. Not only can you create intricate formal or informal designs, but espaliering plants on a heat-absorbing wall gives them enough protection, especially with a southern exposure, that you may be able to grow species that aren't usually hardy in your region. Pears and other fruits are popular espalier subjects, but ornamental species are equally good.

Cotoneaster (*Cotoneaster* spp.)	4, 5, 6
Chinese persimmon (*Diospyros kaki*)	6/7
American persimmon (*Diospyros virginiana*)	4, 5, 6
Hollyleaf sweetspire (*Itea ilicifolia*)	6
Magnolia (*Magnolia* spp.)	4, 5, 6
Crabapple (*Malus* cvs.)	3, 4, 5, 6
Apple (*Malus domestica*)	3/4, 5, 6
Firethorn (*Pyracantha* spp.)	5/6
Pear (*Pyrus* cvs.)	4, 5, 6
Sweet box (*Sarcococca* spp.)	5/6
Viburnum (*Viburnum burkwoodii*)	4, 5, 6

Visiting public and private gardens, especially gardens in your own area, is one of the best ways to discover which plants will do well for you. You'll also get ideas about plant combinations or how to solve problems in the garden, such as planting under a maple or that hot, dry "hell strip" between the driveway and the fence that marks your property line. Most gardeners are happy to share their plants, but snapping off leaves, stems, or seedheads without permission will make you a visitor *non grata*.

FLOWER IN THE CRANNIED WALL

The one thing that most of New England gardens have plenty of is rocks. Stones. Boulders. All those walls that serpentine their way through our woods are a testament to our mineral wealth, and our ancestors' grit. If you've inherited a stone wall—or have built one—enhance it with a few plants. Don't forget that you need to tuck in some soil in the same cranny where the plant roots will go.

THYME

'Bronze Beauty' creeping bugleweed (*Ajuga reptans*)	shade	3, 4, 5, 6
Rock cress (*Arabis caucasica*)	sun	3, 4, 5, 6
Purple rock cress (*Aubrieta deltoidea*)	sun	4, 5, 6
Basket of gold (*Aurinia saxatilis*)	sun	3, 4, 5, 6
Bellflower (*Campanula* spp.)	shade	3, 4, 5, 6
Snow-in-summer (*Cerastium tomentosum*)	sun	3, 4, 5, 6
Perennial candytuft (*Iberis sempervirens*)	sun	3, 4, 5, 6
Creeping Charley (*Lysimachia nummularia*)	shade	4, 5, 6
Moss pink (*Phlox subulata*)	sun	3, 4, 5, 6
Saxifrage (*Saxifraga umbrosa* var. *primuloides*)	shade	2, 3, 4, 5, 6

Sedum/stonecrop (*Sedum* spp.)	sun	3, 4, 5, 6
Hens and chicks (*Sempervivum tectorum*)	sun	3/4, 5, 6
Thyme (*Thymus* spp.)	sun	3/4, 5, 6

A VERMONT COUNTRY GARDEN

Barns, rocky outcrops, and lilacs (*Syringa vulgaris* 'Sensation' is her favorite) are the backdrop for Carol Haddock's country flower garden. A spinner, weaver, and expert gardener, Haddock lives in Jericho, Vermont (Zone 4a), on a twenty-two-acre farm. Busy with 100 Lincoln sheep and her wool business, Haddock likes informal flowers that take care of themselves—no spraying, no staking—and that work well in the large, informal bouquets she is famous for making. The plants in this list that have no hardiness zone information are annuals or are grown as annuals in New England.

Hollyhock 'Single Mixed' (*Alcea rosea*)	
Goatsbeard (*Aruncus dioicus*)	3, 4, 5, 6
Aster (*Aster* spp.)	3, 4, 5, 6
Wild white indigo (*Baptisia alba*)	4, 5, 6
Blue false indigo (*Baptisia australis*)	2/3, 4, 5, 6
Purple coneflower (*Echinacea purpurea*)	3, 4, 5, 6
Snow-on-the-mountain/ghost weed (*Euphorbia marginata*)	
Sunflower (*Helianthus annuus*)	
'Sommersonne' ox-eye (*Heliopsis helianthoides* subsp. *scabra*)	3, 4, 5, 6
Perennial pea (*Lathyrus latifolia*)	3/4, 5, 6
Asiatic and oriental lily (*Lilium* cvs.)	3/4, 5, 6
Flowering tobacco (*Nicotiana alata*)	
Single form peony (*Paeonia* hyb.)	3, 4, 5, 6

"Tall, sturdy plants look at home in a country garden, perennials like goatsbeard, daylilies, purple coneflower, and helianthus. My son built a rustic arbor out of saplings to support bittersweet and honeysuckle vines, which creates an interesting vertical element, and I fill out the garden with annuals to keep it colorful all summer. Sheep that have escaped their pens are my biggest problem: They're especially fond of lilies."
Carol Haddock, Wool Hollow Farm, Jericho, Vermont

FLOAT LIKE A LEPIDOPTERA: PLANTS TO ATTRACT BUTTERFLIES

Different plant species attract different butterfly species. The common checkered skipper and painted ladies fly to hollyhocks; parsley lures eastern black swallowtails. Milkweeds may be the champion come-on, attracting more than fifty butterfly species. The plants listed below are among those that are most popular with the largest number of butterflies and moths.

SUNFLOWER

Don't forget that the best thing you can do to attract butterflies to your garden is not to use toxic chemicals. To protect moths and other night-flyers? Get rid of a bug-zapper, if you have one. Studies show that they kill more beneficial insects than the pests they were designed to control.

The plants in this list that have no hardiness zone information are annuals or are grown as annuals in New England.

Yarrow (*Achillea millefolium*)	3, 4, 5, 6
Milkweed (*Asclepias* spp.)	3, 4, 5, 6
Aster (*Aster* spp.)	3, 4, 5, 6
Butterfly bush (*Buddleia davidii*)	5, 6
Thistle (*Cirsium japonicum*)	4/5, 6
Thistle (*Cirsium rivulare*)	4, 5, 6
Coreopsis (*Coreopsis* spp.)	3, 4, 5, 6
Queen Anne's lace (*Daucus carota*)	3, 4, 5, 6
Garden carrot (*Daucus carota* var. *sativus*)	
Purple coneflower (*Echinacea purpurea*)	3, 4, 5, 6
Joe-Pye weed (*Eupatorium maculatum*)	3, 4, 5, 6
Sunflower (*Helianthus annuus*)	
Marsh mallow (*Hibiscus moscheutos*)	4/5, 6
New England blazing star (*Liatris scariosa* var. *novae-angliae*)	4, 5, 6
Mallow (*Malva sylvestris*)	
Mint (*Mentha* spp.)	3, 4, 5, 6
Bee balm (*Monarda* spp.)	3, 4, 5, 6
Pentas (*Pentas lanceolata*)	
Parsley (*Petroselinum crispum*)	
Phlox (*Phlox* spp.)	3, 4, 5, 6
Black-eyed Susan (*Rudbeckia hirta*)	3, 4, 5, 6
Goldenrod (*Solidago* spp.)	3, 4, 5, 6
Red clover (*Trifolium pratense*)	3, 4, 5, 6
New York ironweed (*Vernonia noveboracensis*)	4, 5, 6
Speedwell (*Veronica* spp.)	3, 4, 5, 6

ON THE MARGINS: PLANTS FOR SOPPY PLACES

All the plants on this list thrive in bogs and/or shallow water—they're perfect for planting along streams or low spots that stay wet throughout the summer. They also belong on the margins of water gardens and ponds, graceful plants that soften the meeting of water and land.

Sweet flag (*Acorus calamus*)	4, 5, 6
Bog rosemary (*Andromeda polifolia*)	2, 3, 4, 5, 6
Bog arum (*Calla palustris*)	3, 4, 5, 6
Marsh marigold (*Caltha palustris*)	3, 4, 5, 6
Tussock sedge (*Carex stricta*)	3, 4, 5, 6
Houttuynia (*Houttuynia cordata*)	5, 6
Northern blueflag (*Iris versicolor*)	4, 5, 6
Soft rush (*Juncus effusus*)	4, 5, 6
'Aurea' golden creeping Charley (*Lysimachia nummularia*)	4, 5, 6
Aquatic crowfoot (*Ranunculus aquatilis*)	4, 5, 6
Arrowhead (*Sagittaria latifolia*)	3/4, 5, 6
Cattails (*Typha latifolia*)	3, 4, 5, 6

FLOWER TALK

The "language of flowers" was a floral game that matched human character traits and emotions with specific plants. It reached its height of popularity during the reign of Queen Victoria, and was "spoken" through small bouquets called tussie-mussies. To wish a friend happy birthday, for example, you sent a bouquet containing basil, rose, lavender, plum, and statice. Since all these correlations have no basis in science and any species or cultivar will do, it isn't surprising that the correlations of traits and flowers differ from one book to another. (A good reference is *The Victorian Flower Oracle* by Patricia Telesco.) Tired of e-mail? Plant a tussie-mussie garden.

Angelica	inspiration	Laurel	success
Bleeding heart	fidelity	Lavender	devotion
Borage	courage	Peony	beauty
Daffodil	respect	Purple coneflower	capability
Dahlia	treachery	Rose	love
Dogwood	faithfulness	Rosemary	remembrance
Fennel	strength	Rue	virtue
Feverfew	good health	Sage	wisdom
Geranium	affection	Spirea	self-centeredness
Holly	foresight	Violet	modesty
Hosta	devotion		

GARDENS TO VISIT

Although this list is far from definitive, it is a good sample of large and small, formal and informal, ornamental and edible gardens that you can visit in New England. Most are public gardens, some of which charge entrance fees. A few are especially lovely display gardens associated with commercial nurseries. Some of these gardens have specialized collections, such as peonies or roses, so you may want to phone ahead to find out the best time to visit.

Connecticut

Audubon Fairchild Garden, Riversville Road, Greenwich; 203-869-5272.

Bartlett Arboretum, 151 Brookdale, Road, Stamford; 203-322-6971.

Bates-Scofield Homestead, 45 Old King's Highway, Darien; 203-655-9233.

Bellamy-Ferriday House and Garden, 9 Main Street North, Bethlehem; 203-266-7596.

Bowen House/Roseland Cottage, Woodstock; 203-928-4074.

Butler-McCook Homestead, 396 Main Street, Hartford; 203-522-1806.

Caprilands Herb Farm, 534 Silver Street, Coventry; 860-742-7244.

Cricket Hill Garden, 670 Walnut Hill Road, Thomaston; 860-283-1042.

Denison Peqyotsepos Nature Center, Peqyotsepos Road, Mystic; 203-536-1216.

General William Hart House, 350 Main Street, Old Saybrook; 203-388-2622.

Gertrude Jekyll Garden and Glebe House Museum, Hollow Road, Woodbury; 203-263-2855.

Greenwich Garden Center Bible Street, Cos Cob; 203-869-9242.

Harkness Memorial State Park, 275 Great Neck Road, Waterford; 860-443-5725.

Harrison House, 124 Main Street, Branford; 203-488-5771.

Hillside Gardens, 515 Litchfield Road, Norfolk; 860-542-5345.

Historical Society of Glastonbury's Welles Shipman Ward House, 972 Main Street, Glastonbury; 203-633-6890.

Hotchkiss-Fyler House, 192 Main Street, Torrington; 203-482-8260.

Institute for American Indian Studies, 38 Curtis Road, Washington; 203-868-0518.

Logee's Greenhouses, 141 North Street, Danielson; 860-774-8038.

Massacoh Plantation, 800 Hopemeadow Street, Simsbury; 203-658-2500.

New Canaan Nature Center, 144 Oenoke Ridge, New Canaan; 203-966-9577.

Noah Webster's House, 227 South Main Street, West Hartford; 203-521-5362.
Pardee Rose Garden, 180 Park Road, Hamden; 203-787-8142.
Pratt House, 20 West Avenue, Essex; 203-767-8201.
Putnam Cottage, 243 East Putnam Avenue, Greenwich; 203-869-9697.
Scott-Fanton Museum Garden, 43 Main Street, Danbury; 203-743-5200.
Stanley-Whitman House, 37 High Street, Farmington; 203-677-9222.
Sundial Herb Garden, 59 Hidden Lake Road, Higganum; 860-345-4290.
Twombly Nursery, 163 Barn Hill Road, Monroe; 203-261-2133.
Webb-Deane-Stevens Museum, Main Street, Wethersfield; 203-529-0612.
Welles-Shipman-Ward House, 972 Main Street, South Gladstonebury; 203-633-6652.
White Flower Farm, Litchfield; 860-567-8789.
White Memorial Conservation Center, Litchfield; 203-567-0015.
Wilhelmina Ann Arnold Barnhart Memorial Garden, Hayden Hill Road and Walkley
    Hill Road, Haddam; 203-345-2400.

Maine
Abby A. Rochefeller Garden, off Route 3, Seal Harbor; 207-276-3330
Asticou Azalea Garden, Asticou Way, Mount Desert Island, Northeast Harbor; 207-276-
    5456.
Beatrice Farrand Garden, College of the Atlantic, Route 3, Bar Harbor; 207-288-5015.
Bernard McLaughlin Garden, Main Street, South Paris; 207-743-7620.
Celia Thaxter's Garden, Appledore Island; 607-254-2900.
Conway Homestead and Museum, Conway Road, Camden; 207-236-2257.
Deering Oaks Rose Circle, Deering and Forest Avenues, Portland; 207-874-8300.
Formal Garden at the Colonel Black Mansion, Surry Road, Ellsworth; 207-667-8671.
Hamilton House Gardens, Vaughn's Lane, South Berwick, 207-384-5269.
Heather Garden, Walker Art Building, Bowdoin College, Brunswick; 207-725-3000.
Heather Garden, Wolfe's Neck, University of South Maine, Freeport; 207-865-3428.
Hedgehog Hill Farm, Route 2, Buckfield; 207-388-2341.
Kennebec Valley Garden Club Park; Augusta Civic Center; Augusta; 207-622-1124.
Leighton Sculpture Garden; Parker Point Road, Blue Hill; 207-374-5001.
Lyle E. Littlefield Trial Garden, University of Maine, Orono; 207-581-2918.
Marrett House Gardens, Route 25, Standish; 207-642-3032.
Merry Gardens, Mechanic Street, Camden; 207-236-9046.
Merryspring, Conway Road, Camden/Rockport; 207-236-2239.
Petit Plaisance, South Shore Road, Northeast Harbor; 207-276-3940.
Rogers Farm, Bennoch Road, Orono; 800-287-7396.
Thuya Lodge Garden, Northeast Harbor, Mount Desert Island; 207-276-5130.
Wadsworth Longfellow Home and Garden 487 Congress Street, Portland; 207-879-0427.
Wild Gardens of Acadia, Off Route 3, Acadia National Park; 207-288-3338.

Massachusetts
Adams National Historic Site, 135 Adams Street, Quincy; 617-773-1177.
Alexandria Botanical Gardens and Hunnewell Arboretum, Wellesley College, Wellesley;
    617-235-0320.
Arnold Arboretum, 125 Arborway, Boston; 617-524-1718.
Bartholomew's Cobble, Copper Hill Road, Ashley Falls; 413-229-8600.
Berkshire Botanical Gardens, Route 102, Stockbridge; 413-298-3926.
Bidwell House, Art School Road, Monterey; 413-528-6888.
Botanic Garden of Smith College and Lyman Plant House, College Lane, Northampton;
    413-584-2700.

Bridge of Flowers, 75 Bridge Street, Shelburne Falls; 413-625-2544.

Chesterwood, off Route 183, Stockbridge; 413-298-3579.

Cushing House, 98 High Street, Newburyport; 508-462-2681.

Edith Wharton Restoration at the Mount, Lenox; 413-637-1899.

Garden in the Woods, New England Wildflower Society, 180 Hemenway Road, Framingham; 508-877-7630.

General Sylvanus Thayer Birthplace, 786 Washington Street, Braintree; 617-848-1640.

Glen Magna Farms, 57 Forest Street, Danvers; 978-774-9165.

Hancock Shaker Village, Route 20, Pittsfield; 413-443-0188.

Heritage Plantation, Grove and Pine Streets, Sandwich; 508-888-3300.

Isabella Stewart Gardner Museum, 280 The Fenway, Boston; 617-566-1401.

Jeremiah Lee Mansion, 161 Washington Street, Marblehead; 617-631-1069.

Longfellow House, 105 Brattle Street, Cambridge; 617-876-4491.

Mayflower Society House, 4 Winslow Street, Plymouth; 617-746-2590.

Mount Auburn Cemetery, 580 Mount Auburn Street, Cambridge; 617-547-7105.

Newbury Perennial Gardens, 65 Orchard Street, Byfield; 978-462-1144.

Nor'East Miniature Rose Inc., 58 Hammond Street, Rowley; 617-948-2408.

Old Sturbridge Village, 1 Old Sturbridge Village Road, Sturbridge; 508-347-3362.

Peabody Essex Museum Oriental Garden, 161 Essex Street, Salem; 800-745-4054.

Plimouth Plantation, Plymouth; 508-746-1622.

Porter-Phelps-Hunting House Museum, 130 River Drive, Hadley; 413-584-4699.

Sedgwick Gardens at Long Hill, 572 Essex Street, Beverly; 978-921-1944.

Tower Hill Botanic Garden, 11 French Drive, Boylston; 508-869-6111.

The Vale (Lyman Estate and Vale Greenhouses), 185 Lyman Street, Waltham; 781-891-4882.

Weston Nurseries, Route 135, Hopkinton; 508-435-3414.

New Hampshire

Aspet (home and gardens of Augustus Saint-Gaudens), off Route 12A, Cornish; 603-675-2175.

The Balsams, Route 26, Dixville Notch; 603-255-3400.

Canterbury Shaker Village, 288 Shaker Road, Canterbury; 603-783-9511.

The Fells, National Wildlife Refuge; Route 103A, Newbury; 603-763-4789.

Fuller Gardens, 10 Willow Avenue, North Hampton; 603-964-5414.

Governor Langdon Mansion Memorial, 143 Pleasant Street, Portsmouth; 603-436-3205.

Lilac Arboretum, University of New Hampshire, Durham; 603-862-2222.

Meadow Pond Gardens, Meadow Pond Road, Gilmanton; 603-267-7232.

Moffatt-Ladd House, 154 Market Street, Portsmouth; 603-436-8221.

Mount Washington Hotel, Route 302, Bretton Woods; 603-278-1000.

Prescott Park, Marcy Street, Portsmouth; 603-431-8748.

Rhododendron State Park, off Route 119, Fitzwilliam; 603-532-8862.

Rundlet-May House, 364 Middle Street, Portsmouth; 603-436-3205.

Strawberry Banke, 454 Court Street, Portsmouth; 603-433-1106.

Urban Forestry Center, State of New Hampshire, 45 Elwyn Road, Portsmouth; 603-431-6774.

Rhode Island

Blithewold Mansion and Gardens, 101 Ferry Road, Bristol; 401-253-2707.

The Breakers, Ochre Point Avenue, Newport; 401-847-6543.

General James Mitchell Varnum House Museum, 57 Pierce Street, East Greenwich; 401-884-1776.

Green Animals, Cory's Lane, Portsmouth; 401-847-6543.

Hammersmith Farm, Ocean Drive, Newport; 401-847-1000.

Heber W. Yongken, Jr. Medicinal Plant Garden, University of Rhode Island, Kingston; 401-792-2751.

Museum of Rhode Island History at Aldrich House, 110 Benevolent Street, Providence; 401-331-8575.

Roger Williams Park Greenhouses and Gardens, Elmwood Avenue, Providence; 401-785-7450.

Samuel Whitehorne House, 416 Thames Street, Newport; 401-847-2448.

Shakespeare's Head, 21 Meeting Street, Providence; 401-831-7440.

Winsor Azalea Garden, 44 Marden Street, Cranston; 401-277-2601.

Vermont

Cady's Falls Nursery, Morrisville; 802-888-5559.

Downtown Ely Gardens, Route 5, Fairlee; 802-333-9906.

Evergreen Gardens of Vermont, Route 100, Waterbury Center; 802-244-8523.

Gardener's Supply, 128 Intervale Road, Burlington; 802-660-3500.

Greatwood Gardens, Goddard College, Plainfield; 802-454-8311.

Hildene, Manchester Village; 802-362-1788.

Horticulture Research Center, University of Vermont, Routh 7, South Burlington; 802-656-2980.

Olallie Daylily Gardens, Marlboro Branch Road, South Newfane; 802-348-6614.

Park McCullough House, North Bennington; 802-442-5441.

Rocky Dale Nursery, 806 Rocky Dale Road, Bristol; 802-453-2782.

Shelburne Museum, Route 7, Shelburne; 802-985-3344.

Vermont Perennial Gardens, Dorman Road; 802-875-2604

Vermont Wildflower Farm, Route 7, Charlotte; 802-425-3346.

RESOURCES

THE MAIL-ORDER GARDEN

Gardening by mail wasn't so easy two centuries ago, even for Thomas Jefferson, who found himself thwarted by British blockades while trying to obtain plants from Europe. In contrast, we have access to scores of local nurseries and garden centers. They're a fine resource, especially those that grow their own plants and/or specialize in particular plants or groups of plants. (Twombly Nursery in Monroe, Connecticut, for example, has a huge and matchless inventory of shrubs and trees.) You can depend on them to sell cultivars that will be hardy in your garden.

If you don't live near a good local nursery, you can take advantage of the hundreds of North American nurseries and seed companies that offer tens of thousands of plants. Listed here are some of the fine firms that can send you anything from ash trees to zonal pelargoniums. Most are located in New England (and welcome visitors), but a few are located elsewhere. Many, but not all, of the mail-order catalogs are free; firms that charge for their catalogs often refund the cost with your order.

As you're shopping—or even if you're just looking—don't forget to ask for information and help. Seed and plant sellers are a remarkably friendly and helpful bunch. We're all gardeners, remember, "comrades of the spade."

Allen, Sterling & Lothrop, 191 U.S. Route 1, Falmouth, ME 04105; 207-781-4142 (herb, flower, vegetable seeds).

Amanda's Garden, 8410 Harper's Ferry Road, Springwood, NY 14560; 716-669-2275 (native woodland wildflowers).

Avant Gardens, 710 High Hill Road, North Dartmouth, MA 02747; 508-998-8819; www.avantgardensne.com (hardy and tender perennials).

Barth Daylilies, 71 Nelson Road, Alna, ME 04535; 207-586-6455 (daylilies).

Bloomingfields Farm, P.O. Box 5, Gaylordsville, CT 06755-0055; 860-354-6952; www.bloomingfieldsfarm.com (daylilies).

Blue Meadow Farm, 184 Meadow Road, Montague, MA 01351; 413-367-2394 (uncommon annuals).

Botanicals, 219 Concord Road, Wayland, MA 01778; 800-432-5535 (trees, shrubs, perennials).

Brent & Becky's Bulbs, 7463 Heath Trail, Gloucester, VA 23061; 804-693-3966; www.brentandbeckysbulbs.com (bulbs).

Briarwood Gardens, 14 Gully Lane, R.F.D. 1, East Sandwich, MA 02537 (shrubs, rhododendrons).

Bristol Mums, Inc., 50 Pinehurst Road, Bristol, CT 06010; 800-582-6967 (chrysanthemums).

Broken Arrow Nursery, 13 Broken Arrow Road, Hamden, CT 06518; 203-288-1026 (rhododendrons, kalmias, woodland trees and shrubs).

Burt Associates Bamboo, P.O. Box 719, Westford, MA 01886; 978-692-3240; www.bamboo.com/users/bamboo (bamboo).

Butterbrooke Farm Seed, 78 Barry Road, Oxford, CT 06478-1529; 203-888-2000 (untreated seeds for heirloom vegetables, some flowers).

Caprilands Herb Farm, 534 Silver Street, Coventry, CT 06238; 203-742-7244; www.caprilands.com (herbs).

Carlson's Gardens, Box 305, South Salem, NY 10590; 914-763-5958; www.carlsonsgardens.com (azaleas, rhododendrons, woody shrubs).

Chappell Nursery, 1114 Trumbull Highway, Lebanon, CT 06249; 860-642-6996 (rhododendrons, azaleas, kalmias).

Completely Clematis, 217 Argilla Road, Ipswich, MA 01938-2617; 978-356-3197; www.clematisnursery.com (clematis).

Comstock, Ferre & Co., 263 Main Street, Wethersfield, CT 06109-0125; 860-571-6590; www.tiac.net/users/comstock (flower, herb, vegetable seeds).

The Cook's Garden, P.O. Box 535, Londonderry, VT 05148; 800-457-9703; www.cooksgarden.com (organic seeds of vegetables, herbs, flowers).

Countryman Peony Farm, RR-1, Box 990, Northfield, VT 05663; 802-485-8421 (peonies).

Cricket Hill Garden, 670 Walnut Hill Road, Thomaston, CT 06787; 860-283-1042; www.treepeony.com (Chinese tree peonies).

The Daffodil Mart, 30 Irene Street, Torrington, CT 06790-6668; 800-ALL-BULB (hardy and tender bulbs).

Daystar, 1270 Hallowell–Litchfield Road, West Gardiner, ME 04350-3571; 207-724-3369 (perennials, shrubs, trees).

Earthheart Gardens, RR-1, Box 847, South Harpswell, ME 04079; 207-833-6327 (Siberian and Japanese iris).

Eastern Plant Specialities, Box 226, Georgetown, ME 04548; 732-382-2508 (native species, perennials, shrubs, trees).

F. W. Schumacher Co., Inc., 36 Spring Hill Road, Sandwich, MA 02563-1023; 508-888-0659 (seeds for trees, shrubs).

Fedco Seeds, P.O. Box 520, Waterville, ME 04903-0520; 207-873-7333; www.fedcoseeds.com (untreated herb, vegetable, flower, grain seeds; many heirlooms).

Fedco Trees, P.O. Box 520, Waterville, ME 04903-0520; 207-873-7333; www.fedcoseeds.com (all fruits, woody ornamentals, perennials, bulbs).

Fieldstone Gardens Inc., 620 Quaker Lane, Vassalboro, ME 04989-9713; 207-923-3836; www. fieldstonegardens.com (perennials).

Forestfarm, 990 Tetherow Road, Williams, OR 97544-9599; 541-846-6963; www.forestfarm.com (shrubs, vines, trees, roses).

Fox Hill Nursery, 347 Lunt Road, Freeport, ME 04032; 207-729-1511; www.lilacs.com (lilacs, roses)

French's Bulb Importer, P.O. Box 565, Pittsfield, VT 05762-0565; 802-746-8148 (hardy and tender bulbs).

The Great Plant Company, P.O. Box 1041, New Hartford, CT 06057; 800-441-9788; www.greatplants.com (tender and hardy perennials, tropicals, lilacs).

Green Mountain Transplants, Inc., 2290 Vermont Rte. 14 North, East Montpelier, VT 05651; 802-454-1533; www.gmtransplants.com (vegetable, flower transplants).

Harris Seeds, P.O. Box 22960, 60 Saginaw Drive, Rochester, NY 14692-2960; 800-514-4441; www.harrisseeds.com (herb, vegetable, flower seeds; fruits, vegetable transplants).

Hermit Medlars Walk, 3 Pierce Street, Foxborough, MA 02035; 508-543-2711 (dwarf bearded iris).

High Mowing Organic Seed Farm, 813 Brook Road, Wolcott, VT 05680; 802-888-1800 (organic, biodynamic heirloom vegetable seeds).

Hill Gardens, 107 Route 3, Box 39, Palermo, ME 04354; 207-993-2956; www.hillgardens.com (daylilies, hostas).

Hillside Nursery, 107 Skinner Road, Shelburne, MA 01370; 413-625-9251 (native wildflowers and ferns).

Jackson & Perkins, P.O. Box 9100, Medford, OR 97501; 800-545-3444; www.jacksonandperkins.com (roses).

Joe Pye Weed's Garden, 337 Acton Street, Carlisle, MA 01741; 978-371-1073 (Siberian and interspecies iris).

John Scheepers, Inc., 23 Tulip Drive, Bantam, CT 06750; 850-567-0838; www.johnscheepers.com (bulbs).

Johnny's Selected Seeds, 1 Foss Hill Road, Box 2580, Albion, ME 04910-9731; 207-437-4301; www.johnny-seeds.com (vegetable, herb, flower seeds).

Ladybug Herbs of Vermont, RR1-Box 3380; Wolcott, VT 05680; 802-888-5940 (herb seeds and organic plants).

Le Jardin du Gourmet, Box 75, St. Johnsbury Center, VT 05863-0075; 802-748-1446 (herb, vegetable seeds; garlic; herb, perennial plants).

The Lily Nook, Box 657, Rolla, ND 58367; 204-476-3225; www.lilynook.mb.ca (lilies).

Logee's Greenhouses, Ltd., 141 North Street, Danielson, CT 06239-1939; 860-774-8038; www.logees.com (tender perennials).

Lowe's Own-Root Roses, 6 Sheffield Road, Nashua, NH 03062; 603-888-2214 (hardy shrub roses, heirloom roses).

Maltais Flower Farm, RD-1, Box 1475, Gilmanton, NH 03837; 603-267-7262; www.maltaisfarm.com (perennials).

Mary Mattison Van Schaik Imported Dutch Bulbs, P.O. Box 188, Temple, NH 03084; 603-878-2592 (hardy bulbs).

Mountain River Flower Farm, 128 Old Route 110, West Dummer, NH 03588; 603-449-2158; www.mrff.com (lilies, Japanese and Siberian iris).

New England Wild Flower Society, 180 Hemenway Road, Framingham, MA 01701; 508-877-7630; www.newfs.org (seeds, plants: native species).

Nor'East Miniature Roses, P.O. Box 307, Rowley, MA 01969; 800-426-6485; www.noreast-miniroses.com (miniature roses).

Nourse Farms, Inc., 41 River Road, South Deerfield, MA 01373; 413-665-2658; www.noursefarms.com (berry and asparagus plants).

Oakridge Nurseries, P.O. Box 182, East Kingston, NH 03872; 603-642-7339 (wildflowers, ferns).

Olallie Daylily Gardens, 129 Auger Hole Road, South Newfane, VT 05351; 802-348-6614; www.daylilygarden.com (daylilies).

Old House Gardens, 536 Third Street, Ann Arbor, MI 48103-4957; 734-995-1486; www.oldhousegardens .com (heirloom hardy and tender bulbs).

Old Sturbridge Village, 1 Old Sturbridge Village Road, Sturbridge, MA 01566; 508-347-0375 (seeds of heirloom flowers, herbs, vegetables).

Paradise Water Gardens, 14 May Street, Whitman, MA 02382; 781-447-4711; www.paradisewatergardens.com (water garden plants).

Perennial Pleasures Nursery, 2 Brick House Road, East Hardwick, VT 05836; 802-472-5104; www.kingcon.com/hyssop/index.htm (heirloom flower and herb seeds, plants).

Pinacle Plants, P.O. Box 857, Essex, CT 06426; 860-767-2819; www.pinnacleplants.com (unusual perennials).

Pinetree Garden Seeds, Box 300, New Gloucester, ME 04260; 207-926-3400; www.superseeds.com (seeds of flowers, herbs, vegetables).

Plainview Farm Fine Perennials, 529 Mountfort Road, North Yarmouth, ME 04097; 800-396-1705; www.plain-viewfarm.com (perennials).

Pleasant Valley Glads, P.O. Box 494, 163 Senator Avenue, Agawam, MA 01001; 413-786-9146 (gladiolus, dahlias).

R. Seawright, 201 Bedford Road, Carlisle, MA 01741-0733; 978-369-1900 (daylilies, hostas).

Raising Rarities, P.O. Box 405, Jacksonville, VT 05342; 802-368-7273 (nursery-propagated native lady's slippers, orchids).

Richters, 357 Hwy. 47, Goodwood, ON L0C 1A0, Canada; 905-640-6677; www.richters.com (herb plants and seeds).

Rock Spray Nursery, P.O. Box 693, Truro, MA 02666-0693; 508-349-6769; www.rockspray.com (heathers, heaths, alpines).

The Roseraie at Bayfields, P.O. Box R, 670 Bremem Road, Waldoboro, ME 04572-0919; 207-832-6330; www.roseraie.com (roses, including heirlooms).

Royall River Roses, 70 New Gloucester Road, North Yarmouth, ME 04097; 207-829-5830; www.royallriver-roses.com (roses, heirloom roses).

Schipper & Co., P.O. Box 7584, Greenwich, CT 06835; 203-625-0638; www.colorblends.com (bulb mixtures).

Seaside Daylily Farm, P.O. Box 807, West Tisbury, MA 02575; 506-693-FARM; http://vineyard.net/daylily (daylilies).

Select Seeds/Antique Flowers, 180 Strickney Hill Road, Union, CT 06076; 860-684-9310; www.selectseeds.com (heirloom flower, herb seeds).

Shepherd's Garden Seeds, 30 Irene Street, Torrington, CT 06790; 860-482-3638; www.shepherdseeds.com (herb, vegetable, flower seeds).

St. Lawrence Nurseries, 325 State Hwy. 345, Potsdam, NY 13676; 315-265-6739; www.sln.potsdam.ny.us (tree fruits, berries, nuts).

Surry Gardens, P.O. Box 145, Rte. 172, Surry, ME 04684; 207-667-4493 (perennials, rock garden plants).

Sylvan Nursery, 1028 Horseneck Road, Westport, MA 02790; 508-636-4573; www.sylvannursery.com (landscape-grade trees, shrubs).

Tranquil Lake Nursery, Inc., 45 River Street, Rehoboth, MA 02769; 508-252-4310; www.tranquil-lake.com (iris, daylilies).

Tripple Brook Farm, 37 Middle Road, Southampton, MA 01073; 413-527-4626; www.tripplebrookfarm.com (perennials, grasses, shrubs, vines, trees, ornamental edibles).

Underwood Shade Nursery, P.O. Box 1386, North Attleboro, MA 02763-0386; 508-222-2164; www.underwoodshadenursery.com (perennials, ferns, grasses and ground covers for shade).

Valente Gardens, RFD 2, Box 234, East Lebanon, ME 04027; 207-457-2076 (perennials).

Van Bourgondien's, P.O. Box 1000, Babylon, NY 11702; 800-622-9997; www.dutchbulbs.com (hardy and tender bulbs).

Van Engelen, Inc./John Scheepers, Inc., 23 Tulip Drive, Bantam, CT 06750; 860-567-8734; www.vanengelen.com (bulbs).

Variegated Foliage Nursery, 245 Westford Road, Eastford, CT 06242; 860-974-3951 (herbaceous and woody plants with variegated foliage).

Vermont Bean Seed Company, Garden Lane, Fair Haven, VT 05743; 803-663-0217 (vegetable, herb seeds).

Vermont Daylilis, Barr Hill Road, Greensboro, VT 05841; 802-533-7155 (daylilies).

Vermont Wildflower Farm, P.O. Box 1400, Louisiana, MO 63353; 800-424-1165; sss.gardensolutions.com (wildflower seeds).

Vesey's Seeds Ltd., York, PEI C0A 1P0, Canada; 902-368-7333 (herb, vegetable, flower seeds for short seasons).

The Village Gardener, 10 Sagamore Farm Road, Hamilton, MA 01936; 978-68-1161 (daylilies).

Walter K. Morss & Son, Lakeshore Road, Boxford, MA 01921; 978-352-2633 (raspberries, strawberries, blueberries).

Western Maine Nurseries, 1 Evergreen Drive, P.O. Box 250, Fryeburg, ME 04037; 800-447-4745; www.western-mainenurseries.com (conifers and deciduous trees, large orders only).

Weston Nurseries, P.O. Box 186, East Main Street, Hopkinton, MA 01748-0186; 508-435-3414 (trees, shrubs, vines, roses).

Wheeler Farm Gardens, 171 Bartlett Street, Portland, CT 06480; 888-437-2648 (zonal and ivy geraniums).

White Flower Farm, Litchfield, CT 06759; 800-503-9624; www.whiteflowerfarm.com (bulbs, perennials, ferns, grasses).

Wild Ginger Woodlands, P.O. Box 1091, Webster, NY 14580 (seeds for native woodland plants).

Windham Wildflowers, P.O. Box 207, Westminster Station, VT 05159; 802-387-4096; www.flowerseeds.com (seeds of wildflowers, perennials).

Windrose Nursery, 1093 Mill Road, Pen Argyl, PA 18072-9670; 610-588-1037; www.windrosenursery.com (woody plants-shrubs).

BOOKS FOR FURTHER REFERENCE

The American Horticultural Society A–Z Encyclopedia of Garden Plants, DK Publishing, 1997.

Bennett, Jennifer. *Dry-Land Gardening,* Firefly Books, 1998.

Bennett, Jennifer. *The Harrowsmith Annual Garden,* Camden House, 1990.

Bennett, Jennifer. *The Harrowsmith Book of Fruit Trees,* Camden House, 1991.

Bennett, Paul. *The Garden Lover's Guide to the Northeast,* Princeton Architectural Press, 1999.

Buchanan, Rita. *Making a Garden,* Houghton Mifflin, 1999.

Buchanan, Rita. *Taylor's Master Guide to Landscaping,* Houghton Mifflin, 2000.

Burrell, C. Colston. *A Gardener's Encyclopedia of Wild Flowers,* Rodale Press, 1997.

Cole, Trevor. *Gardening with Trees and Shrubs: In Ontario, Quebec, and the Northeastern United States,* Whitcap Books, 1996.

Cullina, William. *The New England Wild Flower Society Guide to Growing and Propagating Wildflowers of the United States and Canada,* Houghton Mifflin, 2000.

Cutler, Karan Davis. *Burpee—The Complete Vegetable and Herb Gardener,* Macmillan, 1997.

Cutler, Karan Davis, ed. *Flowering Vines,* Brooklyn Botanic Garden, 1999.

Cutler, Karan Davis, ed. *Tantalizing Tomatoes,* Brooklyn Botanic Garden, 1997.

Dirr, Michael A. *Manual of Woody Landscape Plants,* Stipes Publishing, 1998.

Donnelly, Ruah. *The Adventurous Gardener: Where to Buy the Best Plants in New England,* Horticultural Press, 2000.

Eddison, Sydney. *A Passion for Daylilies,* HarperCollins, 1992.

Eddison, Sydney. *The Self-Taught Gardener: Lessons from a Country Garden,* Viking, 1997.

Ellis, Barbara. *Attracting Birds and Butterflies,* Houghton Mifflin, 1997.

Ellis, Barbara. *Taylor's Guide to Growing North America's Favorite Plants,* Houghton Mifflin, 1998.

Foster, F. Gordon. *Ferns to Know and Grow,* 3d ed., Timber Press, 1984.

Heath, Brent, and Becky Heath. *Daffodils for American Gardens,* Eliott and Clark Publishing, 1995.

Heger, Mike, and John Whitman. *Growing Perennials in Cold Climates,* Contemporary Books, 1998.

Hill, Lewis. *Cold-Climate Gardening,* Storey Communications, 1987.

Hill, Lewis. *Fruits and Berries for the Home Garden,* Garden Way Publishing, 1977.

Hill, Lewis, and Nancy Hill. *Bulbs: Four Seasons of Beautiful Bloomers,* Storey Communications, 1994.

Holmses, Roger, et al. *Home Landscaping: Northeast Region,* Creative Homeowner Press, 1998.

Jones, Samuel B., and Leonard E. Foote. *Gardening with*

Native Wild Flowers, Timber Press, 1990.

Leighton, Ann. *American Gardens in the Eighteenth Century: For Use or for Delight*, University of Massachusetts Press, 1976.

Leighton, Ann. *American Gardens in the Nineteenth Century: For Comfort and Affluence*, University of Massachusetts Press, 1987.

Leighton, Ann. *Early American Gardens: For Meate or Medicine*, University of Massachusetts Press, 1970.

Lima, Patrick. *The Art of Perennial Gardening: Creative Ways with Hardy Flowers*, Firefly Books, 1998.

MacKenzie, David S. *Perennial Ground Covers*, Timber Press, 1997.

Nuese, Josephine. *The Country Garden*, Charles Scribner's Sons, 1970.

Obrizok, Robert A. *A Garden of Conifers*, Firefly, 1999.

Ogden, Shepherd. *Straight Ahead Organic*, Chelsea Green, 1999.

Olson, Jerry, and John Whitman. *Growing Roses in Cold Climates*, Contemporary Books, 1998.

Osborne, Robert A., *Hardy Roses*, Storey Communications, 1991.

Perényi, Eleanor. *Green Thoughts: A Writer in the Garden*, Random House, 1981.

Powing, Beth. *Hardy Trees and Shrubs: A Guide to Disease-Resistant Varieties for the North*, Firefly Books, 1996.

Rupp, Rebecca. *Red Oaks and Black Birches: The Science and Lore of Trees*, Storey Communications, 1990.

Schultz, Warren. *A Man's Turf: The Perfect Lawn*, Clarkson Potter, 1999.

Taylor, Patricia A. *Easy Care Native Plants*, Henry Holt, 1996.

Tripp, Kim E., and J.C. Raulston. *The Year in Trees: Superb Woody Plants for Four-Season Gardens*, Timber Press, 1995.

Verrier, Suzanne. *Rosa Rugosa*, Firefly Books, 1999.

MORE SOURCES OF INFORMATION

The best single source for the names and addresses of seed companies, nurseries, tool and equipment firms, garden publications and organizations, and plant societies is Barbara Barton's *Gardening by Mail* (5th ed., 1997). You also can access the book—which lists more than 900 nurseries, 280 suppliers, 300 societies and organizations, 111 libraries, and 89 publications—on the web at http://vg.com/gbm. Overwhelmed by those numbers? Begin with these interesting and useful resources for New England gardeners.

Organizations

All-America Selections/National Garden Bureau, 1311 Butterfield Road, Suite 310, Downers Grove, IL 60515; 630-963-0770; http://www.all-americaselections.org; http://www.ngd:org (two nonprofit organizations that focus on new and outstanding cultivars for home gardeners).

The Flower and Herb Exchange, 3076 North Winn Road, Decorah, IA 52101; 319-382-5990; http://www.seedsavers.org (members of this national nonprofit have access to seeds of thousands of heirloom and open-pollinated flowers and herbs).

New England Garden History Society, 300 Massachusetts Avenue, Boston, MA 02115; http://www.masshort.org/neghs.

New England Nursery Association, Inc., 8-D Pleasant Street, South Natick, MA 01760; 508-653-3112; http://www.nensyassn.org (good source of information about retail nurseries in New England).

New England Wild Flower Society, 180 Hemenway Road, Framingham, MA 01701-2699; 508-877-7630; http://www.newfs.org (information about using native plants in the garden; the NEWFS can provide addresses of state chapters in CT, MA, ME, NH, and VT; in RI, contact the Rhode Island Wild Plant Society, P.O. Box 114, Peace Dale, RI 02883-0114).

North American Fruit Explorers, 1716 Apples Road, Chapin, IL 62628; www.nafex.org (a free-wheeling national organization of dedicated fruit lovers—trees fruits, berries, nuts, and more; members exhange seeds, cuttings, and information).

Northeast Organic Farming Association, P.O. Box 697, Richmond, VT 05477; http://www.nofavt.org (New England organization of gardeners and farmers committed to organic methods).

Seed Savers Exchange/Flower & Herb Exchange, 3076 North Winn Road, Decorah, IA 52101; 319-382-5990; http://www.seedsavers.org (members of this national nonprofit have access to seeds of tens of thousands of heirloom and open-pollinated vegetables and fruits).

State Cooperative Extension Services

Cooperative Extension Services are information gold mines. In New England, the central office for each state's CES is located at its state university. You can find the office nearest to you in the telephone directory under the listing for your state university; look for "Extension" or "Cooperative Extension." Or access your Cooperative Extension Service through the Web:

Connecticut: http://www.canr.uconn.edu/ces.
Rhode Island: http://www.edc.uri.edu.
Maine: http://www.umext.maine.edu.
Massachusetts: http://www.umass.edu/umext.
New Hampshire: http://ceinfo.unh.edu.
Vermont: http://ctr.uvm.edu/ext.

The website of the mother lode of Cooperative Extension—the USDA Cooperative State Research, Education and Extension Service—is http://www.reeusda.gov.

New England gardeners can search through more than 20,000 Cooperative Extension bulletins and fact sheets from 46 different different universities and government institutions across the United States and Canada from this site managed by the Ohio State University: http://plantfacts.ohio-state.edu. It's a superb resource for the home gardener.

Web Resources

If you're among the plugged-in set, there are hundreds of thousands of garden-related websites (one quick search limited to "English only" turned up a "more than 500,000" response. Website addresses change frequently, however, so rather than list my 100 favorites, here are a few sites that should be around in the year 2002. Remember that most sites have links to still more sites.

All-America Rose Selections: http://www.rose.org (rose information plus email addresses of New England rosarians who are willing to answer your questions).

Andersen Horticultural Library: University of Minnesota: http://vg.com/gbm (database for finding commercial sources of plants and other information; subscription required).

Garden.com: http://garden.com (an electronic garden superstore, but site also has plant finder, garden articles, chat rooms).

Garden Guides: http://www.gardenguides.com (general information about plants and gardening).

Gardening Launch Pad: http://www.tpoint.net/neighbor (well-organized site for links to other garden sites).

Garden Net: http://www.gardennet.com (huge garden website, with many links, bulletin boards, plant information, and an online magazine).

GardenWeb: http://www.gardenweb.com (major garden website with information, links, forums, seed exchange, and more).

NOAA National Weather Service: http://www.nws.noaa.gov (weather archives and more).

Perry's Perennial Pages: http://www.uvm.edu/~pass/perry (information about growing perennials from Leonard Perry, a professor of Plant and Soil Sciences, University of Vermont).

Virtual Garden: http://www.vg.com (site includes a plant encyclopedia, links, forums, and more).

Newsgroups: There are thousands of newsgroups where you can share information, post questions, and more. A good place to begin finding one right for you is http://dir.yahoo.com/Recreation/Home_and_Garden/Gardening/Usenet.

INDEX